NEBRASKA
No place quite like it!

NEBRASKA
No place quite like it!

20 years of memories

by Harold Hamil

Illustrations by James R. Hamil

THE LOWELL PRESS / KANSAS CITY, MISSOURI
1985

FIRST EDITION
Library of Congress Catalog Card Number 85-82088
ISBN 0-932845-10-X
Copyright © 1985 by Harold Hamil

This book was photocomposed in Century Schoolbook and printed on 60-pound Warren's Olde Style, a neutral pH paper with an expected 300-year library storage life as determined by the Council of Library Resources of the American Library Association by The Lowell Press of Kansas City, Missouri

All rights reserved. No part of this book may be reproduced, stored in a retrieval system or transmitted in any form or by any means, electronic, mechanical, photocopying, recording, or otherwise, without the prior written permission of the publisher.

The dustjacket watercolor, "State Capitol Building at Lincoln," and the endsheets watercolor, "High Water on the Platte," by James R. Hamil.

Dedication

"Full many a flower is born to blush unseen and waste its sweetness on the desert air."—Thomas Gray's "Elegy Written in a Country Church Yard"

Flowers by the hundred flit across my memory of the 20 years in Nebraska. Their names run through this book—names of people I lived with, studied with, worked with, argued with, learned from. Some attained a measure of prominence, but many were born to blush unseen, and to them this book is dedicated.

Contents

Foreword ix
Introduction xi
1. Nebraska—Naturally 1
2. Railroad Town 9
3. College Days 26
4. Adam Breede 63
5. A Man Named Smith 79
6. Dave(y) Was a Welshman 109
7. Summer of '34 119
8. First There Was Dust 130
9. The Tri-County Odyssey 139
10. Man in Black 167
11. The Bell Tolls Later There 177
12. Pearson the Poser 200
13. A Medley of Memories 211
14. Fred A. Seaton 228
15. A Year with the AP 248
16. Lincoln Years 257

Foreword

"There is no place like Nebraska..."

This is the first line of a song that spread from the university campus at Lincoln into every corner of the state. It has stirred the hearts of football fans through much of the twentieth century. It has prompted some cynical questions, too—especially during the hard years of the 1930s. For one who spent all those years of drouth and depression in Nebraska there was much to see, much to hear, much to learn. And there were great people to know and observe. Though I left the state more than 40 years ago, I retain pleasant memories of what history tells us were unpleasant times. For me there has been no other place quite like Nebraska. I hope this book bears out my conviction.

HAROLD HAMIL

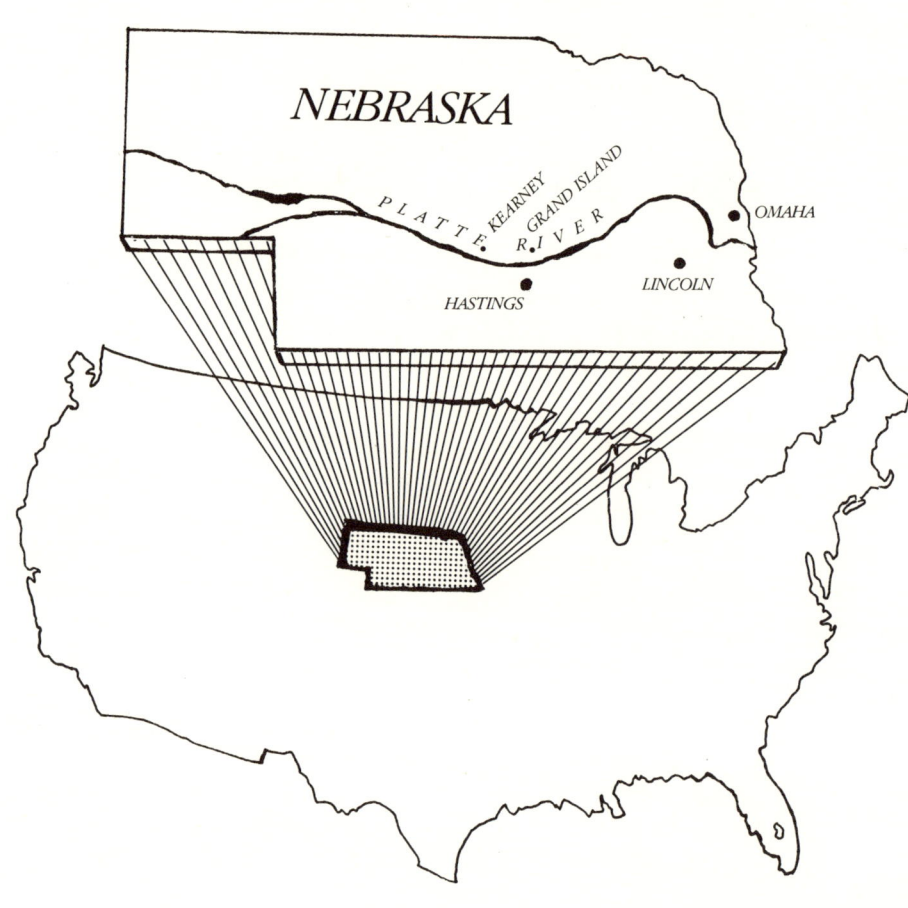

Introduction

Point in Mid-America

Hastings, the seat of Adams County, Nebraska, spreads over a high and gently undulating plain that includes the indiscernible divide between the watersheds of the Big and Little Blue rivers. It is in the transitional zone between the tallgrass hills and prairies of Nebraska's eastern counties and the shortgrass plains that extend westward to the Rocky Mountains. Its elevation, officially 1,920 feet, puts it roughly at 1,000 feet higher than the Missouri bottoms on its eastern border and some 1,500 feet lower than the Colorado border to the west. It is about 50 miles southeast of Kearney, once proud claimant to being the midpoint on a coast-to-coast highway, and about the same distance north of the geographic center of the 48 contiguous states, near Lebanon, Kansas.

Wagon trains on the Oregon Trail came into what is now Adams County near its southeastern corner, following the course of the Little Blue. Leaving the river, they took a northwesterly route to the Platte and Ft. Kearney and missed the site of Hastings by about a half-dozen miles. They crossed dry draws coming from its direction, but they knew enough about the plains to keep from heading up such declivities in search of ponds or springs. It was better to travel hard from river to river than camp in an area where there was no surface water except in the wake of heavy rains. Thus did the early white migrants hurry across Adams County.

Hastings, when I first knew it, was just past its golden anniversary, but people talked more of its future than its past. Farsighted citizens beat the drums of civic loyalty in a variety of ways. They measured each infant step of a little business that showed signs of growing into a bigger one. They assembled statistics. Hastings was big in horse collars and harnesses. For a time it manufactured more tire pumps than any other city. And it was on the way to leadership in pressure-spout oil cans. It had a radio station for several years—a big one with signals strong enough to reach most any part of the country. The station—KFKX—was established by Westinghouse for experimental purposes. Whatever the experiment showed, it was not enough to convince the company to keep the station in Hastings. KFKX went to Pittsburgh shortly before Kool-Aid went to Chicago. Then came the Great Depression.

NEBRASKA
No place quite like it!

1. Nebraska—Naturally

Lured By the Near and the Known

Through my early boyhood in Colorado I had a vague feeling that there were only two other states that counted for much. One was Tennessee, where my parents were born and reared. The other was Nebraska.

All the relatives who came to visit were from Tennessee, and so were many hired men and a growing number of neighbors. But people who identified with Nebraska seemed to be everywhere. This is explained, of course, by geography. We were in the northeastern part of Colorado which, on the map, seems to be caught by Nebraska in a sort of thumb-and-finger squeeze.

Going north from our ranch, one crossed the line into Nebraska after about a dozen miles. Beyond that a few miles was Sidney, a county seat of some historic repute, but not quite so large as our own county seat, Sterling.

Watching the Union Pacific trains go by, we rode with them on fancied trips all the way between Denver and Omaha. Traveling eastward in our dreams, we crossed into Nebraska just beyond Julesburg, then went through such places as Ogallala, North Platte, Kearney and Grand Island and on into Omaha.

From hired men we heard about the wide valley of the Platte beyond the confluence of the north and south branches. It was so wide in places, they said, as to make our own South Platte Valley seem like little more than a big draw. One man described the vast stretches of alfalfa around Gothenburg, Cozad and Lexington as something we couldn't begin to match in our narrow valley.

Some of these nomadic ranch workers had lived in eastern Nebraska, and they were especially vocal on the subject of corn. They would rather have husked corn in the fall than fork clumsy, dirt-encrusted sugar beets onto wagons and haul them to the dump. They grumbled about the hard work of irrigating. They made corn farming seem quite appealing to a growing boy already past the stage of finding fun in the diverting of water from the South Platte into ditches and from ditches onto fields of beets, small grain and alfalfa.

While Father planted some corn on dryland patches every year, it was a chancy crop and rarely matured to the point it could be put through a sheller. Nobody dreamed that with the coming of hybrids eventually there would be corn varieties adaptable to the short growing seasons of Colorado and that irrigated fields along the South Platte someday would produce corn to match anything Nebraska had. And nobody dreamed that Nebraska would hold its own as a corn state only through acceptance of irrigation for millions of acres of the kind of land our Nebraska-trained hired men had never thought of irrigating.

In any event, a lot of my fascination with Nebraska centered on the general observation that farming was better and easier there. That I should have been influenced by things agricultural when my boyhood dreams were of finding some way to break out of a long family tradition and be something other than a farmer seems, in retrospect, to have been a bit contradictory. On the other hand, my whole system of values came from farm people and farm experiences. Nebraska, much more of an agricultural state than Colorado, appealed to me, and the idea of going there for further education seemed natural and comfortable.

My choice of Hastings College, therefore, was affected some by the fact that Hastings was in Nebraska. There were other considerations, of course, not the least of which was that the cost estimates outlined in Hastings literature seemed more in line with what I could afford than did those of Grinnell College in Iowa, for example, or the University of Colorado at Boulder. While my father was lukewarm about the whole idea of college, my mother was encouraging. Both seemed to feel that Hastings' affiliation with the Presbyterian Church was a built-in safeguard against my straying too far from the standards of conduct they expected of me.

Most of what went with me into Nebraska that September night in 1924 was in a small trunk. While I returned to Colorado for Christmas and summer vacations, the trunk never did. It stayed in Hastings until 1940, and after a year in New York, it came back to Lincoln, where we lived three years. I like to think that the whereabouts of that trunk established my Nebraska residence for a full score of years, allowing the year in New York to stand as a sort of sabbatical.

When I left Lincoln in 1944, I was, by most people's standards, approaching middle age. I look on those Nebraska years as a time of many beginnings, many first encounters, of experiences that became benchmarks and lessons that have governed judgments and actions ever since. People I came to know there became people against whom I would measure countless acquaintances and friends in other places.

This book, then, deals with what I consider my 20 years as a Nebraskan. They were good years in that they were the years of my greatest physical vigor, the years of highest hope and ambition, the years of my marriage and the births of my two sons. But they included some bad years for Nebraska, and it's hard for me to look back upon them as easy years for me. My dreams and the dreams of those about me were shattered and reshattered by the Great Depression and the blight of the Dust Bowl era.

William Jennings Bryan was very much alive when I went to Nebraska. He died the following year, but his ghost walked among political personalities for at least a dozen years. Men identified themselves as Bryan Democrats, and some of the front-runners among these seemed to try to emulate the Great Commoner in style of dress and haircut. I heard the last hurrahs for Gilbert Hitchcock, J. H. Morehead, A. C. Shallenberger, J. N. Norton, Edgar Howard and W. J. Bryan's brother, Charlie.

Sam McKelvie, once governor, was much in the news of the late twenties as a member of President Hoover's Farm Board. Through all the years of the thirties, it seemed, Dwight Griswold of Gordon had his mind set on being governor. Twice defeated in the general election and once in a primary, he finally made it in 1940 and was governor when I left the state. I knew Carl T. Curtis as a young man merely hoping for a career in the national Congress.

I was a sort of front-row observer as Fred Seaton came out of Kansas in 1937 and started working his way toward the top echelons of state and national political leadership. His coming was more than a passing event for me. He was my new boss at the Hastings *Daily Tribune,* and from all we had heard there was good reason to expect some changes would be made.

The *Tribune,* aggressive proponent of any and all New Deal programs that offered relief from problems besetting our region, had supported Franklin Roosevelt in the 1936 campaign and had backed a Democrat, Roy Cochran, for governor. The *Tribune* and the Lincoln *Star* were the only dailies that had supported Nebraska's shift to a one-house legislature. The paper had shown a degree of new intransigence, certainly, in its ardent advocacy of the re-election of George W. Norris to the Senate after he had renounced Republicanism and chosen to run as an Independent. It was enough of a shock to learn, in May of 1937, that the *Tribune* owners had agreed to sell the paper; it was almost traumatic to consider that if I stayed on as managing editor I would be suddenly subject to the wishes of a man who had been a member of the campaign team of Alf Landon in his unsuccessful 1936 bid for the presidency. Fred Seaton, still in his twenties, was, from all reports, an orthodox Republican in background and recent commitments. The *Tribune* and I had been on the other side. The adjustment turned out to be less difficult than I had anticipated.

While this book covers the three years I worked with Seaton, it is far more extensive in reporting the personal relationships with Henry G. Smith and David J. Lewis, two veterans of the paper when I went to work there. The two of them, not always together in philosophy or in detailed recollections, filled me in with anecdotes of the years when Adam Breede, founder of the *Tribune*, was in many respects Hastings' most colorful citizen. They also were free with advice on the fundamentals of journalism as they viewed them. Each, in his quite distinctive way, was a teacher.

Men were talking about the possibilities of irrigation on the uplands south of the Platte River when I arrived in Hastings as a student. Later, as a news reporter and editor, I embraced the irrigation idea as the real key to the future of the region. Eventually, the application of supplemental water to hundreds of thousands of acres would transform this whole section of Nebraska. In the beginning, though, all attention focused on the transfer of surface water from the Platte River. As it turned out, there was a more manageable supply 100 feet or so below the ground that could be tapped with wells. For most of my years on the *Tribune* I was an avid chronicler of the hopes, the fears and frustrations of irrigation advocates. The organization that built the dams and ditches of the

Tri-County system got much of its momentum from a small, dedicated group in Hastings. What they said and did was the daily fare of readers of the *Tribune*. I took very seriously the job of dishing it up.

The *Tribune*, in 1940, was the sweepstakes winner among small-city dailies in the annual awards program of the National Editorial Association. While attending the N.E.A. convention in New York, where the awards were made, I visited friends at the Associated Press headquarters in Rockefeller Center and indicated some interest in working for the organization. A few weeks later I had agreed to become a feature editor on the New York staff.

Our family had been established in an apartment just off the Columbia University campus for about six months when an inquiry came as to my interest in becoming director of the School of Journalism at the University of Nebraska. I made a quick trip to Lincoln, agreed to terms and was back there for the opening of school in the fall of 1941.

Three months later came Pearl Harbor, and three years after that came final word that I was permanently ineligible for military service. I decided to get back into active newspaper work, and in October 1944, I left Lincoln for St. Louis. And thus the period covered in this book came to a close.

Looking back on the 20-year period in Nebraska, one doesn't need much imagination to chart it as a meteorologist would chart the weather of a single year. The winds blew hot and cold—economic winds as well as physical—and the social and political winds as well. There were extreme highs and extreme lows and a full quota of the moderate periods that are the accepted rewards for living through the heat of summer and the cold of winter most anywhere in the Great Plains.

Much of the narrative centers at Hastings, because that's where I was most of the time. What happened in that county seat and regional trade center differed only in detail and degree from what happened in countless communities across the land during the years between two great wars—the years of Lindbergh, the New Deal, the Great Depression and the rise of Adolf Hitler.

During my 12 years with the Hastings *Daily Tribune* I never once thought of my experiences as preparing me to write a book. For that particular period and for the kind of book this is, though, not a single individual was in better position to be doing just that. Reporters and editors, if they are worth their salt, are constantly inquiring, constantly examining and re-examining their surroundings. They accost people and ask questions with an air of authority denied individuals in other occupations. More than that, they attract the gossips' offerings and enjoy a certain immunity from suspicion or disdain when trafficking informally in the lowest forms of gossip. Some of the material on the following pages—not very much—can be established as no more than popular gossip. But gossip has a way of maturing into folklore and from that, sometimes, into the accepted annals of a community.

This book, therefore, is one person's record of things seen, things heard and things experienced in Nebraska between 1924 and 1944. It describes people I knew and observed. It recalls reactions to events that were national and international in scope, but it is not an attempt at writing history in the scholarly sense. That there should be some trivia seems wholly justified. For one thing, the ebb and flow of human events can be measured by little things in the lives of little people as well as by the grand pageantry in which states and nations, empires and armies are the actors of record. Trivia can be interesting, and sometimes significant.

The writing was made easy by the encouragement I got from friends and associates of long standing. Thanks to the courtesy of Gladys and Don Seaton and Bob Hunter,

I had access to the files of the Hastings *Tribune*. The same courtesy was extended by the Adams County Historical Society.

Harold Cowan, Ed Wilken and Sue Baker-Josties, all three of whom worked with me at the *Tribune*, read portions of the manuscript.

Two of my most ardent supporters in the early days of this project were the late Dorothy Weyer-Creigh and Charles Osborne. The former was principal author and editor of a monumental history of Adams County that was published in 1972. Osborne, a member of the Hastings College freshman class with me in 1924, lived out his years in Hastings as a businessman with an interest in history that contributed to the growth of both the Adams County Historical Society and the Nebraska Historical Society, of which he was a president.

Judge Robert Van Pelt and Robert Crosby, both of Lincoln, helped find the answers to some questions. Dr. Frank E. Weyer, academic dean at Hastings College during my student years and a historian in his own right, read and commented on the chapter covering my college years. This chapter was one of several that were read and checked by my brother, David A. Hamil of Sterling, Colorado.

2. Railroad Town

Destiny (and Most Everything Else) Rode the Trains

Hastings was a railroad town from the beginning. Its mother, in a figurative sense, was the Burlington and Missouri River, first rail line to reach Adams County. Its sire, to complete the image, was the St. Joseph and Denver City, which had strayed into the county with no clear-cut plan for getting out.

The meeting, or mating, of these lines was a case of unplanned parenthood which produced a city that would take pride in its railroad heritage for the next 100 years.

There was never a formal marriage—or merger—of the parent lines, and both eventually changed their names and developed new relationships with other railroads. But the product of their first encounter remains in the crossing of two main-line tracks a few blocks from the heart of downtown Hastings. One track now is identified as Burlington Northern, and it extends in an unbroken line all the way between Denver and Chicago. The other is Union Pacific, carrying fast freight trains between Kansas City and Gibbon, Nebraska, and to and from there on the U. P.'s double-track rails to Utah and other points west.

Builders of the Burlington, laying out new towns as they moved westward from Lincoln, had named them in alphabetical order, starting with Archer, Burks, Crete, Dorchester, Exeter, Fairmont, Grafton and Harvard. Across Adams County they had designated Inland, Juniata and Kenesaw.

The St. Joseph and Denver City, approaching from the southeast, was also on an alphabetical binge. Starting with Alexandria, it had spotted Belvidere, Carleton, Davenport, Edgar, Fairfield and Glenville. There was a period of hesitation before choosing a location for the "H" town. There was good reason to head from Glenville to Juniata on a sharp veer to the west. Juniata was the county seat and could offer certain benefits not to be found in just any random town. Juniata leaders decided their town had enough attractions that they could turn down the St. Joseph's suggestion that they issue bonds and pay for the privilege of having another railroad.

The St. Joseph people took this as a snub and decided to build along the general course they had been following. This brought them to the Burlington at a point about seven miles east of Juniata. Landowners in the vicinity were quick to start platting a town, and the railroad was ready with the name of a construction engineer, Thomas D. Hastings, to maintain the alphabetical sequence.

The St. Joseph and Denver City, the railroad that had come into the county without knowing for sure how it would get out, had forced on the more purposeful Burlington a townsite that was not in that railroad's original plan. It also forced the Burlington to shift the site of Inland several miles to the east, and it was soon apparent that it had shattered the dreams of Juniata. Hastings, with two railroads, started booming, in a relative sense, and in less than a decade it had wrested the county seat from its older neighbor to the west.

The St. Joseph and Denver City stopped at Hastings for the time being. It eventually became the St. Joseph and Grand Island, and in due time was merged into the Union Pacific and developed into a main link between central Nebraska and eastern Kansas and Kansas City.

It was in the spirit of the times that wherever two rail lines met, as the two had met at Hastings, there was

Railroad Town 11

In the heyday of steam

sound reason to start thinking of a third line, a fourth or a fifth. It was that way in Hastings for many years after its founding.

Two additional companies extended rails to Hastings—the Missouri Pacific from the south and the Fremont, Elkhorn and Missouri River (North Western) from the east. The Rock Island and Santa Fe pointed lines out of Kansas in the direction of Hastings, but neither got farther than Nuckolls County. Hastings investors were active in promotion of the Kansas City and Wyandotte, a line projected across northeast Kansas in the general direction of Hastings, but it, too, stopped near the Nebraska border.

Old men talked on street corners well into the twentieth century about the greatness that might have come to Hastings if its dreams of railroads had fully materialized. With a little bit of luck and all those railroads, it might have become another Kansas City or an Omaha, they said.

But even against this history of shattered dreams, Hastings became a railroad center of some significance. The Burlington mothered it well, making it a division headquarters, the site of various maintenance facilities and the convergence of several branch lines. It shared with Lincoln, Holdrege and McCook the role of support points for a network of Burlington rails that pretty well draped itself over all of Nebraska south of the Platte River. (The Burlington and Missouri River became the Chicago, Burlington and Quincy and then the Burlington Northern.)

While there was passenger service on Union Pacific trains to Grand Island, Kearney and to St. Joseph and Kansas City via Marysville, Kansas, the traffic through Hastings was mainly freight trains after the U. P. built the so-called Gibbon cutoff. By the early 1930s the Union Pacific was moving long trains behind powerful steam locomotives between Gibbon and Kansas City, with extensive yards and other facilities making Hastings an important service point.

The Missouri Pacific and North Western were minor factors in the volume of rail traffic in and out of Hastings, but the Chamber of Commerce and all promotion-minded citizens counted them and the St. Joseph and Grand Island (for years after its merger with the Union Pacific) to support the proud claim that Hastings had five railroads.

My memories of Hastings as a railroad town, however, are more of the sounds, the sights and the scents than of any statistics. They go back to the days of steam and crack passenger trains, days of reliance on railroads and a romance in their functioning that are hard to explain to a generation that didn't experience them.

In the early 1960s, when the first commercial jet

airliners started flying over my house on their way to landing at the Kansas City Municipal Airport, there was drama in each plane's approach. It was an event that reminded me of the arrival every evening in Hastings of Burlington Passenger Train No. 3 in the 1920s and early 1930s.

The time would be a few minutes after eight o'clock. On a still night the first signal would be a low hum or the unmistakable whistle blasts from a point three or four miles across the open farmland to the east. From an upstairs window on the east side of town one could see the headlight at about the time the first sounds came through. The hum would gradually become a roar, and the whistle notes would become louder, more frequent and, seemingly, more frantic.

At a point near the east city limits the engineer would let up on the throttle and the locomotive's thundering would give way to the clack and clatter of iron wheels on rail joints and the rattle of loose boards and metal shields at street crossings. Within five or six blocks of the track the ground sometimes seemed to tremble.

Listeners could tell the train was slowing down by the longer intervals between passage of each set of trucks over the heavy iron frogs where the Burlington crossed the Union Pacific. There was a series of squeaks as the brakes took their final grip on the wheels of as many as twenty mail cars, baggage cars, day coaches and sleepers. In a matter of five minutes the speeding monster of the open country had become a docile mass of some hundreds of tons—mainly steel—and there its lighted windows stretched for nearly a quarter of a mile.

The engine would pant impatiently and hiss a little while travelers from the east poured out of the three or four doors and a comparable number stood, bags and parcels in hand, ready to rush for the better empty seats. A switch engine would nudge up to the rear, a switchman would uncouple the train at the front of the diner. There would be a backward ride for Pullman passengers, then a move forward for the final uncoupling of the dining car on a sidetrack where it and its crew would wait (and sleep) until picked up by an early-morning eastbound train whose passengers would be expecting breakfast. For No. 3 there would be no meals between Hastings and Denver.

In a matter of minutes all new passengers would be in their seats, the mail and baggage cars would have traded their incoming cargoes for things going west. There would be a swinging of lanterns from the open doors, some quick, powerful puffs from the locomotive, and Hastings' most popular train would be on its way. The usual crowd of train watchers would disperse, some to walk to hotels, homes or rooming houses, some to get into parked cars. But they were by no means the only people in town who knew No. 3 had come and gone. The sounds of the straining locomotive, the ringing bell, the precise series of whistle blasts with which the engineer signaled departure—all these were notice to the community that the curtain was going down on another nightly show.

One reason why No. 3's daily visit was a big event was that it was a big train. The *Tribune* in the late 1920s ran a short feature story on it and its eastbound counterpart, No. 2, and referred to them as the longest passenger trains in the world. The claim probably originated with the Burlington, but the fact remains that the 20-plus cars of these trains were rarely matched by trains one saw on other lines, including the Union Pacific, with several "name" trains operating between Chicago and West Coast points.

The fact that people talked more about No. 3 than No. 2 can be explained by the fact that No. 3 had a schedule advantage. No. 2 came in at mid-morning when most people were at work. No. 3 came shortly after most families had completed dinner. It was a good time to be

Railroad Town

out driving, a good time for a brief stop at the station to watch the train come in. It was a good time to listen. There were relatively few autos on the streets between 8 and 9 P.M., very little noise of any kind to drown out the roar of No. 3's locomotive, the reverberation of its whistle and the worried warning of its bell. When No. 2 came in, cars and trucks were moving about, switch engines were puffing and whistling through both the Burlington and Union Pacific yards. It was hard to separate the sound of No. 2's arrival from the other railroad sounds.

No. 3's coming and going were part of the night sounds of a railroad town. These sounds are among my most distinct memories of Hastings. Trains could be annoying, of course, as were the long Union Pacific freights that passed within 100 feet of our back door for the eight months we lived on North Minnesota Avenue. Toiling locomotives shook the foundations, and the rumble and clack of the following string of 50 to 75 cars cut off all conversation in daytime and interrupted sleep at night.

But against such annoyances one had to weigh the full meaning of their sources. The sounds of the railroads were the sounds of a living community.

They took on a special meaning at night, as do the snores of a sleeping companion in a dark room. They came through the night air—the toots of whistles, the clanks of drawbars, the puffs, the hisses, the saucily ringing bell of a switch engine as it chugged from one end of the yards to the other. They spoke soothingly to the lonesome, the sleepless, the worried and the feverish. For a college student in the first throes of homesickness they were a reassuring reminder that the train that brought him was matched by one that ran in the opposite direction—just in case his new circumstances became unbearable.

My first view of Hastings was from a window of the two-coach passenger train that came in from Grand Island every morning about eight o'clock. I had spent most of the night on a larger Union Pacific train and three hours or so in the Grand Island station. For the next 16 years I would travel in and out by rail, and in 1940 my formal departure would be via the Burlington's Denver-Chicago Zephyr. Through the intervening years I would take the railroads of Hastings for granted. I would see and ride a lot of trains, hear the sounds and smell the fumes. I would see coal-burning locomotives supplanted by those whose boilers were fired with oil. I would watch the coming of diesel power and the streamlined passenger trains that were destined to become an endangered species before the original units had worn out.

In May of 1934 Hastings people forgot their worries about unseasonal heat and dying wheat crops to line the tracks and see one of the first Burlington Zephyrs on a test run between Denver and Chicago. There were guards at all the crossings, in the open country as well as in town, and speeds of up to 100 miles an hour were scheduled for straight stretches. The run was made with an average speed of 77.46 miles an hour for the 13-hour trip.

I rode one of those early Zephyrs to Chicago and back later that summer, and in the fall of 1935 I was aboard a similar train that attained a speed of 122 miles an hour between McCook and Oxford. On this occasion the Burlington was demonstrating to newsmen and others the stability of some 50 miles of track that had been completely rebuilt following the Republican River flood of the preceding summer.

The first Zephyrs were small unified trains with no sleeping cars. They were followed on the Chicago-Denver line by longer full-service trains, the Denver Zephyr and, later, the California Zephyr. Alex Barket, Kansas City contractor and banker, bought one of these trains intact after it was retired from service in the 1960s. It stood for several years at the Kansas City Union Station and was used now and then for short promotional excursions

Railroad Town 17

around the city. Still sleek and sturdy, it was an interesting illustration of an institution that had grown obsolete while fully functional. Ultimately, it went back into service—in Saudi Arabia.

The coming of the Zephyrs and other diesel-powered trains changed the sounds of the railroads. On many lines there was a deliberate policy of altering the original air horns to make them emulate the sounds of steam whistles. The Burlington chose to leave the Zephyrs with a sound that resembled a high-pitched steamship horn. This was distinctly the sound of the Zephyrs during my years at Hastings. Arriving after 10 P.M., the eastbound Zephyr replaced No. 3, more or less, as a public attention-getter. The westbound train arrived between 3 and 4 A.M., and its coming and going were noted mainly by light sleepers, insomniacs and night-shift workers.

There was still talk in Nebraska during my years there of the days when the Burlington and the Union Pacific conducted a sort of phantom government. The stories varied, but in their most simplified form they made the Platte River the dividing line between the political domains of the two railroads, with the Union Pacific dictating certain decisions affecting the state north of the river and the Burlington in command of what took place south of the river.

Charles H. Dietrich, it was said, became a United States senator as the designee of the Burlington. He was elected governor in 1900 and had barely taken office when the legislature got into a protracted hassle over the election of someone to a Senate seat that was left open by the death of M. L. Hayward of Nebraska City.

D. E. Thompson, a Lincoln millionaire and superintendent of Burlington lines west of the Missouri, sought the appointment. He was bitterly opposed by the Lincoln *Journal.* Finally, after two months, the deadlock was broken when Thompson stepped aside in favor of Dietrich as a compromise candidate. Dr. James C. Olson, in his *History of Nebraska,* cites this case as one that helped convince the state that the popular election of senators would be an improvement over the system of leaving the choice to the legislature.

Dietrich, a Hastings banker, had been pushed for the governorship by Adam Breede and others at Hastings. There was strong evidence certainly that the push into the Senate was largely provided by Burlington interests after they gave up on Thompson. And in the spirit of the times, why not? Wasn't Hastings the second most important point on the Burlington lines south of the Platte?

More consistent by far than their influence on politics was the influence of the railroads in establishing the patterns of economic and social movement. Trains fanned out from Hastings in every direction on daily schedules (some didn't run on Sundays). The ultimate destinations included the terminal points of branch lines and such places as McCook, Red Cloud, Lincoln, Aurora, Grand Island and Kearney, where connections were made with other trains. Hastings, through its rail services, had close ties with communities all across southern and western Nebraska and sizable areas in Colorado and Kansas.

Everything moved with the railroads—people, goods, ideas and the humorous and bawdy anecdotes that sprang up around presidents, governors, show people and other public figures. Building materials, food staples, home furnishings, shoes, dry goods, newspapers, magazines, bank drafts and packets of currency rode the trains. So did the salesmen, or drummers, some of whom guarded their stocks of the aforementioned stories as jealously as they guarded their bulky sample cases.

With reliable rail service to literally hundreds of small towns where the ultimate purveyor of most necessities was an independent retailer with no commitments to anything resembling the chains and central buying agencies of later years, Hastings was an ideal location for a wide variety of wholesale institutions. Some were locally owned; others were branches of national or regional operations. Such places in Hastings received goods by the carlot and dispensed in smaller shipments by rail and, eventually, by truck.

It was only natural that a city where wholesaling thrived would attract the interest of certain manufacturers. Hastings clay was good for brick making and the products of two manufacturers accounted for a lot of railroad tonnage for several decades. The J. H. Haney Company, manufacturer of horse collars and harness in the beginning, was the predecessor of W. M. Dutton and Sons Company, which became an important hardware wholesaler by the 1920s. As horses gave way to automobiles, the company became a distributor of automotive supplies and for a number of years it manufactured one of Hastings' better known products, the Rose tire pump. New products came with new times, and the company name became Dutton-Lainson.

Railroads that gave much to a city such as Hastings also could sometimes take away. They did that more or less in the case of the Perkins Products Company.

What happened with Perkins is one of the most intriguing might-have-been stories of Hastings industry. Under the leadership and creative genius of E. E. Perkins this company started in Hastings in 1920 as a small-scale producer of spices, flavorings, liniments, toilet preparations and the like. A concoction for curing the tobacco habit was a big seller for a time. In the late 1920s Perkins came up with a powdered soft drink and called it Kool-Aid. This, as much as any single thing in the history of the city, is Hastings' contribution to the list of American trade names (Kleenex, Kodak, Stetson, Levi, etc.) that have attained generic status.

Kool-Aid was off to a flying start before the 1929

market crash, and it gained momentum right through the Depression years. In 1931, with the product well on its way to a place in the stores of every city and hamlet across the country, the Perkins accountants came up with a finding that railroad freight rates, especially on the main ingredient, sugar, were an important factor in the economics of making and selling Kool-Aid. And so the company moved to Chicago because of rate advantages open to it from that city as a central manufacturing and distributing point. Or so the Chamber of Commerce always explained.

Hastings boosters lamented this loss for years. There was eventually a measure of compensation in a series of generous gifts by the Perkins family to Hastings College.

Hastings' role as supplier of goods and services to the businesses of smaller towns made for close personal ties. Bankers, merchants and other business leaders of the nearer of these towns read the Hastings *Daily Tribune*.

Railroad Town

Many came to Hastings for the affairs of the Scottish Rite and Shrine bodies whose memberships extended over much of western Nebraska. It was not uncommon in the 1920s to read or hear about groups of women who had come by train from such places as Alma, Holdrege, Edgar or Oxford to shop at Hastings stores. Hastings lawyers traveled by train to attend court sessions in county seats throughout the western part of the state. Patients came by train to consult physicians and dentists or to undergo treatment in the Mary Lanning Memorial Hospital.

One of the most distinctive of the many railroad-related businesses in Hastings was for more than a score of years the shipment of live chickens. Prosaic as it may sound, it had romantic and glamorous aspects that helped fix it into the folklore of the community.

From the turn of the century until after World War II the farms of Nebraska and other Cornbelt states were a prime source of poultry products marketed in the nation's

major population centers. For many years chickens went to market on the claw, so to speak. Millions of them, collected by the Hastings Poultry Company, were loaded into specially built cars and shipped live to New York, Philadelphia, San Francisco and other cities.

Each car included a compact room near the center doors where an attendant could prepare meals and sleep for the period of several days he was on the road. These attendants fed and watered the chickens and saw to the final acceptance by a purchaser in the city of destination. For literally hundreds of men with limited education and modest resources a job as a "chicken runner" opened doors to an outside world that few men in similar circumstances ever saw. They attended baseball games in New York, and one of them, John "Rowdy" Hopp, came home with stories that may have helped inspire a son, John "Cotney" Hopp, to follow a career that took him to the major leagues.

Some of these chicken runners discovered during the Prohibition era that they could buy in New York or San Francisco what passed as "good stuff" in the illicit liquor trade. As the years went by and they became more talkative about their chicken running years, they told of working their way to the rear of the passenger train on their return to Hastings and of special arrangements for someone to be waiting in the shadows to help with suitcases loaded with their bottled products.

J. T. Oder, owner of the Hastings Poultry Company, had worked for Swift and Company before coming to Hastings in 1909. As his business grew and prospered he became known as the largest independent poultry dealer in the United States. Besides the headquarters at Hastings, there were concentration and shipping facilities at Julesburg, Colorado; Missouri Valley, Iowa; and North Platte and Loup City in Nebraska. He bought from other dealers at many other places.

Railroad Town

Reminiscing about the business in 1978, one of J. T. Oder's sons, A. Dale Oder of New York City, said that the number of carloads shipped from Hastings may have ranged as high as ten a week. Dale recalled that his father had an interest in a poultry company in San Francisco and that some of the best chickens were selected for the one to two carloads a week that went there. He said that while his father's facilities in Hastings were on Burlington trackage, he was always friendly to the Union Pacific and seemed to favor that line when there was a choice.

The end of the live chicken shipping business in Hastings was heralded in the mid-twenties when Swift and Company announced plans to build a dressing plant on the site of a one-time ballpark just west of the downtown business district. Swift and other major companies literally dotted the Midwest with plants of this kind. While these regional plants seemed to provide a protective efficiency for the chicken business that had been a sideline of grain farmers of the Midwest, they didn't save it from a new force that was taking root in other parts of the country. Before these regional dressing plants were 25 years old they became obsolete in the face of a steady shift of poultry production from the Midwest to Georgia, Alabama, Mississippi, Arkansas and other southern states and, in the case of eggs particularly, to huge production facilities near population centers on both the East and West Coasts. What had been a sideline for farmers in Nebraska and neighboring states became an industry for big integrated corporations in other parts of the country. And all this took place before men with vivid memories of their chicken-running days were barely beyond upper middle age.

Railroads influenced the decisions of uncounted individuals and families to abandon smaller communities and live in Hastings. Farm boys and girls watched the trains go by and built up their dreams of the towns and cities from which the trains came and went. For rural boys there was a natural yearning to sit someday as the man at the throttle or to hang from the rear of a caboose and wave instructions to the front-end crew.

One little town on the Union Pacific, Hanover, Kansas, seemed to have been at one time the home of an unusually large number of Hastings people. One of them was D. G. Neuman, for several years a member of the staff of the Chamber of Commerce. His explanation was that the Union Pacific was an important part of life around Hanover. It was near the point where trains moved up a steep grade on the eastward pull out of the valley of the Little Blue. A pusher engine had been stationed at Hanover for a time, and the very presence of a sort of hometown locomotive added to the glory of railroading in those parts. Some Hanover boys became trainmen. Neuman, a bookkeeper by training, worked for years as a Union Pacific rate clerk. He joined the Chamber of Commerce staff in the early 1930s as a sort of watchdog over freight rates. Local industry was ever alert to the possibility it might be the victim of a rate change that would be adverse to its interests and the interests of Hastings as a manufacturing and distribution point.

Twice during my four years in college I returned to Hastings from Sterling in the caboose of a freight train. Father, always interested in helping any of us to save a few dollars and involved at that time in the buying and selling of livestock, had arranged in each instance to ship a carload of cattle to Omaha at the time I would be traveling in that direction. (The railroads provided for one person to accompany a load of livestock to market. A shipper of two or more loads was entitled to a return ticket.) I really didn't get to Omaha with either carload. On the first occasion we shipped over the Burlington, by way of Brush. We pulled out of Sterling in the early evening, spent a couple of hours in Brush and a couple in

Railroad Town 25

McCook and got to Hastings in the late afternoon of the next day. The second trip was by Union Pacific. I left the train at Grand Island—without even saying goodbye to my cattle—and took a bus to Hastings.

In the fall of my freshman year in college the Hastings football team played Doane at Crete on a Saturday afternoon. Enough students and townspeople were interested in seeing the game to induce the Burlington to take team and fans to Crete and back on a special train—two coaches, a baggage unit and a steam locomotive, as I recall. Once, in the early 1930s, the North Western took the team, the band and fans to Fremont for a game with Midland College. A special train took a couple of hundred persons from the Holdrege-Minden-Hastings area to Lincoln once in connection with some Tri-County project promotion. After construction was started on the Kingsley Dam (Tri-County), a train of at least six coaches took interested persons from Hastings to Ogallala one summer day via the Union Pacific.

Railroads remained important to Hastings through the years of great change following World War II. The service, however, underwent drastic revisions. Passenger service dwindled down to a single Amtrak train each way daily on Burlington Northern tracks. During the writing of this book I spent a number of nights at the Clarke Hotel, still sturdy and well kept after more than 65 years. The night sounds were still there, but different in several respects, including the tones of the whistles. What may have impressed me as much as anything about railroad life in the late 1970s was the number of freight train crews who were sleeping, as I was, in the city's biggest hotel. Most of them were assigned to the unit coal trains that were moving west through Hastings and McCook after dumping their loads from Wyoming at power plants in Kansas City and points south and east of there. In the old days train crews never stayed in the big hotels.

3. College Days

Golden in a Sense, But Not Exactly Glittering

It was about 9 A.M. on September 10, 1924, when I got off the St. Joseph and Grand Island train at Hastings. I still wonder how I could have spent most of the next 16 years at a place where the impressions of that first day were as consistently discouraging as mine were.

Dry, hot weather had plagued the region for weeks. The corn I saw from the train on the final run into Hastings was stunted and brown. In town the lawns were parched, and the gutters had collected little drifts of withered leaves as they floated down from trees that had lost all love of summer.

In Colorado the night before there had been a feel of fall in the air. By mid-morning of that first day in central Nebraska the temperature was moving into the eighties, and the higher humidity at the lower altitude was an unfamiliar depressant. I was physically tired from an almost sleepless night on a day coach and badly worn mentally and spiritually from wrestling with the anxieties over this major move of my life, the first one that was largely of my own choosing.

I had come to Hastings to attend college. It was to be a new experience, not just for me, but for my whole family. I was committing four full years to education beyond high school. I had to look to the levels of second and third cousins on either side of my family to find anyone who had done that. There was no push or inspiration, certainly, from the thought that mine might be the role of a pioneer. I was plainly unsure of myself and worried.

I thought of those four long years ahead of me as the train squeaked to a stop. What I had seen of the city hadn't impressed me. What I would see of the little college would not undo, in that first day, any of the haunting misgivings.

I was spared being completely alone on the final leg of my journey by a chance conversation with a young fellow who changed trains with me at Grand Island. He, too, was on his way to enroll as a freshman at Hastings College. His parents lived at Venango, Nebraska, and he had boarded the train at Julesburg. He had been at Hastings during the previous year, living with two sisters and attending high school. His name was Don Broughton, and for the next three years I would know him as classmate, football player and part-time member of the Hastings police force. Eventually he would qualify as an Army Air Force cadet, go through training in Texas and, in due time, become a commercial pilot for United Airlines. He came to an untimely death in the crash of a private training plane at Salt Lake City.

Don and I walked from the railroad station to the Alcott School, where one of his sisters was a teacher. After his brief visit with her, he directed me to the college campus and went his way.

The college, on first view, along with just about everything else on that hot, windy day, fell short of my expectations. Four modest buildings dominated the campus. Three of these, with considerable open space between them, were in a line on the east side of what amounted to an extension of Elm Avenue through the heart of the campus. From north to south, they were McCormick Hall, Ringland Hall and the Carnegie Science and Library Building. Looking south on the same open space that these buildings faced from the east was

Alexander Hall. Among the less prominent structures was an all-wood gymnasium that would burn during the coming year and, southwest of Alexander Hall, the basement portion of a projected women's dormitory, Taylor Hall. This had been roofed over and would be for many years the college dining center.

Founders of the college had included men and women with the powerful propensity for tree planting that had become a Nebraska tradition, and by 1924 the open sections of the campus included sizable elms and other varieties. But even with its trees, the campus failed to fit any ideas I had of either a physical or academic oasis on that hot September day.

Within a matter of thirty minutes I had registered for 16 hours of ancient history, English, mathematics and Spanish and was $200 poorer after writing checks to cover a semester's tuition ($40), a semester's meals at the dining hall and some minor fees. I had been guided through the registration process by the dean of the college, Frank E. Weyer, and had yielded meekly to his every recommendation. The dormitory spaces for some 30 men in Ringland Hall long since had been filled, he told me, but there would be plenty of rooms in homes near the campus. Within an hour I had found a room to my liking at the home of Dr. and Mrs. E. A. Thomas, on the corner of East Seventh and Ash Avenue. (Dr. Thomas, a dentist, conducted some night classes in biology at the college.) I paid the full $15 for one month's rent, but by mid-afternoon I had agreed to share the room with Howard Kelso, a junior from Unadilla, who had accosted me on the campus after learning from Mrs. Thomas that I might welcome a roommate.

At some point in the middle part of the day I started for the railroad station to claim my luggage. I was saved about four blocks of walking when a tall, thin and stern-visaged man stopped his Model-T Ford at the edge

College Days 29

Hastings College in the 1920s

of the campus and offered me a ride. He introduced himself as Robert McDill, mathematics professor, and I explained I was registered for one of his classes in college algebra. From his house on East Seventh I walked to the station, arranged for a taxi to haul my luggage and rode out to my new quarters.

My memories of Hastings College cover events spread over four years, but the impressions of that first day form a kaleidoscopic pattern that has held together without loss of major detail. Faces I saw and voices I heard have stayed with me in hard line and clear tone. The flaw in my memory is the lack of any clear reason why I must have spent two hours or more visiting with other confused and uncertain freshmen around the front steps of the library. I have mental pictures of several groups and individuals, always with the steps or columns of the library in the background.

The only familiar face I would see all day showed up there. I remembered it as belonging to a fellow from Brush, Colorado, who had attended some kind of conference in Sterling during my junior year in high school. He had more or less dominated that conference with his quickness of opinion and ability to speak. His name was Harold Turpin, and I was to learn that he was back at Hastings for his sophomore year. Visiting with him on the library steps was a girl who attracted my attention to the extent I found out that she, too, was from Brush. Her name was Mabel Keplinger, and seven years from that week we would be married. Harold Turpin went into the Presbyterian ministry.

I recall seeing Eugene Staley as central figure in an animated discussion. Someone told me he was a senior but no older than the average freshman. He would earn a doctorate at the University of Chicago before his twenty-second birthday. His studies in international economics would crop up in comments on world events from the 1930s to the 1960s.

Many of the fellows I talked with referred to their jobs. Some would be waiters or dishwashers at the dining hall. Some would do janitorial work in the college buildings. Several had part-time jobs downtown, and Howard Kelso, my roommate, explained that he would spend several hours each night setting type at the *Tribune*.

I suddenly realized that checks written that first day used up half the money I had left in the bank at home. I wondered if I had made a mistake in not exploring the job situation more thoroughly. I soon learned that the market was limited, that most jobs downtown and on the campus had been arranged for months earlier. It came home to me, too, that there was a sort of seniority system in the allocation of campus jobs. Upperclassmen got first choice, and seniors could be expected to have worked their way into better jobs than sophomores should expect. Peeling potatoes at the dining hall would be my job as a senior, not for prestigious reasons, certainly, but because it took less time than did the jobs as waiters, dishwashers or janitors, and the pay was the same—three meals a day.

I went early that first night to the dining hall for the first of the meals I had paid for. There were only a few of us in the waiting room when a tall, strong-featured fellow wearing a denim apron came out of the kitchen for what appeared to be a sort of survey of what would be showing up for this first dinner of the semester. His name was Don Warner, someone explained. He had been a winner in the high hurdles as a freshman member of the track team the previous spring.

For some reason I took note of him, especially of his aloofness as he surveyed us huddled newcomers in the waiting room. He was getting set to take over the scraping table, where all the dirty dishes were dumped by the waiters as they cleared the dining room. His domineering manner, I would learn, was essential to survival in a job where one had to be always on guard against being buried in garbage and messy dishes. A year from that date I would take over from Warner and become for nine months the lord of the grapefruit rinds, the smeared plates and saucers and the squashed and oozing dishes of uneaten creamed dried beef and chocolate pudding.

At the Thomas house that night I got acquainted with the four students, besides Kelso and me, who would occupy three rented rooms on the second floor. Verne and Marion Young lived on a farm near Trumbull. Verne, a senior, had managed earlier in his college career to become the Hastings distribution agent for the Omaha *World-Herald*. He and Marion would get up every morning between 3:30 and 4 o'clock, ride their bicycles to the Burlington station and, with the help of Tony Consbruck, a halfback on the college football team, deliver several hundred copies of the paper.

In the third room were Fritz Poor and Guy Edmondson, both from Kenesaw. Fritz had come straight from a neighborhood threshing rig, and my first encounter with him was in his room as he shook new oats from the cuffs of his overalls. Verne Young, always quick with descriptions, definitions and opinions, had described Fritz as a sort of superstar of the previous year's football team. A latecomer to the sport, he had blossomed in his junior year into a phenomenal catcher of passes from Bobby Stephens, who was, in turn good enough to earn a letter as one of the quarterbacks on the University of Nebraska team in 1925. (He transferred to Nebraska after two years at Hastings.)

It was obvious after the first exchange of words with Fritz that it was easier to learn about him from Verne Young than to extract personal views in an informal conversation. He would go through his senior football season with a good record, but the team would not match the one of the previous year. He would be a forward and captain of the basketball team. After graduation he all but disappeared. The word was out that he had enrolled in medical school in the Boston area, but nobody seemed to know which school. There were reports that he would play some more football, despite the possibility his years at Hastings would make him ineligible under the rules of most collegiate sports organizations. There were reports also that he played professional football while in medical school, but when he showed up in Hastings in the middle 1930s in search of a place to open a medical practice, he was at his laconic and secretive best in responding to my questions as to whether he had furthered his athletic career in those years in the East. I am not sure that I extracted from him the name of the medical school from which he was graduated. It was generally agreed in sports circles at Hastings that most any university coach would have had to look hard in those days for anyone matching his talents as a catcher of passes.

The young men around me at the Thomas home seemed deadly serious about going to college, and the hard work and sacrifice did not deter them. Fritz Poor and the Young brothers cooked most of their meals in their rooms. They brought milk, butter, eggs and other food from their farm homes. Howard Kelso, whose father was minister of a small Presbyterian church at Unadilla, seemed strictly on his own. He took most of his meals at downtown restaurants and probably paid his tuition in installments. Howard took his degree in 1926, and I heard very little from him until he showed up in Hastings in the mid-1930s on a vacation from his job as typesetter for the *New York Times*. I would lose track of him again until after he retired from the *Rocky Mountain News* in Denver. Verne Young went into teaching and held important administrative posts in Iowa. Marion took over the *World-Herald* distributorship and carried on for several years. Clyde Edmondson dropped out that first year.

In renting a large portion of their home to college students, Dr. and Mrs. Thomas were doing what scores of families on the east side of Hastings did at that time. There were dormitory rooms for some 30 men on the campus and about twice that number for women. The rest of the out-of-town students lived in private homes. Some did light housekeeping, as the Youngs and Fritz Poor did at the Thomas home. Many took their meals at the college dining hall, and some took meals in the homes where they lived or in one of the boarding houses of the neighborhood.

Contrary to practices that eventually would be a standard part of administering colleges and universities, the practice at Hastings in 1924 was to limit the college's involvement in student housing to a sort of advisory role.

In this role the college did on rare occasions give a sort of blacklist status to some places that offered housing. To the best of my recollection the administrators were more concerned with protecting students from temptations of the flesh than from exposure to the physical austerity of some rooms that were offered at bargain rates.

Hastings College in the mid-1920s was one of literally scores of little church-related colleges across the country that were on the borderline of survival. Two such institutions in Nebraska—Grand Island (Baptist) and Cotner (Disciples of Christ)—would close within the four years I was at Hastings.

Calvin H. French, the president, spent a lot of time in travel to eastern cities in search of funds. His white hair and mustache signaled the fact that he was past middle age. His experience as president of two other colleges, Rollins (Florida) and Huron (South Dakota), and as associate secretary of the Presbyterian General Board of Education, stood him in good stead as he made the rounds of individuals, foundations and trusts that might contribute to a modest little college in Nebraska. His major accomplishment during my four years in college was completion of a campaign to add $470,000 to the college endowment fund.

Returning from one of his solicitation journeys, he usually made a brief report at the daily chapel period. He referred in casual ways to having stayed at YMCA dormitories while on visits to Pittsburgh, Philadelphia and other cities. He rode the trains, of course, and usually chose a day coach when it meant saving a few dollars. His navy blue suits often reflected hard wear, but his appearance always was that of poise and dignity. More than anything else, he was gracious and considerate, a Christian gentleman in the full sense of that term. When he presided over the chapel service we sang his favorite hymn, "Lead On, O King Eternal."

Vice-president of the college was Donald D. MacKay, professor of philosophy and psychology and a veteran of teaching and administrative responsibilities in other small colleges. He filled in for Dr. French during the latter's frequent absences, but he seemed not disposed to exercise authority beyond the routine requirement of a given situation. This modest stance was in some ways a contradiction, because he was a proud man—proud of his Scottish ancestry, proud of his Presbyterianism, proud of his advanced degrees. If he had any feelings about his shortness of stature, he kept them to himself. He stood erect, walked erect, urged members of his classes to do likewise. His suits were carefully tailored to his protuberant midsection, and once when he advised students to think positively, throw out their chests and face the world, his demonstrating gesture popped a vest button.

There were some who questioned his use of William James' *The Principles of Psychology* as the basic text in his beginning course. The book had been published in the 1890s, and new texts had replaced it on many campuses. When we got to James' chapter on habit, Dr. MacKay assured us it would explain the behavior of many people we would come in contact with. For me it has, and for me the course was worth the time I spent reading James and listening to a plump little man who believed in walking tall and talking tall.

Frank E. Weyer, the dean, was the managing officer of the college in the eyes of most students. He was beyond question the watchdog over student conduct, which by the standards of a later day was strictly limited. No smoking on the campus, no dancing (by out-of-town students), no drinking, of course, but that was a lesser problem. The local and state laws of the prohibition era were pretty well respected by the kinds of young people who attended Hastings. At each Tuesday chapel session the dean's office distributed cards on which students were expected to report their church attendance of the previous Sunday.

Dean Weyer, a graduate of the college, had spent a few years in public school work. He taught courses through which students qualified to teach in secondary schools and was without question responsible for the decisions of a high percentage of students to prepare themselves for teaching. As a strong advocate of teaching as a career, he had on his side the trends of the times. New high school buildings had sprung up all over the rural Midwest during World War I and afterward. Rural school districts had been consolidated to make some of these high schools possible, and farm boys and girls who would not have attended high schools if they had been born a generation earlier were swelling attendance, playing on the basketball teams and making the schools important centers of activity in hundreds of communities throughout Nebraska and neighboring states.

The surge of interest in high school education was interlocked, more or less, with a trend toward college attendance by a rising percentage of the population. Many of us at Hastings in the mid-1920s were among the first in our families to grace the halls of a college or university. Some of us could not claim parents who had earned high school diplomas. The companion increases in both college and high school attendance fed each other. With me on the campus at Hastings were numerous graduates of new high schools who would go back to become teachers, coaches, principals or superintendents in the burgeoning systems from which they had come.

I was troubled during my first days at Hastings by the fact that my new surroundings, while formally exemplifying an upward step on the educational ladder, did not reflect a comparable advance in physical trappings. The two principal classroom buildings—Ringland and McCormick Halls—were older by many years than the high school building I had left a few months back. The total floor space in all buildings where teaching took place at Hastings was about the same as that of my high school. Total enrollment that freshman year would be lower than the total of the four classes in my senior year of high school. The total number of faculty members was about the same.

I had left high school with a distinct interest in history, English and Spanish. I was vaguely committed to pursue all three in college, but my first choice was history. My enthusiasm for majoring in history was dimmed by my early encounters with the head of the history department, Horace M. Cunningham, under whom I studied that first year. By the end of the first semester I had lost interest in history as a major study. I was uncomfortable in Cunningham's classes, and the best explanation I have after some 50 years is that he was a very insecure person who resorted to bombast and exhibitionism out of sheer fear he could not build or sustain a reputation by more conventional means. He knew his field, but his classes were better known for his histrionics than his history.

My freshman English teacher, Elizabeth Bowen, was on a par with the best English teachers I had in high school. Clara Altman, my Spanish teacher, was a change—something of a relief—from Dr. Camille Werling at Sterling High School. But in her second-year Spanish class I found myself well ahead of those who had had only one year of college Spanish. Miss Altman taught college Spanish with some of the popularizing techniques of a high school teacher, whereas Werling had taught high school Spanish with the exacting demands of a traditional college instructor.

Ultimately, I decided upon English as my major and Spanish as my first minor. The momentum of my two years of Spanish study in high school along with some practical use of the language while working with Mexicans during the summers, enabled me to build up my Spanish credits with a minimum of effort. Looking back on my good grades in Spanish, I feel a slight tinge of guilt for having taken full advantage of Clara Altman's persistent efforts to make fun and games a part of the study of Spanish. We learned to sing in Spanish, and eventually our class was sounding off with Miss Altman's translations of the college fight songs and a popular air or two.

The student body of my freshman year numbered about 360. It would be considerably beyond 400 by my senior year. Where did these students come from? Between 25 and 30 percent gave Hastings as their home address. Most of these had graduated from Hastings High School. But there were a few each year whose families had moved to Hastings at or about the time the oldest child was ready for college. Except for the Hastings contingent, the student body came mainly from the farms and small towns of Nebraska. There was practically no representation of Omaha or Lincoln. There was a notable number of sons and daughters of Presbyterian clergymen, including several from outside Nebraska. They were attracted to Hastings, in part at least, by a college policy of charging only half the normal tuition rate to children of ministers and missionaries. Presbyterian missionaries were responsible for the presence of a scattering of students from Korea and at least one, as I recall, from Puerto Rico.

There were some students for whom the choice of a college had not been dictated by lack of money to attend a larger or more prestigious school. Some of these lived in Hastings, sons and daughters of doctors, lawyers and established business leaders. They stayed in Hastings for convenience or out of sheer preference for the modest approach to higher education that Hastings College represented. There were some from families of means outside Hastings whose parents had insisted on their being at Hastings. In certain cases one could speculate on the possibility the parents saw need for close personal contact with instructors—for academic reasons—or the likelihood that Hastings would afford fewer off-campus distractions and more supervision of personal conduct than, say, the University of Nebraska at Lincoln.

The number of automobiles on the campus was never enough to suggest that the time had come for parking spaces in the quantities most campuses would be thinking about 15 years later. Students living in Hastings sometimes drove their family cars to classes. No more than five out-of-town students had automobiles at any given time in my four years. Mrs. Ida Capps, librarian in my freshman year, sometimes came to the campus in her electric car.

From the foregoing one can hardly draw a picture of the student body of the 1920s that would be different in outward characteristics from what would have been found on many Midwestern campuses. We were products of our time and our predominantly rural surroundings. There was an atmosphere of modesty—and maybe insecurity—on the part of students who, in the main, were hesitant to proclaim ambitions beyond the normal promises of heredity. The spirit of the country bumpkin ran deep in some of us, and we took delight in cracking wise about bird watchers, artists, musicians and most anyone else whose cultural and esthetic aspirations seemed to look beyond the levels of the communities that had spawned us. But along with the many outward shows of crudity, vulgarity and irreverence there were outcroppings of sensitivity, respect for learning and for the religious formalities that were imposed by the college. As I look back on some of this behavior I have to concede that we tended to fall into postures of ambivalence or equivocation as a cover of our uncertainties as to where we were and where we were headed.

In my sophomore year the college employed a new

business manager, J. Edwin Pasek, who had been a student at Huron College when Dr. French was president there. He moved into the financial problems of the college with a brusque efficiency that was as offensive as it was startling to many students who were struggling to meet their financial obligations. Somewhere along the line a sort of whispering campaign against Pasek reached the point a student committee was named to carry complaints to the board of trustees. I was a member of the committee. The only others whose names I recall were Laurens Williams of Gothenburg and Charles Osborne of Bayard. The latter had to deal with the delicate fact he was a nephew of A. H. Jones, chairman of the college board of trustees.

We chose Williams as our spokesman, and his presentation to the executive committee of the trustees forced on all of us a realization that he was not fooling when he voiced hope he might someday be a trial lawyer. He described in general but graphic terms the complaints against a man who was being called a Shylock. Then he went specific, detailing the experiences of Reuben Zieg, a tall, rugged fellow from York County who apparently had failed to make certain payments on time. None of the rest of us had seen serious reasons to pity Reuben, but our indifference was pricked by Williams' recital of the "sad case of a poor Russian boy" who had come up short of as much money as the college's financial spokesman was demanding. There was pathos in the appeal, and drama. Trustee Neil Dunn, president of the First National Bank of Hastings, seemed more entranced by Williams' oratory than by the case against J. Edwin Pasek. The crowning incident in a campaign that stretched over more than a year was the removal of a large frame outhouse from Heartwell Park one night in April of 1927 to a spot in front of the administration building, where it was properly designated with signs and banners as "Joe's Palace." (A part of the anti-Pasek campaign had been a popularization of his first name. He no longer was J. Edwin in student circles. Just plain Joe, or "Bohemian Joe.")

I doubt that anyone ever told Reuben Zieg just how sad his case had sounded in the hearing room. He might not have liked the manner in which he was thrust into the role of martyr. By the time school opened the next September, it was generally known that J. Edwin was in his last year. But there was a new instructor on the campus by that time who managed to offend some of the students who had been active in the campaign to discredit Pasek. This time there was direct action. The offensive one was seized on his way home from a movie one night and deprived of half of his mustache as he lay wriggling under a blanket in an alley a few blocks from the campus. Justice came quickly in this case, but not to the satisfaction of the instructor.

I couldn't help thinking of these uprisings against authority as I observed during the 1960s the various expressions of unrest on campuses all across the country. And I couldn't help reminding my friends that two of the individuals engaged in the waylaying of the teacher with the mustache eventually became trustees of the college. As a senior with a variety of campus responsibilities and a feeling that physical assault was a bit beyond what the rather vague charges against the man could justify, I refused to join in the action. It could have been said, nevertheless, that the dormitory room I shared with Paul Stuckey was a sort of communications center or command post for what went on that night. One of the more amazing aspects of the incident was that Dean Weyer, knowing pretty well where this kind of student intrigue centered, called in two students the next day and had their confessions in a matter of minutes. The professor, for reasons that nobody seemed to want to discuss, was the only one who paid a price. He was summarily dismissed. Dean Weyer arranged for him to be paid for the spectacles that he lost in his encounter.

I detail the foregoing incidents to make sure that my narrative does not gloss over what some might look upon as rather crude and primitive digressions from our pursuit of the liberal arts. But having mentioned them, I suggest that they symbolize something basic in our educational experiences. In the substance of these actions there was recognition of the fact that in a fair and wholesome society the concerns of the few often should become the concerns of the many. It can be argued certainly that our collisions with authority were true-life exercises on a campus small enough to constitute a laboratory for on-the-job study of a vast range of human relationships. Nobody thought of it that way at the time, I am certain, but I have had occasion to think of it that way many times in recent years.

Our student body came together without benefit of the sifting and sorting that were standard with larger and better known institutions or with the fraternities and sororities that were supposed to provide group-living experiences on larger campuses. Financial barriers to enrollment were all but non-existent, despite the vigilance of J. Edwin Pasek as guardian of the college's accounts. Few ever were denied admittance for sheer lack of a credit or two or for low grade marks on the credits submitted. Some who came without credentials earned in high school could enroll in the so-called academy and take whatever high-school-level work was required and be enrolled in some college classes at the same time.

There was an inescapable mixture of the bright with the dull, and I have had reason over the years to conclude that this was sometimes more of a break for the bright than the dull. The lazy mingled with the ambitious and seemed at times to gain inspiration therefrom. The poor and the hard-pressed rubbed shoulders with the few from affluent homes, and the results often benefited both. One's daily associations on the campus most certainly did not insulate one from the realities of the broad social and economic spectra that would be encountered in the world for which we were preparing ourselves.

Higher education of the kind offered by a struggling little church-related college has been both touted and derided. While Hastings was short of many things from which I might have benefited, I must say that it offered opportunities that would have been denied many of my generation if such institutions had not existed.

Going to college at Hastings in the 1920s was for most of us more of an experiment or adventure than it would be for succeeding generations there or in other American institutions of higher learning. We were carried along by individual will and personal choice more than by convention or tradition. We were front-runners without a spirit of rebellion or a stomach for upsetting the system. Considering our general acceptance of the moral, social and political standards of the time and of our upbringing, I find it hard to illustrate that ours was the spirit of the pioneer, the visionary or the romanticist. But to some extent it probably was. We liked what we saw of the rewards of hard work and hard study and what came with the attainment of some degree of leadership in the white-collar society that seemed to be waiting for us.

We were in tune with Victor Herbert, Sigmund Romberg, Jerome Kern and Irving Berlin. We didn't talk much about such things, but we liked the way the skilled baritone in the company that brought *The Student Prince* to Hastings told us that ours were the "golden days in the sunshine of our happy youth." The second-hand phonograph that some of us installed in the third floor of Ringland in 1927 rang out through the early evening with such songs as "What'll I Do?," "Always," "Remember," and "Look for the Silver Lining."

We took Calvin Coolidge for granted and heard no challenge of his declaration in 1925 that the "business of America" was business. We thought we were preparing ourselves for true-to-life experiences, but we anticipated nothing like the stock market crash of 1929 and the shock, the cynicism and the despair that followed. Things were happening in Berlin, Moscow, Tokyo and other far-away places that would lead to events that would dominate our thoughts and actions through the prime middle years of our lives, but they provoked no forebodings that I can recall. We were still to learn that history does not prepare us for all the surprises.

One thing about our generation of Hastings graduates is that we went forth with little to sell beyond ourselves. There were only a few hundred degree-holding alumni in the whole world. Many of these were still in Nebraska, but the rest were widely dispersed. We heard much in our student days of the alumnus who had become president of the University of Colorado and the one who was a member of the Interstate Commerce Commission. There was mention now and then of two mathematics professors, a pastor of a large church in Seattle and the president of a bank in Spokane. These few scattered reputations were hardly enough to justify for us what a graduate of an Ivy League college did at about the time of our graduation. He armed himself with a neat packet of personal cards that listed his name, his college and his year of graduation. What else did people need to know? For those of us who went into the world from Hastings College in the 1920s there was little thought we might establish who we were by explaining where we had been.

Where did we go and what did we do? I have mentioned already the directions some took after leaving college. A complete survey would be a sociological study far beyond the scope of these pages. But an answer in sample, if not in detail, seems in order, even though it must come from my

College Days

memory, a few clippings and letters and such publications as the 1925-28 editions of the college yearbook, class reunion memos and recent issues of *Who's Who in America*.

The president of the senior class of 1925 was Beth Newell, daughter of a physician at Alexandria, Nebraska. Majoring in economics, but interested also in literary studies and history, she was one of the prettiest and most personable women on the campus. She would remain in Hastings, marry Archie D. Marvel, raise a family, take part in a wide range of community affairs, attain a sort of professional status as a reviewer of books and eventually be elected national president of the Young Women's Christian Association. After the death of her first husband she would marry Lloyd J. Marti, also a Hastings graduate, and live in Lincoln. Few friendships have been more rewarding than has been ours of more than 50 years with this gracious, intelligent lady.

The president of the junior class was H. Vance Greenslit, son of a Burlington yard superintendent at Hastings. Handsome, athletic, a capable singer, dramatist and debater, he was president of the student association as well as his class and captain of the track team. After graduation from the college of law at the University of Nebraska he would become a claims attorney for a budding bus line. Eventually his company was merged into the Greyhound system, and he closed his business career in Chicago as president of Greyhound Lines. While living in New Orleans, he instituted legal proceedings and cleared the name of an ancestor who had been found guilty in one of the notorious witchcraft trials of Massachusetts Colony in the seventeenth century. He may have got more national news coverage from this than from his considerable success in the bus industry.

Checking the 1925 *Bronco* with the 1968-69 issue of *Who's Who in America,* I found that these senior and junior class presidents of 1924-25, plus at least one other person from each class, were among the 66,000 listings. The others were Eugene Staley, with the Stanford International Development Educational Center, Palo Alto, California, and Eugene Perry, chemical engineer and industrialist, Wilmington, Delaware. Recognition by *Who's Who* is by no means the only measure of achievement in America, but the presence of these four out of roughly 100 members of those classes seems worth noting.

The president of the sophomore class in 1924-25 was Fred Kuykendall of Nunn, Colorado. He taught at Leadville and Eaton in his home state, but in due time he entered the school of medicine of the University of Colorado. He practiced at Eaton for a number of years and closed out his career as staff doctor in the student health service on the university campus at Boulder.

Freshman class president was Alden Berquist of Hastings. He transferred to the University of Nebraska after one year and went from there to the First National Bank of Chicago, from which he retired in 1971 as senior vice-president in charge of the bond department.

Captain of the football team in my freshman year was Carl Schneider of Plattsmouth. He returned to Plattsmouth after graduation, joined his father in the banking business and made that his career. George Armstrong of St. Paul, graduating with the same class, also went into banking and was president of the Overland National Bank of Grand Island when he died.

The football captain in my sophomore year was Wayne Binfield, whose home was on a farm in southern Hall County. He had no objective but to be a coach. His success in several western Nebraska high schools was such that an athletic facility at Scottsbluff bears his name. He came close to fame of a different sort in a game against Kearney. There was a fumble, and after a confusing series of grabs for the ball, Wayne came up with it and headed

College Days

for the goal. If Tony Consbruck, Hastings halfback, hadn't tackled him, he would have scored for the opponents, because he was running in the wrong direction. A University of California center (Binfield played center) did the same thing in a Rose Bowl game a few years after that. His name was Roy Riegels, and his wrong-way run became a legend.

The football captain in 1926 was Robert Latta, son of a Hastings physician. He taught and coached at Geneva and Beatrice, managed chambers of commerce at Beatrice and Casper, Wyoming, got into trade show promotion and management and was associated with the Chicago Amphitheater and McCormick Place (Chicago) before "retiring" to California, where he became involved again in show management.

The 1927 captain was Laurel Lewis, who, with a brother, Ancel, came from Osceola. He taught and coached at Butte, Nebraska, was superintendent of schools there for four years. He spent four years as an educational adviser with the Civilian Conservation Corps and four as an investigator with the U. S. Civil Service Commission. He was in the insurance business in Colorado when he died in 1965.

The 1928 captain following my graduation was Thurlo McCrady, one of the all-time great athletes of Hastings College. He coached at Superior and at Hastings College and was athletic director at South Dakota State and Kansas State before moving into professional sports, first as an executive with the American Football League and later with the American Basketball Association.

The first man I saw wearing one of the heavy red sweaters with the big block "H" of the championship football team of 1923 was Warren Steinbach of Hartington. He taught in the high school at Nelson, earned a doctorate and ultimately was on the chemistry faculties at the University of Arkansas and Miami University in

Florida. From teaching in high schools to graduate study, to university or college teaching or to administrative positions in the educational field went a sizable number of students of that period.

George Bruntz, class of 1925, taught in California schools to begin with, but ended his career on the faculty of San Jose State with several books to his credit.

Herbert Wood, 1927, taught first in private schools in Hawaii and China; came back to the United States and earned a doctorate at Wisconsin. He was on the faculty of MacAlester College for a time and then went to Washington State, where he taught history and held the title of acting vice-president for one year and acting dean of social sciences and humanities for another.

Kenneth Browne, president of my class in our sophomore year, taught in Nebraska schools, earned degrees at Stanford and the University of Pennsylvania and served deanships at Doane College, Illinois Wesleyan, Wayne State in Nebraska and Towson State in Maryland.

Ralph Becker of Glenvil, another member of my class and a three-letter man in sports, taught and coached at Curtis, did advanced study at Columbia University and eventually became superintendent of schools at Evansville, Indiana. He wound up his career with the Department of Health, Education and Welfare in Washington.

Lyle Ashby of Guide Rock and Hastings and a member of the class of 1927 taught briefly at Kearney and joined the staff of the National Education Association in Washington. He retired as deputy executive secretary of that agency with a doctorate earned as he went along.

Grant Koontz of Fairbury, class of 1927, skipped the high school teaching and started immediately toward earning advanced degrees—a master's from the University of Nebraska and a doctorate from Yale. He was on the team of scientists assembled at the University of Chicago early in World War II for the Manhattan Project (atomic bomb). He was professor of physics at the College of Wooster for a number of years and rounded out his career on the staff of the Los Alamos Scientific Laboratory in New Mexico.

Louis Douglas of Bloomington, class of 1931, took a rather circuitous route through the teaching field, including some time as acting dean at Hastings College, and ended his career as professor of political science at Kansas State University.

Ronald Thompson of Doniphan, a freshman with me who took his degree with a later class, advanced himself from mathematics teacher to university administrator and ended up as registrar at Ohio State University.

Laurens Williams, previously mentioned, studied law at Cornell, went into practice in Omaha and eventually served a term as president of the Nebraska Bar Association. He went to Washington as an assistant to the secretary of the treasury in the Eisenhower administration and was in private practice in Washington until his death.

Howard "Dutch" Welch, who lived at Berwyn but had gone to Gothenburg for his senior year of high school, had won the mile in the 1924 national high school track meet in Chicago. A three-letter man in sports, he went into teaching and coaching and then to ownership of an automobile agency in Kearney. He and Genevieve Greenslit, sister of Vance, were married shortly after graduation.

William Snyder of North Platte, fellow sprinter on the track team for two years, transferred to the University of Nebraska College of Agriculture. His younger brother, Bruce, roomed with me in Ringland Hall one year. The brothers eventually became farmers and purebred cattle breeders at Paxton.

Paul Stuckey of Lexington was my roommate in our senior year. He spent a year at Cornell and returned to the family banking and livestock interests at Lexington. He was for many years chairman of the board of the Lexington State Bank. He and Grace Pressley of the class of 1930 were married in 1931.

Lawrence Hagood of Arcadia, seated next to me in many classes and the daily chapel service, remained a close friend until his death. He went into teaching and school administration, but he and his wife, the former Ramona Duxstad, settled on a farm near Broken Bow after World War II.

Charles Osborne of Bayard and I discovered early in our freshman year that we were among the few who could converse in the vernacular of the sugar beet country. He dropped out of school for two years and was graduated with the class of 1930. He joined his uncle, A. H. Jones, in the automobile business in Hastings, served as an officer in World War II, returned to Hastings and established himself as a self-trained historian as well as businessman. His special interest was the Oregon Trail. Long before Tom Osborne would stir the hearts of University of Nebraska football loyalists as a successful coach, the name was known to some of us as that of Charles' father, also a graduate of Hastings, as young Tom would be before going into his coaching career.

Lois Atwater would spend only one year with us, but we remembered her after her marriage to Carl T. Curtis of Minden and his rise through the House of Representatives to the United States Senate.

Blues-singing Lucille Christopher of Trumbull left college to enter medical technician training. While attached to a hospital at Scottsbluff, she met James E. Jensen, plant pathology graduate of the University of Nebraska. Eventually they were married, and he became president of Oregon State University.

Reed Heckenlively, several years older than the average of those in classes with him, was a fully qualified

College Days

railroad fireman who made daily runs to Kearney and back during his last two years in school. He roomed in Ringland Hall one year with Eugene Perry, previously mentioned, and talked wistfully of an academic career. After graduation in 1927, though, he gave greater weight to his seniority with the Union Pacific than to his diploma. Ultimately he attained the rank of engineer, and reports of his death mentioned that he had piloted crack passenger trains for several years in and out of North Platte.

Walter Scott, another member of the class of 1927, had accumulated considerable seniority with the Burlington in jobs that included some time as fireman on a switch engine in the Hastings yards. He went into teaching, but within a few years he had joined the police department in San Diego. His report to classmates on the occasion of their 50th reunion was a long narration of lively and sometimes bizarre experiences.

Paul Hansell, who transferred to Carnegie Tech after three years, brought his Carnegie credits back to Hastings to qualify him for graduation with the class of 1927. He took a job with Westinghouse in public relations and was laid off in St. Louis in the early days of the Great Depression. Returning to Hastings, he worked with me as a reporter on the *Tribune* for several years, went to the Omaha *Bee-News* and then to the Associated Press. (His starting salary at the *Tribune* was $15 a week.) He retired in the early 1970s after having been head of the AP Bureau in Miami, Florida, and manager of a heavy flow of news from and about Castro's Cuba for more than a decade.

Thomas M. Kealy, whose family home was a few blocks from the campus, made his way through four years of close and friendly association with a predominantly Protestant student group and headed straight for several years of special preparation for the Catholic priesthood.

Ultimately he became vicar general of the diocese of Lincoln. His popularity as a student was not hurt by the fact that he had a Model-T Ford and took other students with him on occasion to distribute "special delivery" mail as it arrived at the post office.

The freshman class president in 1926-27 was David A. Hamil, my younger brother. He returned to Colorado, and after getting established in farming and cattle feeding, he ran for the state legislature and served 16 years there, including six as speaker of the house. He tried twice for the governorship, was head of state institutions for six years and administrator of the Rural Electrification Administration of the U. S. Department of Agriculture for 14 years.

Robert Crosby of North Platte, freshman president in 1926-27, finished his undergraduate work at the University of Minnesota, studied law and served a term as governor of Nebraska. Secretary of his freshman class was Alice Criswell of Hastings. She married Floyd Dominy of that class. He transferred to the University of Wyoming and went from there into a career that led eventually to his appointment as commissioner of the Bureau of Reclamation in the U. S. Department of the Interior.

Two fellows who were earning high school credits in the academy during my senior year were Clarence M. Pierson, who had tried farming in his native Polk County and decided to prepare himself for something else, and Seiriol Williams, native of Nanaimo, B. C., who had tried selling shoes in Chicago and decided he would rather be a doctor. Pierson earned his degree, sold insurance for a while, married Margaret Branagan of the class of 1932, studied law at the University of Nebraska and was a prominent member of the bar in Lincoln until his death in 1978. Williams earned his bachelor's degree at Hastings, took his medicine at Harvard, married Wilma Kibben of Curtis, and practiced until retirement in Nanaimo.

College Days 53

In our time and for many years afterward, Hastings College ranked high among small colleges in the quality of instruction it offered in the field of music. This reputation centered on the personality, the talent, the drive and dedication of one man—Hayes M. Fuhr, head of the music department, or conservatory, as it was formally designated. He was a voice teacher and choral director with powerful impulses to manage anything with which he was involved. His wife, Ruth, taught piano. The two of them had been the backbone of the department since early World War I days.

A native of Illinois, Hayes Fuhr had attended Western Illinois College at Macomb and taught one year at Culver Military Academy. Coming to Hastings when barely out of his teens, he and the music department had grown together. He ran his little part of the show with an air of command unmatched by the president or dean or any other department head. He spoke with an eloquence and conviction that few, if any, other faculty members ever displayed. His vocabulary was extensive, and he chose and emphasized words that sometimes dazzled his listeners. He could be brusque and biting in some of his comments, but his emphasis on excellence appealed to the serious student. Among those of my time who followed him into full-time careers in music education were William Tempel of Goehner, who taught at Beatrice and the University of Nebraska and was head of public school music at Lima, Ohio, when stricken by cancer; Horatio Farrar of Hastings, who taught voice at Kansas State and later was professor of music at Southwest Missouri State in Springfield; Boyd Bohlke of Kenesaw and Hastings, who became a sort of Mr. Music in the school system of Sioux Falls, South Dakota.

Among the many surprises awaiting me when I enrolled at Hastings was the coach of athletics, August Holste. His football team had won the state college championship the year before, and most students spoke respectfully of him. Nobody, though, seemed to know him. He was referred to as a one-time quarterback under Amos Alonzo Stagg, famous coach at the University of Chicago. Some said he was a second-string quarterback, behind the legendary Walter Eckersall, who played at Chicago four years.

In any event, he had coached at Hastings for a time prior to World War I and had come back after an absence of several years. He was a dour and sad-eyed individual, hard of hearing and disposed to speak in screeching tones that seemed always to convey complaint or criticism. At the state track meet in 1925 I mistook a trackside post for the finish line, slowed down too soon and almost missed qualifying in the preliminaries of the 220-yard dash. In something less than a complimentary tone he observed to someone as we walked to lunch, "That Hamil—he don't know if he's afoot or on horseback."

In the fall of 1925, just as football practice was getting under way, Holste resigned. Within a matter of days, President French had discovered that W. G. Kline of Lincoln and Falls City, a former coach at several schools, including the University of Nebraska, was available. He was promptly hired to take over the athletic program. Kline was a man of striking appearance, jovial and gregarious. He possessed a vast store of stories about coaches and the general field of collegiate athletics. Just why he had not stayed long in any of the several jobs he had held was a question. The answer, in due time, was apparent to some of us: He had a hard time sticking to the details and he talked a better game than he coached.

His talking, nevertheless, may have been his biggest contribution to those of us who longed for at least a reasonable record of achievement in our athletic specialties. When the spring of 1926 rolled around, he announced he would take some of us to the Kansas Relays and, maybe, the Drake Relays. That was beyond anybody's expectations. He said we were good enough to win in those meets. We hoped he was right. He hadn't seen any of us run in competition.

In due time we headed for Lawrence and the Fourth Annual Kansas Relays. It would be "mid-spring" in Kansas, the promotional literature told us. It was still cold at Hastings, though, and rain kept us from the kind of workouts we should have had. We really weren't ready for the big time.

"Wild Bill," as he sometimes was called by sports writers, had arranged with Carl Pratt for transportation in the latter's Cadillac touring car. Pratt, an alumnus of the college, was the prospering president of the Hastings Business College. There were seven of us in all—Pratt, Kline, Howard Welch, Butler Isaman, Malcolm Keiry, Ned Greenslit and I. Welch was entered in the open 1,500-meter run. The rest of us made up a mile-relay team entered in the college division.

We left Hastings in early morning the day before we were to run. Neither Kline nor Pratt had a clear idea of the route we would take, and there were discussions at almost every town as to the best road to the next one. Most of the roads were dirt and gravel. Some were rough. I remember going through Geneva and Belvidere in Nebraska, and Marysville, Blue Rapids, Frankfort, Wamego and Topeka in Kansas. In all or most of those places we repaired a tire. By the time we had fixed the last flat, Pratt had bought at least three new tires. Seven adults and a lot of luggage were far more than the car or tires were built to carry. This had become very obvious to us rear-seat passengers. One of us had to sit on the floor between the seats and rest his feet on the running board. This meant keeping the door open, and that meant there was little protection from the raw winds even though the so-called side curtains were in place.

For the five of us from the track team this was our first

visit to eastern Kansas. Somebody noted the prevalence of stone houses and barns along the way, and Kline launched into a typical discourse. There was much limestone in Kansas, he said. It was important enough to the state that the University of Kansas yell, with the phrase, "Rock Chalk, Jayhawk," was a reference to that fact. Rock chalk, he said, was limestone. And the yell—"best college yell in the country."

Our troubles with Carl Pratt's tires kept us on the road until almost midnight. We were scheduled to sleep at the Sigma Chi fraternity house, where beds were waiting. But what beds! There was little sleep that night and little enthusiasm next morning for the challenges of the day.

Howard Welch placed third in the 1,500-meter run, but our relay team finished fifth or sixth. I got some satisfaction from having stayed at the head of the field to the end of my lead-off lap in the mile relay. One reason was that Kline had warned me that if I didn't hold the pole position at the first turn, I might be shoved off the track by bigger and heavier runners. Between his confidence and his warnings, he forced me into running the fastest quarter-mile I ever had run.

Bill Kline's big talk and his willingness to take teams to the Kansas and Drake relays were his contribution to a new era in track at Hastings. In my junior year, under Kline, our distance medley relay team won third at Drake. In my senior year, after Kline was gone and T. C. "Brigham" Young had taken over the athletic program, we won the sprint medley at Drake with a time record that stood for several years. I was the only senior on the team. The others, Francis Kemp of Fairmont, Clarence Bierman of Hastings and Ed Lindell of Arnold, would be joined by Elmer Baruth of Indianola in 1929 to compose a team that gave Hastings one of its years of great recognition in track, with victories in the Texas Relays as well as the Kansas and Drake meets.

College Days

On an August morning in 1940 I saw the unmistakable features of Bill Kline coming toward me in a mass of rush-hour pedestrians on Sixth Avenue in New York. I stopped him, we visited a moment and made a date to attend a pre-season professional football game the following week. (I was working for the Associated Press and could get complimentary tickets.) He had separated from his wife and was living in a men's residence establishment in the heart of Manhattan. He was vague as to any employment or source of livelihood, but he was writing a book, he said, one that would open eyes and run up a lot of sales. He had talked about writing a book back there in the 1920s. He was enthusiastic in those Hastings days about everything, it seemed, but the nitty-gritty of his job. He was a dreamer with a strong body that had given him athletic status at the University of Illinois. He told me I should set my sights on the Olympics. He told all of us a lot, and some of what he said was effectively inspirational.

Midway through my junior year—the second and last of Bill Kline—I was more or less pressed into taking over the paper work of the athletic department. The job had been handled by Dean E. Shaffer, graduate with the class of 1925, who had stayed on to take care of several such chores and teach some classes in journalism. It was my job to list the entrants in the conference track meet in May, and one of my most distinct recollections is of having entered two sprinters whose names Kline did not recognize when I submitted the entry list for his signature. On my recommendation, he let the entries stand. The men were Clarence Bierman and Elmer Baruth, both of whom had been working out regularly. It was this kind of oversight that marred Kline's record.

All this reference to athletics might suggest that my interests that year revolved around the gymnasium and the track. The truth is that I took the athletic department chore against my better judgment. I was up to my neck in the responsibilities of editing the 1927 *Bronco,* the college yearbook, along with a full schedule of classwork.

Editing the *Bronco* made that year my best by all means in terms of finances. It was custom that the editor and business manager of the yearbook took on the project not just for the honor, but also for any money they could make. From my experience as business manager of my high school yearbook I knew how editorial efficiency could cut costs by speeding up the production schedule and result in big discounts on the purchase of photo engravings. I knew also that somebody had to pound the pavements to sell advertising. Pretty much at my insistence, Laurens Williams agreed to be business manager. He called on Hastings businessmen with a very careful plan to let them know he was the son of a banker. He sold more lines of advertising than ever had been sold for a *Bronco.* I speeded up the picture-taking and got most of our engravings into the plant at St. Joseph, Missouri, before Christmas. Some of the discounts ran as high as 33 percent. When the book was out and all bills were paid, Williams and I split a profit of almost $1,000 that had been netted on a project where total budget was less than $4,000. I went into my senior year with more money in the bank than I had when I enrolled as a freshman.

That senior year was in many ways what a senior year in college should be. It afforded some relaxation from demands and uncertainties of the earlier years and participation in activities and pursuits that until then had seemed beyond my reach. With most required subjects out of the way, I had more choice as to classes I would enter. Some of us who had enjoyed the advanced composition classes of Miss Janet Carpenter, head of the English department, had talked her into offering a still further advanced class in writing. This class of not more than a dozen and meeting only once a week, as I recall, was

College Days   59

probably the most stimulating and gratifying of my four years in college.

Janet Carpenter had come to Hastings from Sturbridge, Massachusetts, with her family when she was approaching her teens. She was graduated from the college in 1892 and had taught Latin and Greek as well as English at several places, including colleges in Highland, Kansas, and Kansas City, Missouri, before she became head of the English department at Hastings in 1906.

She was small of stature, sharp-featured and given to rather set styles in hairdo and dress. She had a ready smile for any situation or comment meriting it, but she was serious and sometimes cutting in her response to what she might consider frivolous or non-scholarly. She was prim, proper and precise, and the alliteration could be extended to cover some students' feeling that at times she was a bit prudish. She was an institution within an institution and largely responsible for a relatively high percentage of English majors among Hastings graduates of my time. I never have regretted being counted among those who studied under her, although she seemed always to encourage me to accept my grades as reflecting a practicality in use of the language rather than a talent that might lead to a literary career.

She was a practical person herself. While she wrote an occasional piece for publication, she was content to accept her reputation as a good teacher as adequate proof she had used her abilities properly.

Once a year in her composition classes she devoted a period to a theme to be written on the spot. She permitted students to choose one of about three topics. One of these topics always was "Keeping Up With the Joneses." She was careful not to write the topics on the board. Students seemed to choose "Keeping Up With the Joneses" over the other topics, and that was what she wanted them to do. Discussing the themes at a subsequent session, she would disclose that the whole idea was to center attention on the fact that most Americans never had learned how to pluralize a name ending in "s." She would cite illustrations of how, with such names as Evans, Williams, Davis or Jones, people tried to use apostrophes in one way or another to make a plural form. She would start her discussion by writing "Keeping Up With the Joneses" on the blackboard. Even the best of such lessons sometimes goes unheeded. I would recall some 30 years later when receiving a Christmas card from the family of one of my classmates in advanced comp whose name ended in "s." He or his wife had insisted on an apostrophe in the printed family signature.

One day in our little advanced-advanced composition class Miss Carpenter suggested she had before her one of the best themes that ever had come across her desk. She read it through, and the class sat in awed silence. This was the blossoming of a talent far beyond anything we had detected. All I remember about the piece is that it included a description of what went on behind the soft-drink fountain at a typical American drugstore. The description of the pumping process whereby various flavors were applied to sundaes and sodas had just the kind of imagery Miss Carpenter had been urging us to seek. The nouns were vivid, the verbs fairly flew.

Miss Carpenter never divulged authorship of the themes she read in class. The writer of something getting special attention usually managed a gesture to attract any compliments that seemed in order. On this day, though, there was no move by anyone that might disclose authorship. After class, of course, we cleared up any mystery, and some of us were a bit surprised by the seeming modesty of the fellow on whom all attention focused.

We talked about that theme for days. We remembered the better words and phrases. One member of the class remembered them well enough that several weeks later he recognized whole paragraphs in an article he came upon while thumbing through a back copy of *Harper's* Magazine. The author of the original was Simeon Strunsky, a *New York Times* columnist and a better writer on form, certainly, than any member of our class.

Gradually, the word was passed. There was shock and surprise, of course, but also there was resentment. It wasn't fair that a member of the class should have a sort of double-A grade for having been clever enough to adapt somebody else's writing to a class assignment and leave the rest of us with our B's and C's. Two members of the class finally chose to confront the author. He was embarrassed and contrite. He went to Miss Carpenter, confessed everything and agreed to accept whatever punishment or penalty she might impose. To the best of my recollection, she gave him zero for the day and agreed to forgive and forget. He passed the word to some of us, we passed it to the rest of the class, and the chastened one went on to graduation and considerable distinction in his career.

A somewhat similar incident of that senior year involved those of us who constituted the governing body for the 30-plus men living in Ringland Hall. We had elected Ed Lindell of Arnold to the office of mayor, and when word came that one of the residents had lost about $15 from his room under conditions that pointed to one of our first-year residents, Lindell called his deliberative body together. We decided to call in the suspect for questioning. The session went on for hours, with his denials of involvement weakening just enough that Lindell held to his contention that we had to settle the issue in one session or we never would. Finally, we exacted a full confession. We accepted his offer to make restitution, and the matter was forgotten. (Lindell, when asked in 1980, conceded he literally had forgotten.)

The great disappointment of that final year came in

early spring when I pulled a hamstring muscle during a workout and went into the season as a track captain who would limp through every race. I had won the 440 in the conference meet the year before. I didn't even qualify for the 440 as a senior. I did run the 440 lap with our relay team that won the spring medley at the Drake Relays.

By the first of January we seniors were talking seriously of what we would do after graduation. I was having trouble with my eyes, and a doctor discouraged the idea of graduate study of any kind. I had been thinking about going to law school.

I applied for a teaching job at Kearney and was preparing to make a personal appearance there when Henry G. Smith, the new general manager of the Hastings *Tribune*, sent word he wanted to talk with me about a possible job on the newspaper. It was early April, perhaps, when we struck a deal. I would start as a reporter at $20 a week as soon as I received my diploma in June.

With my first paycheck I bought a $5 meal ticket at Carl's Cafe (for $4.50) and paid the $2 I owed the college for my diploma. (At commencement several of us in the class received blank rolls of paper with notes attached to tell us that our diplomas would be held at the business office until payment of this fee.) That $2 debt, the bank account of about $400 with which I left home in 1924 and notes covering the borrowing of $400 from my mother enabled me to say that I had earned all my expenses while going to college except for $802.

4. Adam Breede

His Paper Was His Flag and Trumpet

When Adam Breede died on March 1, 1928, a fellow editor wrote in the Lincoln *Journal* that his life had been "almost as romantic as the tales that unwound themselves from his pen."

The fitness of that tribute is hard to challenge. Adam was a rare mixture of talents, tastes and postures. He was restless, adventurous and whimsical, but never without appreciation of the prosaic and practical. He was not yet 20 years old when he bought the *Independent-Tribune*, a weekly, mostly on credit. He was still in his early thirties when he launched the *Daily Tribune*.

He was an avid hunter and could recount close calls with bears in Alaska and lions, elephants, rhinos, pythons and the like in Africa. He was versifier and philosopher, and when the Fourth of July caught up with him once in East Africa, he could stand up and sing "America" and follow it with his own composition, "Nebraskaland."

When he found time from his first newspaper operation to attend Hastings College, it was not enough that he attend classes. He joined the football squad, where his zest for physical contact and movement made up for any lack of talent. He was a gregarious bon vivant, but he maintained enough reserve to seem mysterious at times to people who thought they knew him.

The word *romantic* suggests chivalric or passionate love, but to the best of my knowledge there was little of either in Adam's record. He was a bachelor to the end.

Nebraska editors in the second and third decades of the twentieth century frequently referred to Hastings as "Adam Breede's town." Some residents, of course, resented the proprietary implications, but there were old-timers who insisted for a dozen years after his death that the *Tribune* and Hastings could never quite make up for the loss of him.

I started working for the *Tribune* as a cub reporter three months after Adam's death. I had met him and seen him often, but I could not call him a personal acquaintance. What I write about him comes mainly from anecdotes and comments of his associates on the *Tribune* and elsewhere in the community, and from his writings.

On the word of Henry G. Smith, I can refer to my hiring as a direct result of Adam's death. Smith, who had been the working editor of the paper for many years, had been designated general manager in the Breede will, and his plan, as he explained it, was to bring onto the staff a young man or two with ambition to take over eventually his old job as managing editor. I was the first of two reporters he added that year.

While all my negotiations for the *Tribune* job had been with Henry Smith, I realized after the first week or two that I was subject to the influences of two other persons on the editorial staff, David J. Lewis and Mrs. Marie Herrin.

Lewis, a native of the Trumbull community, was graduated from Hastings College in 1900 and had worked on the weekly *Tribune* for Adam Breede while in college. His years after graduation had included some time in Wales, where he worked on a Cardiff daily, a year or so as reporter for the Omaha *Bee* and a shorter time as editor and publisher of a weekly at Sutton. By the time I knew him he was considered an old-timer with the *Tribune*. He viewed himself as a reporter above all else and seemed

World's biggest front page.

never to have had any desire for the responsibilities of editorial management or supervision.

Breede's will had specified that the *Tribune* ownership be shared by his brother, David Breede, his sister, Louise Engel, Smith and Lewis, with the first three each to hold a two-seventh interest and Lewis a one-seventh.

Smith and Lewis had agreed that there would be new emphasis on locally-written editorials and that Lewis would be primarily responsible for the writing. During my first weeks on the job, Smith spent part of each day in Breede's former office, attending to his duties as general manager. But he was in the newsroom for the start of the day. He counted on Marie Herrin, a widow in her thirties, to direct the news staff in his absence, and somewhere through that first summer she assumed the duties of city editor.

David Breede and Louise Engel were not active in the management, but for several months after Adam's death the former had a desk in the proof-reading room. One of the tasks with which he occupied himself was going through the files and selecting bits from a personal column, "Tribune Tips," that had appeared under Adam's byline. For some time these selections were reprinted under a headline to indicate they were from past issues of the paper.

The columns were liberally sprinkled with quips from other editors and columnists. Among non-attributed paragraphs and jingles appearing about the time of Adam's death were these:

"Yes, any ass can press the gas."

"He quickly ate and Kept his cake, So everything is Now in Jake."

"It's easy to be good when there is no temptation."

"How well we remember the things that should be forgotten."

"Just because they dress alike, it's no sign they are twins."

My first months on the *Tribune* seem in retrospect to have been marked by the concerns of Smith and Lewis—especially the former—that came with the sudden realization that until Adam's death they had been directing the editorial policies of the paper behind the protective curtain of his dominant personality.

While Adam may have made things hard for them at times—with his long absences, his big spending on hunting trips and his wisecracking way of explaining some policies of the paper—the Adam Breede mystique sheltered them from a public that was amazingly conditioned to think that everything at the *Tribune* started and ended with him.

I don't know whose decision it was to start a column of

warmed-over bits from Adam's "Tribune Tips," but it was an obvious part of a plan to prevent a too sudden conclusion by readers that the spirit of Adam Breede was no longer present in the pages of the paper he had founded. I cannot recall how the decision to discontinue rerunning the "Tips" was arrived at, either, but my memory is clear as to my own lack of enthusiasm for them in their resurrected form.

Mrs. Herrin left the staff in 1931 at the time of her marriage to Ray R. Damerell. Smith and Lewis left in 1937 after sale of the paper to the Seatons of Manhattan, Kansas. The community's memory of Adam Breede had dimmed considerably by then, but from the *Tribune* of my final days with the paper in 1940 his face still looked out over a line saying, "Adam Breede, Founder." This was in type of the same size that listed Fred A. Seaton, Fay N. Seaton and Richard M. Seaton as owners, Fred A. Seaton as general manager, J. Harold Hamil as managing editor, E. Homer Hewins as advertising manager and W. J. McGonegal as circulation manager.

As I reconstruct events between my start with the *Tribune* and my departure in 1940, I can't escape the observation that my 12 years there were years of transition, a sort of hiatus. They bridged a period between personalities—between Adam Breede and Fred A. Seaton. Breede had dominated the paper from its founding in 1905 until his death in 1928. I came into the picture while the community was mourning Adam's death. I left after Fred Seaton had had three years to get acquainted with the paper, the community and the state of Nebraska. He would pretty well dominate the paper for the next 35 years, but with a somewhat different style from that of Adam Breede. He was more the businessman and politician than Adam and less the flamboyant editor. For Adam the paper was flag and trumpet. For Seaton it was more a base of operations.

I shall reserve for a later chapter any further recollections of Fred Seaton as publisher or employer. I shall also save for later chapters any detailed comments on my *Tribune* years with Smith and Lewis. Their stories and observations over our years together, however, are basic to the picture I am trying to draw of Adam Breede. They knew him as well as anyone outside his family, certainly, but they also knew how to be loyal without being idolatrous. Lewis, especially, seemed to look at Adam and his ways with the same cool objectivity that characterized his generally competent reporting of the news.

My first glimpse of Adam Breede was on a fall afternoon in 1924. He had joined a group of 20 to 30 persons along the edge of the Hastings College practice field to watch the football squad go through its daily routine. He stood out there as he stood out in most any crowd, because of his distinctive dress. Most noticeable was his flowing black bow tie. The brim of his large hat dipped over one eye, and his gray suit was perfectly tailored to his trim figure. I cannot recall ever seeing him in any but a gray suit.

Whether he wore a flower on his lapel that afternoon I cannot recall, but I was soon to learn that he started each day with a fresh red carnation in honor of his mother. I was to learn later that he never left the *Tribune* office in the morning without placing a new one-dollar bill, flat and uncreased, in the breast pocket of his jacket. His first purchase probably would be a cigar, and drugstore clerks looked forward to having a part in this little drama in the daily life of a prominent citizen. They talked among themselves about those crisp dollar bills that came from a supply that I. R. Beedle, long-time *Tribune* cashier, maintained.

Adam's natty suits and jaunty hats, his carnation, his insistence on starting each day with a brand-new dollar bill—these were major contributions to his high level of visibility. People knew who he was when they saw him. They gathered around him sometimes at a street corner. He listened to their questions, comments or complaints. There would be an occasional jibe at the *Tribune* by a person dissatisfied with something he had read. Bits of talk I picked up two or three years after Adam's death convinced me that he was not beyond apologizing for the way the paper might have handled a given story or leaving the impression, at least, that "they" back at the office hadn't handled a situation to his complete liking.

I often thought how fortunate he was to have as his back-up man and his willing foil, and sometimes his apologist, an intelligent, poised and articulate person named Smith. When I joined the staff, Henry G. Smith was the new general manager. For many years prior to that he had sat at the central news desk, organizing each day's paper and handling the flow of copy. He was really in charge much of the time, but he played the role with superb anonymity. People out on the beats—at the courthouse, the city hall, the police station, the chamber of commerce and elsewhere—barely knew that such a person existed. It was hard for them to believe that a man with the plain name of Henry Smith was succeeding the colorful, popular and fast-moving Adam Breede.

It was said around the office during my first year that the *Tribune* was not supposed to spare any of its own people from publicity if ever they ran afoul of the law. I hadn't been there a week until Mrs. Herrin told me how Adam had lectured staff members frequently about treating him exactly as they might treat anybody else. If he were to be hauled into police court for drunken driving or something akin to that, he had said, the story was to be printed. Recalling this in a conversation with a veteran policeman a year or so later, I got from him a comment that ran about as follows:

"Adam could have said that was the rule and still have

felt quite safe. If ever I had found him drunk, I would have piled him into my car, taken him home and seen to it that he was safe in bed before I left. Any other policeman would have done the same thing. Nobody was ever going to arrest Adam Breede—nobody in his right mind."

The importance attached to Adam's personal image as a basic asset of the *Tribune* is no better illustrated than in the story Dave Lewis told about how Adam became a correspondent in Europe during World War I. Lewis was never convinced that the situation was critical, and he implied that Smith's worries were more a factor in the ultimate decision than Breede's were.

Adam was a single man of German descent. People around Hastings had developed the kind of anti-German sentiments that were common all across the country after war was formally declared. Adam was in his forties and well beyond the range of the first draft call. But the fact remained that people talked about single men with German names who were not in uniform, regardless of their ages.

Somebody in one discussion mentioned that feelings of this kind had resulted in the throwing of yellow paint on business buildings and even some bombings. The *Tribune* could very well be the target of such acts.

In any event, after there had been some inquiry as to the availability of a commission in a special branch of one of the services where there would be none of the drilling and other tedium of normal preparation for military duty, Smith came up with the idea of Adam's going to one of the war zones as a correspondent. There was the hope he might line up with one of the national syndicates or wire services. As a last resort, it was agreed, he could go as correspondent of the *Tribune*.

While one finds mention of the fact that his writings were available to some 200 newspapers besides the *Tribune*, the widely expressed view among *Tribune* personnel in my day was that Adam's own paper footed most of his expenses.

Whatever the arrangement, Adam made the most of his status as correspondent. He made friends among some of the best-known news writers of the day and, some said, he was never one to avoid a convivial evening with fellow journalists. This leads to what I always have considered Dave Lewis' best story about Adam Breede.

It starts with arrival at the *Tribune* of a cablegram from Paris that read as follows: "PLEASE SEND GRAY PANTS.—ADAM."

This, according to Lewis, prompted Smith to call a high-level conference. Smith was convinced Adam was trying to tell him something. Somebody suggested this might be a message in code. It fell to Smith, then, to send the text of the cablegram to the government decoding office in Washington. After a few days the office replied, and Dave Lewis insisted that these were its exact words: "HAVE STUDIED CABLEGRAM FROM EVERY ANGLE STOP MUST CONCLUDE GENTLEMAN WANTS GRAY PANTS."

That was all *Tribune* people heard about the pants until Adam came home. Lewis or someone else asked him just what he was thinking about when he cabled the request, and his explanation was that he looked down at his olive drab correspondent's uniform one night and suddenly thought it would be good to get back into something gray. He rounded out his explanation with a confession that on the night in question he and other correspondents had been whooping it up, so to speak.

The *Tribune*, when I started working there in 1928, was housed in an aging three-story building that faced east on Burlington Avenue between First and Second streets. About two-thirds of the top floor was strewn with the dried hides, horns, hooves and bits of tails and hair from animals Adam had killed in Africa and India on a round-the-world tour in 1925.

This wall-to-wall collection was as unorganized as the site of a building just demolished by a tornado. Huge slabs of elephant and rhinoceros skin, thick and hard, could have passed as pieces of shattered walls. Some skins were warped into weird shapes that stood out like crumbled sheets of roofing. Here and there among the remains of big animals were smaller bits of skin that had come from snakes, antelopes and other creatures that had fallen before Adam's guns. Frayed and faded shipping tags still stuck to some of the pieces.

The idea was that these trophies would go to the University of Nebraska Museum, but for several years the university was in no position to commit itself to the expense of preparing a display of this kind of material. Finally, after some lobbying in which Henry Smith was quietly involved, the legislature came up with the money, and by 1932 two of Adam's elephants stood clean and lifelike as the dominant figures of a dramatic display at Lincoln.

Whether in the museum or in the dust, confusion and strange smells of the *Tribune's* third-floor storage room, these trophies symbolized a notable economic achievement for the *Tribune* as well as a great adventure for Adam. Nothing much was said around the *Tribune* about how much Adam's world tour might have cost. Dave Lewis, talking freely about such things some ten years later, assured me it cost a lot. He told about serious conferences among those left in charge of the paper about the startling amounts of money Adam's travels were requiring. At some stage—and it may have been after Adam got home—there was a hike in the advertising rate that Dave Lewis ascribed directly to the high cost of Adam's trip. There was also a report that Stein Brothers made an advance payment on a year's advertising.

It seems almost incredible that a small-city daily in

Adam Breede on Safari

Nebraska could support its owner in an undertaking as pretentious as Adam mapped out for himself. In his book on his travels, *Adventuring,* Adam described his four-month safari in Kenya as requiring a "head man," an interpreter, a chef, a head skinner, two assistant skinners and 60 porters. That was a staff roughly twice as large as the one that was putting out the *Tribune* back home.

It is a matter of record, of course, that African natives could be hired in those days at pretty low wages. But the advertising and circulation rates at the *Tribune* were pretty modest by the standards of half a century later. To the best of my recollection the annual cash flow of the paper had not exceeded $200,000 by 1937.

While Adam's months in Kenya were the high point of his trip, he had laid out an itinerary that called for some hunting in India. On board ship from Africa to Bombay he came down with what was called "black water fever" and was near the point of death when he was taken from the ship to a hospital in Bombay. The American consul cabled word of his illness to Hastings, the final words of the message being, "Recovery doubtful."

Just how long he was detained by the illness is not made clear in his written report, but he did not leave India until after a hunting foray that netted at least one tiger.

Adam's book, published in 1926 by Frederick H. Hitchcock and the Grafton Press, includes reports of wild-animal slaughter that would have shocked great segments of American society if the incidents chronicled had come along 50 years later.

He devoted a chapter to the stalking and killing of two bull elephants and another to the killing of what he considered an unusually large bull giraffe. He shot zebras, buffalos, gazelles, hartebeests and varieties of deer and antelope. He described a close call with a rhinoceros, and one of the photographs he brought back shows an African boy astride the shoulders of one of those rhinos (dead) displaying a Hastings *Tribune* paper carrier's bag that Adam had brought along for some such purpose.

Adam appears in several of the pictures, including one with him standing on the shoulder of a dead giraffe and one with a group of bare-breasted African women. In every picture he is wearing his flowing black Windsor tie—sometimes with jacket, sometimes without, sometimes with a pith helmet, sometimes with a broad-brimmed felt hat. In one picture he stands with gun in hand at the head of his entourage, which trails in single file to some barely distinguishable porters, each with a bag or box on his head.

Adam's narrative makes it clear that he managed the

Adam Breede 75

expedition with a firm hand and that he was the one who did most of the killing. H. R. Stanton, a young British engineer, acted as interpreter and stepped in with his gun on occasion to help bring down a dangerous animal.

Nowhere in the book is there anything to suggest an accurate count of animals killed or animals shot at and allowed to get away. It is obvious, though, that some creatures that were not brought down by a first shot escaped into the jungle. One can only surmise how much destruction of game took place beyond that accounted for in the inventory of hides that lay for several years on the third floor of the *Tribune* building. Thoughts of this kind never ran through my mind as I stepped over and around the trophies when making my way from the top of the stairway to the door that separated the hide storage from the engraving and photography departments.

Few individuals in those days cared much about the slaughter of animals in Africa, and Adam Breede, proudly calling himself a hunter, wrote of his expedition as an acceptable and laudable achievement of his time—as it truly was in the minds of most Americans.

Adam's book was far more interesting to me in 1978 than at the time I received a copy in the early 1930s as a Christmas gift from the author's sister and brother, Louise Engel and David Breede. I can't recall that Henry Smith ever discussed the book with me in any detail. Dave Lewis did, and he tended to credit Smith with responsibility for the book's having been written. He implied that Adam acted under some pressure from Smith and also that Adam might not have completed the book had it not been for Smith's urging—and some actual help with the writing and editing.

Henry Smith, amazingly self-effacing for a man of his talents and experience, was ever ready to project Adam's personality and activities to the glory of the *Tribune*. The world tour in itself was an event worth trumpeting. It was something unusual for a small-city publisher to undertake. It was even more unusual for him to write a book about his experiences. The Henry Smith I knew would have sensed all this. But if he tried to convince Adam and the publishers that *Adventuring* should reflect Adam's relationships with a daily paper in Nebraska, he failed. The book runs some 300 pages without a single reference to Hastings, the *Daily Tribune* or much else in Nebraska. (There may have been something on the dust jacket to identify Adam with his newspaper, but there is nothing in the body of the book to indicate specifically where he came from and what his occupation was when not traveling or hunting.) It is hard for me, therefore, to credit Henry Smith with much influence on the form in which the book appeared.

In an opening chapter dealing with the sea voyage from New York to Naples, Adam described a number of traveling companions. Rather than list them by proper names, he characterized them as Gum Shoe, Miss Golden Glow, Sliver, the Sheik, the Philosopher, the Newlyweds, Fat Mamma, the Cornfed and Mr. Gallagher ("but no Mr. Shean").

Several of these were fellow passengers all the way to the East African port where Adam disembarked. A mysterious "queen" boarded the ship at Port Said, and Adam devotes a chapter to the efforts of many on board to determine just who she was. He suggests she was a "queen of Abyssinia" but doesn't come up with proof that this was not mere gossip.

His chapter on Seattle is little more than a report of an encounter with Sliver and Golden Glow, whose traveling together had led to marriage. They reported on what had happened to several others in the group out of New York, including the details of another shipboard romance that had led to marriage. Adam's descriptions of shipmates, his nicknames and his reviews of conversations, including one with the Philosopher on the meaning of life, suggest he may have been trying to recapture some of the flavor of Geoffrey Chaucer's writing about those who traveled with him to Canterbury. It's hard for me to believe that in some of these fringe accounts he wasn't fictionalizing.

The book was no best-seller. If Adam had left out some of his opening chapters, including an attempt to characterize his shipmates, and if he had omitted some of his brief chapters on places he saw but had little time to explore (Burma, the Philippines, Hawaii, Greece, Turkey, Egypt, etc.) and concentrated on his hunting experiences and the country in which these took place, he would have come up with a much smaller book, but it most certainly would have been better received. His chapters on his safari are still good reading.

Accounts of Adam's death noted that he never had thrown off some of the effects of his bout with "black water fever" on his way from Africa to India. He suffered an attack while watching a basketball game at Hastings College and had to be helped from the gymnasium.

His health was not so bad, however, that he could turn down an invitation to join a group of Missouri editors for a tour of several southern states and a trip to Mexico City in late winter of 1928. He became ill while en route from Hastings to St. Louis, where the editors were to assemble. Whether he had planned a stop in Kansas City is not clear in the reports, but he took a room at the Commonwealth Hotel there and called for medical help. First reports apparently were that his condition was serious. Henry Smith and Lawrence Kohl, a nephew of Adam and at that time the business manager of the *Tribune*, went to Kansas City, where Adam was already being looked after by two local friends, Otto P. Higgins and Roy E. Churchill. The latter had once lived in Hastings, and Higgins was a Kansas City political figure of some standing.

Funeral services on March 5 were in the home at 1502

West Seventh Street. While relatively few persons could crowd into the home, the whole community took note. Mayor William E. Nelson called for a general closing of business.

Two of the city's leading clergymen were in charge of the service—Dr. George E. Newell, colorful pastor of the First Presbyterian Church, and Dean Francis R. Lee of St. Mark's Pro-Cathedral, Episcopal.

On the front page of the *Tribune* that afternoon there was a dispatch from Red Cloud telling of the death of C. F. Cather, 80 years old and the father of Willa. The coincidence would have been wholly gratifying to Adam.

5. A Man Named Smith

And His On-The-Job Training Program

Henry G. Smith was by no means a salesman type. But he sold me on the future of the Hastings *Daily Tribune* in our first interview. He kept up a steady flow of promising talk during my first year under his tutelage, and when at the end of that year he announced I was to have the title of city editor, I felt I had passed the test.

As I look back, however, I must concede that I may have been more sold on him than he was on me. For more than three years he kept me guessing as to just how well he rated my performance. One day in my fourth year with the paper somebody pointed out that my name was in the masthead as "managing editor." It had been there two or three days, but I hadn't seen it. There had been no word from Smith as to a new title or new responsibilities. He had gone to the composing room and ordered the insertion without bothering to tell me. Such were the subtleties of a man from whom I learned much about newswriting, news management and the emotions, egos and prejudices of those who deal with the news media, sometimes as critics, sometimes as would-be manipulators.

Smith had emerged as general manager of the paper after long years of deliberate subordination of his personality, his ambitions and his considerable talents to permit the public an uncluttered picture of a newspaper completely dominated by its owner, Adam Breede.

Breede had been dead less than a month when Smith

and I had our first visit. He painted bright pictures of the future of the *Tribune*. He was about 50 years of age, but he seemed to look ahead to the years of his greatest opportunities. He implied that a young man joining him had every reason to aspire to succeed him in the management of the paper—and possibly to acquire some ownership. The city of Hastings, enjoying a surge of industrial development, had a bright future, he said, and the *Tribune* would share in it.

I spent only a few days pondering his offer. On my next visit to his office I agreed to go to work as a reporter on or about June 1 at a salary of $20 a week.

It was arranged that in the interim I should come to the *Tribune* as my schedule permitted and start getting acquainted with the job by going with Dave Lewis on his morning news beat. It also was agreed that I should spend an evening with Smith—the start of a long series of his lectures to which I would be exposed during the coming year. The first of these was during dinner at a downtown cafe, and it included points he would repeat time and again and drive home with practical illustrations.

Learning to write a clear and interesting news story was a never-ending process, he explained. The best way to learn newswriting was to read what others were writing in other papers. He recommended the New York *World*. In due time I subscribed to that paper and read it regularly for at least six months. Walter Lippmann was then editor of the *World,* but I can't recall that Smith made any more than passing mention of him. My instructions were to read the news stories and columns. There was no mention of the editorials. I was fascinated by some of the tricky first sentences *World* reporters used to get readers' attention and adapted one or two to stories I eventually wrote for the *Tribune*. While it was hard to measure any specific benefit derived from my reading of the *World,* I have never had reason to challenge Smith's theory that anyone wanting to learn to write can benefit immensely from reading, in great variety, what others have written.

Smith's lectures included detailed and timely illustrations of what readers of the *Tribune* were entitled to get from the paper. He insisted, for example, on careful reporting of the weather. Our part of Nebraska, he emphasized, was heavily dependent on its annual wheat crops. And each year's wheat crop—if it had survived the winter—was dependent on the spring rains.

Some of the local merchants, he pointed out, had the *Tribune* sent to their hotels in New York or Chicago when they were in those cities to buy merchandise. A report of good general rain at the right time, he insisted, would change a buyer's view as to how much he should order for the coming season. And so it was a *Tribune* policy to publish rainfall reports in detail. What we didn't get through our wire service we got from railroad offices and the Lincoln Telephone and Telegraph Company, which received weather reports from all its local exchanges.

Smith's emphasis on running a newspaper that could be counted on to tell how much rain had fallen on the new wheat around Holdrege or the sprouting corn around Clay Center was just one variation on a theme that would be consistent with him through the next nine years. He was constantly on the lookout for ways to make the paper serve the city and the region which sustained it.

Any appraisal of this emphasis on a detail of the news-gathering function must take into consideration that if the people didn't get weather reports through their newspapers in those days, they didn't get them. It was a matter of some amusement to us newspaper workers back there in the third and fourth decades of the twentieth century that we could hear the folding and creasing of newspaper pages as certain radio announcers undertook rather clumsy reporting of such things as the baseball scores, the stock market listing and the weather. A competitor was on the horizon, but we were slow to recognize it.

Those indoctrination sessions with Smith extended over a period of six weeks perhaps and included at least one dinner together after I had been on the job for a week or so. They were a factor, certainly, in my acceptance of Smith as guide and mentor for the next nine years. While I would learn much from Dave Lewis and others, Henry Smith, by the time I was on the payroll, had established himself as counselor, guide and critic against whose standard of judgment I would measure the merits of countless issues and opinions for all my years in occupations related to the writing and editing of news. He was the kind of man with whom it was easy to reason when one could document one's case to his satisfaction. He was a man of principle, but he made his points with a minimum of preaching.

A native of Philadelphia, he had spent his boyhood and early manhood in Lincoln, where his father was the founding dean of the University of Nebraska College of Law. He worked as an apprentice printer in Lincoln and as a reporter for the Lincoln *Evening News* and the Omaha *Bee*. He was a reporter on the Washington *Post* when Charles H. Dietrich of Hastings was appointed to the United States Senate. He served several years as Dietrich's secretary and was married to the senator's niece, Caroline (Lena) Meyer. The Smiths returned to Nebraska at the conclusion of Dietrich's Senate service in 1905, and sometime in that year he became managing editor of the *Tribune*.

Sue (Baker) Josties, looking back on her four years as his part-time secretary and handler of various reportorial and editorial assignments while going to college, recalled in 1981 that he was "patient and firm." It was obvious to some of the rest of us then that he appreciated her skills in shorthand, typing and the use of language.

A Man Named Smith

Rarely did he engage in nostalgic reminiscing, but on more than one occasion he spoke with some pride about the number of individuals of future prominence who were residents of Lincoln during the turn-of-the-century years when he was there. He would mention William Jennings Bryan, of course. But he was more interested in persons lesser known at the time. John J. Pershing was commandant of the ROTC unit at the university. Charles G. Dawes, later to be vice-president under Coolidge, was a young lawyer. Roscoe Pound was in the early years of a career that would lead to the deanship of the Harvard Law School. Willa Cather was winning her first recognition as a writer of fiction. He felt a sort of kinship with all of them.

Lena Smith's relationship to Senator Dietrich gave the couple easy entree to the higher social circles in Hastings, but their names rarely appeared in the society columns of the *Tribune*. Lena enjoyed social ties with several women, most of whom were in one way or another involved in the activities of St. Mark's Pro-Cathedral, Episcopal.

In contrast to the practice of Adam Breede, Henry avoided developing a circle of cronies. Until his final years with the *Tribune*, when he had been forced more or less into open participation in the affairs of the chamber of commerce and into the reorganization of a bank, he avoided involvement in community organizations. His excuse for not belonging to Rotary, Lions, Kiwanis or any other luncheon club was that their noon meetings conflicted with the hour of final decisions as to the content of an afternoon paper. I don't recall his ever making a straight declaration on this point, but I got the message in more ways than one that it was easier to edit a paper when one's personal affiliations were not likely to interfere with one's judgment.

Every now and then he would organize a Sunday outing on the Platte River. These usually were restricted to the Smiths and from one to four of us younger folk from the *Tribune* staff. One of the more memorable of these expeditions was in midwinter. Coming out of church that blustery morning, I found the Smiths, with Sue Baker, then a college student and Smith's part-time secretary, waiting to see if I could join a party that would include Marie Herrin and members of her family. After I had changed clothes, we headed for the vicinity of Lowell and ended up on a frozen sandbar. We pitched a tent the Smiths had brought and built a fire in front of it. We never quite came to agreement as to whether it was better to stand by our wood fire in the sub-freezing wind or sit on the canvas floor of the tent, which was little warmer than the frozen sand beneath it and very little softer. The meal Henry and Lena prepared included items long since forgotten, but the quality was bound to be good. It was always that way when the Smiths were hosts.

During my second or third summer with the *Tribune* the Smiths invited me to join them for a weekend trip to a rather primitive hostelry on Enders Lake in Brown County. We left Hastings in mid-afternoon—after the final edition of the Saturday paper had gone to press—and drove more than 150 miles, with a stop for dinner at the hotel in Broken Bow. After breakfast Sunday morning, we put a rowboat on the lake and tried fishing in several locations. Our catch was limited to some sickly perch, victims of a disease that had hit the lake that summer, and by noon we were ready to start for home. Henry and Lena seemed little concerned that we were taking no fish. Fishing for them, I was beginning to suspect, was an excuse for expeditions of this kind. Before the afternoon was over, I was convinced that their interest in the eastern sandhill country was not in its fishing lakes but in the man-made national forest near Halsey. Henry Smith knew the story of the forest, created by President Theodore Roosevelt under pressure generated by Dr. Charles

E. Bessey, University of Nebraska botanist. From his newspaper days in Lincoln and his years in the office of Senator Dietrich, he knew about the doubts and questions that had countered Dr. Bessey's insistence that trees would grow in the sandy lands where nothing but grass had grown before. And so we spent part of an afternoon inspecting the test of Bessey's theory. There were pines with trunks up to six inches in diameter along auto trails kept usable by heavy layers of hay that filled the unstable ruts on all the slopes.

About three years later my wife made the fourth in another trip to Enders. Again we tried fishing on Sunday morning; again we packed up and left shortly after noon, and again we stopped at Halsey and toured the forest and the adjacent tree nursery.

From these trips came an understanding of Henry Smith that might not have come to me from relationships restricted to the office. Both he and Lena seemed to undergo a change of mood the moment he shifted the Reo Flying Cloud—and later Studebakers—into high gear. They started talking. When Lena had her turn, she would almost invariably close her narrative with this question: "Isn't that right, Henry?" And when he had his say, which was most certainly a fair amount of the time, he almost invariably talked about lakes and woods and flowing streams. Getting into the open country was something he yearned for more than he ever divulged through those six-day weeks at the *Tribune*. There was no office talk on a Smith-managed trip to the country.

While an undersized ashtray took in one smoldering cigarette butt after another, Henry described lakes and rivers in Minnesota, Wisconsin, Canada and elsewhere. He mentioned fishing in these places, but there was no emphasis on the kind or size of the catch. Gradually over the years I began to see in Henry Smith a sort of frustrated outdoorsman.

Though Smith did enjoy fishing under the right conditions, he definitely was not a hunter. He visited easily with men who dropped into his office to report on trips to choice fishing spots or on hunting expeditions to Colorado, Idaho or Alaska. Never, though, did he boast of his own kill or catch. He brought choice lake salmon back from Minnesota on several occasions and shared them with some of us at the *Tribune*. But when he talked about his trips to fishing lakes, it was not what he caught that got first attention; it was the joy and pleasure of being alive and able to ride in a boat across the lake where the trout abounded in the early days of autumn. And thus I came to understand the change of mood that seemed to come over him the moment we headed out of Hastings, even when the destination was no more than that lonely little boarding house on the treeless edge of a sandhill lake. We would cross the Platte, two branches of the Loup and the clear and sparkling Dismal River. Next day was Halsey and the controversial experiment in forestry. These were modest recompense for a man who seemed to yearn for the best in woods and streams and lakes. To understand Henry Smith in these situations one had to remember, I eventually concluded, that for more than a quarter of a century he had lived and worked in a city laid out on a treeless plain a dozen miles or more from a flowing stream.

It was a rule of the *Tribune* that we never ran pictures of the collected kill of hunters or fishermen. For us editorial employees this was a convenience in dealing with the many persons who came with snapshots of themselves or others holding long strings of fish or posed in the midst of a pile of dead ducks, geese or pheasants or alongside a deer's head with dead eyes on the camera. We would agree routinely to the newsworthiness of such pictures and then state the paper's policy. The idea, we explained, was to avoid any suggestion that we lent the pages of our paper

A Man Named Smith

to any sort of competition that could serve only to encourage unnecessary slaughter and waste. This rule was initiated, I am confident, by Smith rather than Adam Breede, the *Tribune's* founder. Adam liked to hunt, and when he killed an animal in Africa, say, a picture of him and his trophy justified breaking the rule that applied to the fish and game of Nebraska.

In the hay and wheat fields of eastern Colorado, in the college dining hall where I worked for my meals, in classrooms and on athletic fields, I never had found it difficult to understand the person running the show and giving the orders. I had been at the *Tribune* no more than two weeks when it dawned on me that there were many things about Henry Smith that I should analyze and understand if I wanted to win and hold his confidence.

The very complexity of his personality was a challenge. He was reserved and non-committal in many situations. His likes and dislikes frequently had to be judged from actions rather than words. He was dignified in posture and speech, hesitant in either praise or criticism, but quick to the point in any discussion of office policy or practice.

He was a physically dominant person, standing about six feet tall and broad enough in the shoulders that the extra weight he carried in his mid-section was barely noticeable. He was almost always in shirtsleeves around the office, and he wore bow ties. His face, even in repose, carried a sort of built-in scowl, accentuated to some extent by bushy eyebrows. He generally avoided light and flippant comment in the opening of any conversation, and he looked his listeners in the eye. In all my nine years with him at the *Tribune* he would have been picked as the general manager by almost any stranger watching the complement of some 40 employees march by.

I learned much from Henry Smith, but the lesson that may have stood me in good stead more than any other was what I learned about the importance of knowing who one's boss is and how his (or her) mind and emotions react to given situations. What I learned from Smith in this regard I practiced assiduously in my relationships with at least a dozen men under whose supervision I would find myself in the years ahead. None was more complex than Henry Smith and none, within the bounds of his responsibilities, was more capable.

Studying Smith the outdoorsman was only a part of the job, of course. I had to understand him as editor, publisher and student of public affairs, or I might not qualify to take over editorial duties he was ready to relinquish as the pressure of general management came more and more to demand his attention. I was in for a series of tests of my patience and understanding. Smith didn't always explain his surprises.

Within less than a month after I started with the *Tribune*, a young man named Robert F. Kelley came in from Kansas City and started work as a reporter. Smith hadn't told me about him, and I pondered for several days the question of whether there was really a place for me on the staff. Kelley, it developed, had been a reporter on the Kansas City *Journal-Post*. He had interviewed Smith at the time the latter was in Kansas City to be with Adam Breede in his final illness. Smith had offered Kelley a job, apparently, and after some months he had decided to take it. I always suspected that Kelley's appearance came as a surprise to Smith. In any event, I suddenly found myself in a competitive situation that had not been part of the original plan. Kelley, graduate of Rockhurst College in Kansas City, had worked for the *Journal-Post* about three years and could demonstrate skills and experience far beyond what I could offer. He was an immediate hit with Walter Crow, the county attorney, and various others on his news beat. Not only could he handle the news professionally; he could regale his sources with stories of a reporter's life in Kansas City.

When Smith first talked with me about working at the *Tribune* he implied, certainly, that he was looking for someone who eventually would qualify to take over the supervision of the news staff. By midsummer my chances for advancement seemed to be blocked by the presence of an able, experienced man from Kansas City. In due time, though, I sensed that Kelley was getting restless, and within about six months of his coming he had decided to accept a job with the Associated Press at Topeka. At about the end of my first year Smith called me in one day and said he was giving me the title of city editor and responsibility for organization of the local news.

He did not gloss over some built-in problems. Dave Lewis, who was about 50 and a part-owner of the paper, would be taking some news assignments from me. So would Marie Herrin, a personable, aggressive individual in her thirties, who seemed to have absorbed almost every word of opinion and instruction to come from Henry Smith over a period of ten years. She had helped Smith with almost every phase of news management as he shifted his attention to general management of the paper. Dave Lewis was writing editorials as well as covering a news beat. One thing he did not want, though, was responsibility for organizational detail. Mrs. Herrin, on the other hand, would move almost instinctively into any organizational vacuum. She was knowledgeable and capable, and Henry Smith had placed great confidence in her. She had functioned as both city editor and managing editor, as well as women's editor, but to the best of my recollections her name never appeared on the masthead. As a sort of alter-ego for Smith, she functioned about as effectively as if full authority had been spelled out in a title. She bucked the handicap, of course, of being a woman in a world where men were reluctant to bestow titles on women, regardless of abilities or ambitions.

For me as a new and insecure city editor she was a pipeline from which poured a steady stream of advice and reminders of past experiences. She had taken literally—too literally, I sometimes thought—some of Smith's cautions and warnings. As in any community, there were in Hastings the usual share of exhibitionistic and promotion-minded individuals who would use the paper to the fullest in forwarding their personal projects or salving their egos. There were avowed enemies of the *Tribune*, including a couple of lawyers who had threatened libel suits. Such people were on Marie Herrin's taboo list. They were to be played down in the news, if not completely ignored. It bothered me occasionally to realize that what such people did sometimes was interesting or entertaining, if not especially significant. I bit my tongue now and then and deferred to her judgments in such matters rather than appeal to Smith for an interpretation of what she looked upon as his rules.

My initiation into the city editorship was just a few months along when the stock market crash of 1929 signaled the start of the Great Depression. The impact of Black Friday (October 24) itself was hardly noted in Hastings. Nobody said "This is it." The date became important in retrospect, but the disastrous turn of the market on that single day became fully significant only through the steady succession of events over the years ahead. In Hastings the full force of the depression would not be felt until 1931.

Whatever was happening to the national economy back there in 1929 seemed minor to me as I wrestled with the problems of organizing and directing the little news staff at the *Tribune*. It was not easy to argue with Dave Lewis or to insist that he cover stories he looked upon as trivial or unimportant. He owned an interest in the paper. Fritz Daly had come fresh from the University of Nebraska as sports editor. He and I developed a good rapport, but I felt

A Man Named Smith

some responsibility for helping him get around a tendency to use all the worn and trite phrases of the time. I remember arguing that it was great for the first writer to refer to the linemen of a football team as the "forward wall," but over-use of the term had made it objectionable in my eyes. Fritz was slow to agree.

A problem that haunted me for weeks during that first year of editorial responsibility centered on another male member of the staff. He had come on as a reporter especially trained to write about agriculture, and Smith and I agreed we needed to upgrade our agricultural reporting. The women in the office, though, developed an immediate dislike for him. They complained to me, but they also got the word to Smith—via Marie Herrin. Finally, it was agreed we couldn't afford to maintain the position (one of the first concessions to the economic downturn). It fell to me then to engage in my first firing. I went through all the negatives, including the letup in advertising sales, but I never mentioned the complaint that the women had voiced most. They didn't like the smell of this man's feet and had suggested that I advise him to wash his socks more often. I never had accepted this as grounds for firing. As a matter of fact, it was hard to pinpoint any kind of odor in the *Tribune* newsroom—especially on a hot day. From the open windows came the smells of everything from locomotive smoke to horse manure, and from the composing and press rooms came the pungent odors of hot lead, scorched mats, printer's ink and stacked newsprint. In cold weather, with all the windows closed, the air was blue and acrid with cigarette and cigar smoke. I never believed one man's feet should have caused me the anguish of having to fire him without telling him why.

On May 8, 1930, near the end of my first year as city editor, a tornado swept across Hastings and put me and the rest of the news staff to a stiff test.

I was in the room of my brother, Dave, on the third floor of Ringland Hall, on the college campus, when the storm struck. Lights went out, windows came crashing in, and the air was thick with plaster dust. The aging structure seemed to sway, but its walls held up, as did most of the roof. We groped our way downstairs, and, still fearing the possibility the building would collapse, we hurried through fallen tree branches and other debris to a point some distance from it. Someone had suggested we seek shelter in the tunnel that carried steam pipes from the central heating plant to the various buildings. But I can't recall that we ever found an entrance. Rain poured down for some time after the funnel had passed, and much of the damage ultimately was attributed to the water that had come through ripped roofs. A heavy wooden manhole cover from the roof of Ringland Hall had grazed my Model-A Ford, landing just a few feet away. A direct hit would have wrecked my first automobile. Within two blocks of the campus, to the south and east, were several houses without roofs.

Power and telephone lines were down in many places, and streets in all parts of the city were blocked by tree limbs, abandoned cars and varieties of litter. My memory is unclear as to just how I communicated with Henry Smith and Marie Herrin. In any event, the staff assembled early the next morning to report the disaster. By that time we knew there had been only one death directly attributable to the storm. The extent of the property damage was hard to estimate, but by press time we were agreed it was in the neighborhood of $1 million for the city—ignoring losses of farmers whose buildings were in the storm's path as it came from the southwest and left the city in a northeasterly direction.

There was some question in the early morning as to whether we would have power for our typesetting and printing machinery. Representatives of the Kearney *Hub*

A Man Named Smith

and the Grand Island *Independent* appeared in person, as I recall, to offer use of their equipment if ours didn't work. In the end, our machines functioned, and we reported the tornado's damage in almost painful detail. (I had yielded early to Marie Herrin's insistence on describing the damage on a street-by-street basis—home-by-home in some instances—rather than stick to the big picture.) We got many reminders in the days to follow that while we had reported the damage to Mr. Doe's property, we had overlooked Mrs. Roe's place, where the damage was even greater. It would be that way, of course, through all my years in daily newspaper work.

My memories of how the *Tribune* reported the storm itself are far less vivid than those of my involvement in what happened to the courthouse trees. The county board of supervisors had employed an itinerant crew to cut the damaged limbs out of the large elms and other trees that surrounded the building. The treatment of some of the trees was drastic, as it was in other parts of the city. Art Lawson, hardware dealer and native son with a special interest in all things dating back to his father's arrival as one of the first merchants, became spokesman for those who thought the trimmers more destructive than the tornado. He came to the *Tribune* and demanded that I view the damage and write about it.

My first story was confined to a report of Lawson's alarm, of course, but that was not enough. He called in an extension forester from the University of Nebraska. That gentleman found himself in an uncomfortable position, to say the least. He could be critical of some of the ways the trees were trimmed, but he was hesitant to say the crew had botched the job to the extent Lawson thought it had. Touring the grounds with a sizable crowd, the forester pointed to one of the trees and observed that the trimmers had left some "stagheads." Lawson grabbed my arm, pointed to the tree. "See," he said, "stagheads," implying that this was something awful that I should report. It was the first time I had heard the term, and I am still wondering just where it applies in the rules of trimming a damaged tree.

The tree trimming crew involved in this incident was only one of the many itinerant groups that poured into Hastings to tackle the many tasks the storm created. Insurance adjusters came in by the score, along with carpenters, roofers, electricians, telephone crews and the like. Restaurants and rooming houses were crowded. The flow of insurance money into the community, some of us estimated in later years, delayed the arrival of the Great Depression in Hastings by as much as a full year.

About the time I completed my first year as city editor—not long after the tornado—Smith called me in to talk about a change of jobs. I would leave the editorial department and move to the business office. My responsibility would be to promote and sell the services of what Smith had termed the graphic arts department.

For many years the *Tribune* had maintained a small commercial printing service. The equipment was limited to a battery of hand-fed presses and the essential tables, folders and other materials for handling letterheads, handbills, small booklets, business forms and the like. Type was set in the newspaper composing room.

In 1926 the paper had won national attention with an announcement it was establishing a photoengraving department and would be printing local news pictures on a regular basis. This was a bold move for a small daily. There were newspapers several times its size that never had considered offering such services and taking on the fixed costs. Smith, for whom this was a dream come true, had plans to make the new service pay for itself by doing photoengraving for commercial printers and other newspapers throughout the region. The nearest photoengraving services were at Lincoln.

It was obvious from the beginning that a photoengraving shop needed the support of photography and art. Francis Robertson was hired as a full-time photographer on his graduation from Hastings College in 1926. Charles Wicker, sports editor who had studied art in high school and had drawn a few cartoons for the *Tribune,* was converted into a full-time artist and sent away for several weeks of concentrated experience in the use of the airbrush and other techniques.

By 1930 the novelty of all these new services had worn off, and the economy was faltering. Smith faced the fact that some way had to be found to increase outside sales. Oris Fearn, manager of the printing department, had been handling commercial sales of engraving, art and photography. Smith proposed that I give full time to a campaign of promotion and sales of these lines. I would handle all orders and spend several days each month calling on prospective customers in other parts of the state and in northern Kansas. This was what Smith wanted, and I saw no reason to question him. I wondered if I had been a failure in his eyes after two years of reporting and editing. He reassured me that I hadn't.

There is some confusion in my memory as to just how much Smith had said about replacing me in the newsroom before my actual transfer to the business office. Despite his reassurances that I was doing him a favor by taking over the graphic arts sales responsibilities, I wondered if he was giving up on me as a prospective editor. He already had had some discussions, I would learn later, with a young reporter on the Omaha *Bee-News* named Jack Bisco. Within a few weeks after I took over a desk in the business office near the front door, Bisco was established in the newsroom with what seemed a more authoritative position than I had held. He was for all practical purposes the managing editor.

A graduate of the school of journalism at the University of Missouri, Bisco was an aggressive, free-wheeling sort, self-confident and outgoing. He was fresh from reporting one of the early incidents of the Great Depression—the revolt of farmers against low milk prices that had led to the blocking of roads around Omaha and the dumping of trucks and the manhandling of drivers. There was little in the daily news at Hastings to match this as stimulation of the instincts of a reporter. I could see in Bisco a somewhat early realization that life moved more slowly in Hastings than in Omaha and that the sacred cows of a small city were more obvious and frustrating than in a larger one. I knew from my own experience that Marie Herrin would not hesitate to throw up caution signals against some Bisco suggestions, and I felt certain that Bisco would bridle at these more quickly than I had.

From my new desk near the front door on the main floor I was merely an observer, though a somewhat jealous one, of what went on in the news department. My job was to rustle new business for the graphic arts department. I traveled to county seat towns in all directions, prepared promotional materials and handled the walk-in customers. Meanwhile, I was doing what I could to improve my knowledge of the technical aspects of the printing business, especially as it involved the use of engraved copper and zinc plates for reproduction of photography and art.

One day in late September that year (1930) Smith proposed an assignment that would mean a trip to Kansas City. Mrs. Smith's niece, Josephine Mickel, and her husband, Ross, newly married and living on a ranch in North Dakota, had been invited by the Smiths to accompany them to the American Royal Livestock Show in Kansas City. The plan was that the Mickels would come to Hastings and ride with the Smiths to Kansas City in the Reo Flying Cloud. They were to leave on Friday, see the Royal on Saturday and return to Hastings on Sunday. Henry had discovered that he was expected to be in Hastings on the chosen Friday, so he proposed that I join the party and drive the car to Kansas City. Here was an opportunity, he reasoned, for me to visit some places in that city and get advice on how to handle my new job.

We set out early Friday morning, ate lunch at the hotel in Falls City and were settled in Kansas City's Robert E. Lee Hotel by dinner time. (We would pay for the rooms with a due bill accepted by the *Tribune* in payment for advertisements of the hotel.)

Mrs. Smith had mentioned several times as we traveled along that she hoped we could see a good stage play that night. After scanning the evening paper she settled for Mae West in *Sex*. I recall no distinct impressions of the play beyond the fact that it included some lines that would be quoted in stories of Mae's death almost exactly 50 years from that date.

Early the next morning I met a friend of high school days, Marvin Martin, and he and I visited the Kansas City *Star* and the Art Institute, where he had been a student. I visited with photoengravers and artists at the *Star* and talked with a commercial artist in a downtown studio. The purpose of this last visit was to arrange for sending him some art jobs that were pending at the *Tribune* and help develop some standards of quality against which to measure the work of our own artist, Charles Wicker. For the next eight months I would quote the prices of that Kansas City artist when customers balked at the quotations I gave for Wicker's work.

We saw the Royal horse show Saturday night, spent some time Sunday morning visiting the new Country Club Plaza and adjoining residential areas, then headed home to the *Tribune* and, in my case, to the pressing problems of the graphic arts department.

Recalling that trip to Kansas City some 50 years later, I can't help wondering about the fact that it inspired no visions of future years. I never dreamed that I would spend more than a quarter of a century as a resident of that city, would sit on its governing council for more than a decade, attend hundreds of meetings in the building at 20 West Ninth Street, where I met with the artist, and serve on the board of the American Royal.

The key man in the *Tribune* graphic arts department, from a production standpoint, was Bernard Good. The son of a former lumber merchant at Cowles, he had gone through high school in Lincoln and had learned the photoengraving trade as an employee of the Nebraska *State Journal.* When he came to the *Tribune* he was still in his early twenties, but he was a master craftsman, and under his supervision the *Tribune* shop was turning out zinc and copper halftones the equal of anything that could be purchased at Lincoln or Omaha. Good was joined by at least two former *Journal* employees, and one of these, Myron Springer, stayed with the *Tribune* until retirement.

My memories of those 13 or 14 months I worked as the *Tribune's* graphic arts salesman include few flashes of triumph or success. Thanks to my experience in putting out high school and college yearbooks, I sold yearbook contracts to the high school at Ravenna and the school of nursing at the Mary Lanning Memorial Hospital in Hastings. Most everywhere I went, though, I encountered the thickening gloom of depression. It was hard to become enthusiastic about selling when nobody seemed to want to talk about buying.

I went to Smith early in the summer of 1931 to tell him I was planning to be married in the fall and wanted to make sure I was getting along well enough to expect continued employment. Not only did he encourage me to go ahead with marriage plans; he hinted that he might want me to return to the news department. It turned out that Jack Bisco and Fritz Daly had announced plans to leave the *Tribune* and join in a business venture. On top of all that, Marie Herrin would be married in the fall to R. R. Dammerell and was planning to resign. Smith had decided I should return to the newsroom, and with Marie's leaving I would be head of the department, in fact as well as in title, even though no title was mentioned.

In mid-September I headed for Colorado and marriage. I expected to be gone two full weeks, but a message from Smith suggested he would appreciate my getting back to the *Tribune* a few days early. Mabel and I made our way across eastern Colorado and southern Nebraska with her cedar chest extending out of the trunk of our Plymouth coupe, and I reported back to the newsroom on or about September 25.

I can't recall Smith's reason for interrupting our honeymoon, but it could have been some early warnings that bad news was generating, and he wanted to make sure the *Tribune* had the staff to cover it. The news was that the First National Bank was in trouble. First move was toward reorganization with new resources and a new charter, but in the end the bank went into receivership with a thud that shook the whole community. Before the end of October the Clarke-Buchanan Company, its investments mainly in farm mortgages, filed for voluntary receivership. In March of 1932 Hoeppner and Uerling Company, another real estate investment firm, went into bankruptcy. Three major financial institutions had collapsed in less than six months.

George B. Cronkleton, who came from Scottsbluff to be receiver of the First National, was already acting as receiver for nine other banks in Nebraska. For the next two or three years it would be said with varying degrees of approval that Cronkleton had managed to keep open a long list of businesses that a more relentless receiver might have wiped out. In any event, the First National eventually paid out 60 percent on its deposits, including my Christmas savings account of less than $50.

While the closing of banks and investment companies made news, and news was my primary interest and responsibility, it's hard to look back on those late months of 1931 and most all of 1932 without recalling some of the anguish I suffered in dealing with the news. The side effects of a community's financial collapse are best understood only when there is direct and personal association with the victims. At police headquarters, the courthouse, the city hall, the chamber of commerce—most anywhere I went in performance of my duties—I was witness to personal tragedies, grief and despair. These things get lost sometimes in the headlined reports of institutional failures. Proud men who had walked the streets with heads high and with what some thought unnecessary haughty glances at others, were ruined by mistakes in their judgment, mistakes in their investments, mistakes of a whole society. Some pleaded with editors and reporters to skip the unpleasant facts, some plotted to avoid public exposure of their downfall. Some took their medicine without a whimper.

I covered two jury trials that came one after the other in district court. The stories were the same, it seemed to me. There had been bad judgment, failure to cover falling prices. One man went free, the other went to the penitentiary. I overheard a strong-minded juryman explain proudly that he had made sure somebody paid for what he had lost in one of Hastings' failing institutions. The man tried before his jury had gone to prison.

Fallout from the financial failures of 1931 and 1932 would make news for several years. Directors of the First National Bank, for example, were faced with double liability. Some of them had to scratch to come up with the receiver's demands. Each settlement with a director became a matter of record at the courthouse, and there was considerable quibbling over our policy at the *Tribune* that these settlements made news.

In this general climate of disappointment, distrust and frustration the promoters and managers of the county fair started thinking of ways to make something worthwhile of the fair they were planning for August of 1932. Agriculture was in the doldrums, along with the rest of the economy. But it was trouble of another sort that seemed to start the thought processes that led to a truly innovative approach to the annual exposition.

Hastings for years had been proud of its municipal electric plant. Rates were low and service was good, but there were men of some stature in the community who disliked the man who had planned and developed the power plant over a period of at least two decades. His name was W. S. Watson, and among those who had sought his ouster was William Madgett, elected mayor of Hastings in the spring of 1931. Watson resigned under pressure and eventually was replaced by a young man from Missouri, E. S. (Ed) Howard.

Somebody came up with the idea that the county fair could be used to restore confidence in the municipal electric plant, and the idea appealed to the fair board. What was finally agreed upon was a fair that would feature all that was new and novel in the field of electric gadgets and services. Westinghouse had sponsored such a show at Atlantic City, and the company was ready to bring its major exhibits to Hastings for the fair.

Ed Howard, fully conscious of the fact that he was on trial, was a quick and ready participant in the planning, and it may have been his idea that the fair should feature a spectacular lighted fountain. The fountain was obtained and temporarily set up in front of the grandstand for nightly demonstrations. Eventually it was placed in Highland Park near the electric plant and officially established as a memorial to a former mayor, Jacob Fisher.

Henry Smith's interest in the electrical show was solicited early in the planning stage, and he pledged the *Tribune's* unqualified support. He went so far as to authorize the hiring of a full-time reporter to write articles about the fair over a period of several weeks prior to its opening. This was a break for me, because it brought to our staff a man who added materially to our ability to cover the news after the electric show was duly, and quite satisfactorily, staged. Paul Hansell had grown up in Hastings and had taken his degree from Hastings College after three years there and one year at Carnegie Institute of Technology in Pittsburgh. He had been laid off his job on the public relations staff of the Westinghouse Corporation in St. Louis. He was quick to accept the *Tribune's* offer of a temporary job through the electrical exposition and just as quick to accept a permanent spot when the exposition was over. For the next four years he would be a mainstay of my reportorial staff and eventually would be city editor. He left in 1936 to join the staff of the Omaha *Bee-News*.

While Hansell had worked in public relations with Westinghouse, his interest was in things mechanical much more than in the fine points of communication. He had been less than outstanding in his English studies in college. His writing, at the outset, was often awkward. But he stands far above anybody else among a score or more men and women for whom I have acted as teacher during their trial periods in the writing field. Reading his copy, I would make changes and then explain each change to him. After some weeks of observing his amazing ability to remember every such lesson, I made a sort of game of trying to catch him in the repetition of an error in sentence structure or word choice. To the best of my memory he won with an almost perfect score. I sometimes thought he learned to write by rote rather than by rule.

Through the fall of 1932 the national news was dominated by the presidential campaign. Smith and Lewis, with backgrounds of general loyalty to the Republican party, were slow to blame Herbert Hoover for the Great Depression, and neither seemed enthusiastic about Franklin D. Roosevelt. I was confused by the seeming presumption of some of my best Republican friends that a change of presidents was bound to help the national economy. In any event, the *Tribune* maintained a neutral stance through that period of preparation for shifts in public philosophy that would affect the national government for the rest of the century. I recall going to Grand Island one Sunday to hear Herbert Hoover speak from the back of a train. We got close enough to observe the tired eyes and rash-splotched face of a man who was obviously under great strain. Mabel and I voted for Hoover.

By the time of the March 4 inauguration there were signs that Henry Smith was impressed by some of the things Roosevelt had been saying. When the paper came out with quotes from the inaugural speech, Smith read it and called me in. He was critical of the way we had treated some parts of the story which summarized the speech. He argued that there was one sentence that should have been printed in bold-face type. It was the sentence in which Roosevelt told the American people that "the only thing we have to fear is fear itself." This may have been my first warning that Smith and the *Tribune* were moving into the Roosevelt camp and that the *Tribune* would some day be rated as one of the few "liberal" papers in Nebraska.

The Roosevelt inaugural set off a chain of events that shook the community and, as much as any incident, marked the start of positive moves toward coping with the Great Depression. The new president was barely settled in his office when he ordered the closing of all banks. While we in Hastings wrestled with a community-wide cash shortage, we also speculated as to whether one of the banks would be allowed to reopen without an infusion of new money. The Hastings National reopened within the 10-day period that had been set for a close look by government officials at the total banking structure. The Nebraska National was placed in the hands of a conservator, W. C. Fisher.

Smith, in a matter of days, found himself on a special committee to supervise reorganization of the Nebraska National. His emergence as an active participant in affairs outside the *Tribune* was definitely affecting his attitudes at the office, and for me there was a growing feeling that I was on my own in many of the kinds of situations in which I had relied on his final judgment. He would continue to make suggestions and outline general policies, but the day-to-day content of the paper was becoming more and more my personal responsibility.

The message came through with certainty the day I discovered he had quietly ordered that my name be placed in the masthead with the title of managing editor.

Some months following my designation as managing editor, Smith called me in and outlined an unpleasant task. It was time, he said, to replace George Brown, the telegraph editor since shortly after I had joined the staff. I had handled the termination of two or three employees up to that time, but telling George Brown he had to go was a challenge to my conscience. He was well into middle age, with at least one child still in school, and jobs were hard to find. He had come to the *Tribune* in the late 1920s at the invitation of Adam Breede. It was obvious that sentiment had figured in offering him a job, because George's father, A. H. Brown, had given Breede his first newspaper job and had sold him the weekly *Independent-Tribune* under the easiest of conditions.

I had considered Brown's work acceptable and found him easy to get along with. We played tennis together through several summers. Smith, it was obvious, had found little to convince him that Brown was essential to the new *Tribune* he was trying to build.

Many months—maybe a year—transpired from the time I told Brown that he should be looking for another job and his final decision to join a son in a publishing enterprise at a town to the west of Hastings. Through his final months at the *Tribune* it was quietly understood by him and me that Smith had initiated the move.

Smith continued to keep an eye on the people I hired, but never again did he order a dismissal or in any way veto my choice of someone to fill a vacancy. He dropped little hints now and then of things I might do but made no attempt to monitor each day's paper.

It did not escape some of us that George Brown's going fitted the pattern of a youth movement that Smith had seemed quietly to have initiated after becoming general manager. While Smith and Lewis were in their fifties, along with Brown, the average age of all *Tribune* employees probably was under 35. Several of us on whom Smith had placed administrative responsibilities were still in our twenties. Newcomers to the staff, with few exceptions, were younger than the persons they replaced.

While I am a bit hazy as to the exact sequence of replacements on the telegraph desk, I do recall that James McWhorter came straight out of Hastings College and had developed into a competent telegraph editor in a matter of months. Harold Cowan came directly from college, as did Marvin Cruse. Ed Wilken spent some time selling insurance and made his entry to the news staff by way of the proof desk. He went on to be our agricultural specialist after Oliver DeWolf, from the University of Nebraska, had established the pattern of the job. Margaret Reckmeyer came from the Holdrege *Citizen;* Lucille Furman (sister of Bess, who was eventually to cover the White House for the *New York Times*) came from the family newspaper at Danbury. Vaughn Herrin, from whose mother, Marie, I had learned much in earlier years, spent several hours each day at the *Tribune* while attending college. Sue Baker was both newswriter and secretary to Smith while in college.

Cowan, with whom I worked longer than with any other staff member, came on as sports editor in 1931. He demonstrated from the beginning a writing talent that could be applied to many things besides football games and golf matches. When we needed to treat some subject in light vein, we turned to Cowan. In due time he started addressing some of his humorous articles to "Dear Boss." The device seemed to attract readers and, from my point of view, it was important that Smith liked it.

One day in 1935, shortly after the death of Will Rogers, Smith and I were discussing the question of replacing Rogers' daily column. It had appeared on our front page for years. "Why not," Smith asked, "give Cowan a try at writing a column to appear under the 'Dear Boss' heading?" "Why not?" I responded, and Cowan accepted the challenge. The level of excellence and writing style and the wide range of subjects addressed made this daily column a feature that few small-city papers anywhere in the country could match. Smith knew it, and I knew it. Whether Cowan ever felt he was underpaid I do not know. But at something in the neighborhood of $32.50 a week he probably was.

There came a time in the mid-1930s when I could look over the news staff and consider it competent to handle any situation. Other editors, it turned out, were appraising it, too. Gertrude McLaughlin, who had been writing society news when I came to the paper, was attracted to the Omaha *Bee-News.* Paul Hansell, mentioned earlier, followed her in late 1936. Oliver DeWolfe was attracted to another job, and by 1938 Margaret Reckmeyer had gone to the regional Farm Security Administration office in

Lincoln. From there she moved through other bureaus and closed out her career with the CIA in Washington.

A face on the obituary page of a Kansas City paper one day in the late 1970s caught my eye. It was that of Robert F. (Bob) Kelley, looking much as I had known him as a young reporter up from Kansas City to join the *Tribune* staff a few weeks after I had joined it in 1928. We had lived within a few miles of each other in Kansas City for more than 25 years and hadn't seen each other. He had worked for the Associated Press and a Kansas City publishing company.

Jack Bisco, who headed the *Tribune* staff during my year as graphic arts salesman, became a vice-president of the United Press in New York. Fritz Daly, who quit as sports editor to join Jack in a business venture that failed to materialize, served as secretary of the chamber of commerce and secretary to the board of the Central Nebraska Public Power and Irrigation District before leaving Hastings for a job with the Omaha *Bee-News* and, later, the *World-Herald*. He was secretary of the University of Nebraska Alumni Association for a time and died while still in his fifties after working on newspapers at Scottsbluff and Torrington, Wyoming.

It seemed quite natural that Henry Smith, with sale of the paper in 1937, should yield to his long-suppressed desire to be closer to woods and streams. He and Lena eventually bought a home near the Mississippi River south of the Twin Cities. A winter of low temperatures and snow-blocked roads forced a reconsideration and a decision to return to Nebraska. My last visit with them was at our home in Lincoln in 1943. Henry seemed to take some personal pride in the fact that the University of Nebraska had considered my *Tribune* training sufficient to qualify me to head its school of journalism. He was as relaxed and informal as ever I had seen him.

It came to me then that he had been to some extent a

dreamer of improbable dreams and had charmed me with them. For me they were the dreams of untested youth. For Smith, probably, they had been a renewal of hopes and ambitions that had been shattered by events beyond his control. The great plans he outlined in 1928 were interrupted by the Wall Street collapse, the Great Depression, by drouth and flood in Nebraska and by the sheer obstinacy of people standing in the way of innovation and change. What he taught me, I surmise, was the importance of adjusting to obstructing events and accommodating to uncooperative people. Subsequent chapters recall some events, situations and people we dealt with together.

6. Dave(y) Was a Welshman

A Gentle Iconoclast, Too, and the House Intellectual

I had trouble now and then understanding David J. (Dave) Lewis, who was close behind Smith as guide and mentor through my first nine years with the *Tribune*. While he owned a one-seventh interest in the paper and shared with Smith certain policy actions, he abhorred the responsibilities of management and avoided as much as possible the appearance of command. For several years his reportorial work was under my supervision, but the two of us understood that I was not to order him around. I never tried.

In the eyes of most *Tribune* personnel he was the house intellectual. He read books and periodicals some of us had never heard of and would give up most anything else he might be doing for a discussion of literature, history, politics, philosophy or the future of Nebraska's agriculture. I don't know that anyone ever accused him of being an iconoclast, but he cast himself in that role on occasion. The status quo, in his view, was never immune to intelligent challenge.

Small of stature, soft of voice and generally a patient listener to the details of complaints or problems, he startled friends and associates occasionally with vigorous outbursts of dissent. He could be cruelly critical of someone's sweeping assertion. He called for proof or documentation and could speak scornfully when a bold talker failed to produce it.

Smith confided to me that this belligerence in debate might easily be traced to Dave's boyhood in the Clay County farming community where he was born in 1877. Never physically strong, he had been picked on by other boys and had been especially hurt by taunts that made reference to his Welsh ancestry. Smith recalled Dave's telling him once of the hurt that came with other boys' recitation of these lines from an old nursery rhyme:

"Paddy was a Welshman, Paddy was a thief;
Paddy came to our house and stole a leg of beef."

Lewis most certainly could not have been classified with the book burners of our society, but it's a safe guess that he would not have been troubled by a banning of all books in which that rhyme appeared. It was to his credit certainly that any scars picked up in his boyhood did not keep Dave Lewis, the man, from proclaiming proudly that he descended from Welsh coal miners. He had gone to Wales while in his twenties and had worked for some time as a reporter on a daily paper at Cardiff. He was especially proud of having interviewed David Lloyd George, the native of Wales who became Britain's prime minister during World War I.

The record seems clear enough that he went out of his way to reaffirm his pride in his Welsh ancestry. After Smith told me the Paddy story, I developed the theory that Lewis' behavior reflected pride also in his mental agility. I can't help believing that he came to enjoy demonstrating a quicker mind than one might have found among those better-muscled farm boys he grew up with around Trumbull.

In the writing of news stories he adhered to the rules of objectivity, and his editorials were generally quite restrained. There were times and situations, though, when he could not cover his built-in prejudices. His editorials in criticism of William Madgett as a candidate for mayor in 1931 went beyond the sound logic of which he was capable. I cringed as I read some of them, and I am certain Smith was tempted on more than one occasion during that campaign to pull Dave down from the perch of outrage from which he assailed the candidate. It was my opinion at the time that the *Tribune's* attacks on Madgett contributed to a sympathy vote that helped him defeat the incumbent, Joe Davis.

I couldn't help feeling that in his striving to make sure he had no reason to apologize for his Welsh ancestry he developed a sort of pro-Britain stance. On at least a dozen occasions I heard him hold forth on the better quality of beef one ate in England as compared to beef in the United States. He would concede, of course, that most of the British beef had come from Argentina. But the British knew how to prepare beef, he would argue, how to age it and cook it. Such talk, of course, was in direct contradiction of the popular comments of the time about how the British cooked everything to the point of tastelessness. He would argue at length in defense of his position that the people of England and Canada were more polite than Americans. For proof he would cite differences in treatment he had received when going through customs on his travels to and from both countries.

Victim of a depressing assortment of afflictions over the years, he studied his physical weaknesses with scholarly diligence. He seemed almost to make games out of them—all perhaps but an addiction to cigarettes. He seemed to view this as a right and privilege that neither medical authority nor moralist should meddle with. He talked about his ailments less as a hypochondriac than as a man sharing new adventures with his doctors. During our first years together he made regular visits to the Kellogg Sanitarium at Battle Creek, Michigan. As his troubles became more baffling to Hastings doctors, he started going to the Mayo Clinic at Rochester, Minnesota. In due time he was found to have myasthenia gravis.

There was very little literature on this disease of nerves and muscles and very few known cases, but Dave read what reports and comments he could find and spoke proudly of the fact that a Dr. Boothby at Rochester considered his a sort of landmark case. Complications related to diabetes required the amputation of a leg in the late 1930s.

My visits with him before I left Hastings in 1940 were always stimulating. He was still reading and listening to the radio and he welcomed opportunities to review what Elmer Davis, Gabriel Heatter and others had been saying about the preliminaries to World War II that were taking up more and more time and space in the flow of news through the air and the printing presses. He would die of a heart attack without ever knowing the full extent of United States involvement in the war or the final outcome, but he was interested to the end.

The first five years I worked with Dave may well have been the best years of his life. A bachelor until well into his forties, he was married in 1925 to Ada Garver, whom he had known for many years. They had built an attractive home on East Ninth Street and were involving themselves in various community activities. Ada introduced Dave to the YWCA, and he was surprised, I think, by the social consciousness and intellectual breadth of one or two of the professional secretaries who served the organization. The Lewises were charter members of a new book review club, the Fish Fry, which took its name from lines in Marc Connelly's drama, *The Green Pastures.* Within a year or two of the founding of the club, Dave had reviewed the autobiographies of Lincoln Steffens and Clarence Darrow. Club members talked about these reviews for months, and people who never really had known Dave Lewis spoke almost in awe of his friendly interpretations of these sharp critics of things in the American system that many had considered almost sacred. I did not hear either of his reviews, but his talk at the office substantiated his agreement with more of what Steffens and Darrow had written than some of his listeners cared to hear. The Darrow book gave him opportunity to take some shots at William Jennings Bryan, for whom he had little respect since the Great Commoner's involvement in the Tennessee litigation over the teaching of evolution. Among the many topics Dave liked to discuss with his literary acquaintances was the decline of the Book-of-the-Month Club. He had dropped his membership after finding little of merit in the succession of books the club had sent him. He had joined the Literary Guild and liked its book selections much better.

Dave's interest in critical writing had been with him a long time. He had read the early works of Upton Sinclair and Ida M. Tarbell, and while he may have disagreed with some of what they wrote, he was quick to defend the role of the so-called muckrakers in a democratic society. He loved to tell of the time Joseph G. (Uncle Joe) Cannon of Illinois caught him reading Tarbell's *History of the Standard Oil Company*. The setting was a railroad coach somewhere in southwest Nebraska during a political campaign. Cannon had come to the state to speak for Republican candidates. Lewis was traveling with the campaigners as a reporter. Cannon, noting the title of the book Dave was reading, pointed to it and said, "Young man, you shouldn't read that trash." Dave insisted that his response was to the effect that he would make his own decisions as to what books he should read. He was always quick to expand his report of the incident with a comment that among the Republican candidates for Congress in Nebraska that year was George W. Norris, who eventually would get credit for breaking the power of Joe Cannon as speaker of the House.

One Sunday in the spring of 1932, Dave, Ada, my wife Mabel and I journeyed to Cozad in the Lewises' disk-wheeled Packard sedan. We loitered an hour or so along the Platte near Lowell and watched the vast flocks of sandhill cranes at one of the popular rest stops of their annual northward migration. At Cozad we spent some time with my brother David, who had wintered there as custodian of several hundred fattening cattle. We also visited a beekeeper's farm that the Lewises knew about and purchased several cartons of the "spun honey" produced there for a special clientele, including the dining car service of the Union Pacific.

Ada died in 1933, but with the help of a competent housekeeper who had come into the home while Ada was alive, Dave adapted to the loss and kept his spirits remarkably high. The housekeeper, Dorothy Hedgecock, served as practical nurse and chauffeur and ultimately became the second Mrs. Lewis.

Dave continued to write editorials and do some reporting, but his illnesses and his retreats to Michigan and other northern states during a series of hot summers kept him away from the office for long stretches. With the sale of the paper in 1937, he cleaned his desk and we saw no more of him at the *Tribune*. His home, however, was just a block from mine, and I saw him on an average of at least once a week until the summer of 1940.

I like to think of my first day with Dave Lewis as my introduction to what has become an American institution—the morning coffee break. Smith had warned me that Dave might take me to the Millionaires' Club and made it clear that, in his view, it would be a waste of time. In any event, Dave led me straight from the *Tribune* to the Yager Bakery on Second Street. He explained on the way that a dozen or so men made it a practice to stop there around 10 o'clock each morning and that I would benefit from meeting some of them. There were various stories as to how the club got started. Some said it came about because leading men of the community had reason

Dave(y) Was a Welshman 115

to take regular samplings of the wisdom of Jacob Fisher, who had operated the bakery for many years before turning it over to his nephew, Phil Yager. Fisher was a former mayor, but by the time I attended a session of the club he was approaching 90 and was limiting his visits to the downtown area. The club got its name, according to one report, from a comment by a member, Dr. F. C. Babcock, to the effect that "if riches grant time for leisure, then these mortals who knocked off work for morning or afternoon coffee were millionaires indeed." The only two members I recall seeing at the bakery my first morning were H. J. (Bob) Dunn, Ford dealer, and John Stanley, insurance man. The only conversation I remember had to do with Stanley's experiences as a seller of federal bonds during World War I and how he overcame the prejudices encountered in communities with heavy German populations. Of the Millionaires' Club as an institution I have to say that despite all the explanations it was no more than a euphemistically labeled progenitor of the morning coffee break that would become more a right than a privilege among employers and employees everywhere in the United States. Dave Lewis in this instance was the breaker of tradition. Henry Smith never gave in to the idea that any employee, even one who owned a share of the paper—as Dave Lewis did—was entitled to take time out for idle talk and coffee. It is significant, I think, that all the Millionaires' Club members I knew were so situated in their businesses or professions that they could knock off work without asking anyone's permission. In due time the coffee break would be a part of the recognized routine of business and professional life. It wasn't in 1928.

As city editor in the 1929-30 period I had to deal with a sort of covert competition between Dave and Marie Herrin. Both were senior to me in every respect, but they seemed never to challenge my right to make assignments and organize the news beats. Once in a while, though, one of them would express some disagreement with the way the other might have handled a story. I recall faintly that Marie took exception to a sort of office rule that when anything was to be written about Willa Cather and her occasional visits to her old home at Red Cloud, Dave would get the assignments. Dave had a kind of seniority right. In all probability he had read every story Willa Cather had written.

One summer day Dave returned from covering proceedings at the courthouse, wrote about two pages of copy and handed them to me with a satisfied look on his face. His comment ran about as follows: "This is a good story. There are some touchy angles, but I know how to deal with such things. I'm glad Marie didn't get onto this. She would overdo it and stir up a lot of trouble. There won't be any trouble with it if you print it the way I wrote it."

The story was about a marriage annulment in district court. There had been a hearing just before closing time at the courthouse, and it was obvious that the plaintiff's lawyer had arranged the time in the hope the whole proceeding could be disposed of while no reporter was around. He hadn't reckoned with Lucia Dillenbach, clerk of the district court, and her assistant, Forrest Hughes. Both had sat in on the hearing, and when Dave asked next day what had been going on in court, neither could resist telling him what had happened in the quiet of the preceding afternoon. They remembered in detail.

The bride was asking for the annulment, and the groom was offering no objections. The two had met at the University of Nebraska and both had attained some prominence in student activities. They were married near the close of the school year and had gone to New York. The groom was supposed to have a job in a South American branch of a corporation there. He went forth each day from the couple's modest room in Manhattan, ostensibly to the headquarters office of his new employer.

Dave(y) Was a Welshman

It hadn't been that way. He actually was seeking work of any kind. The South American branch job hadn't materialized. His funds were running out. Times were hard; jobs were few. Finally he told all to his frustrated bride. She packed her things and headed home to Hastings and annulment.

The whole affair was embarrassing to the bride as well as the groom, of course, and the bride's mother reacted pretty much as I had expected. Near mid-morning of the day after the story appeared, the mother and daughter came into the newsroom, and neither was smiling as they started telling me they didn't like what the *Tribune* had printed the day before. I hustled them into Dave's cubbyhole of an office. (He had assured me he would explain everything.) The voices of the women were loud and harsh at first, but eventually the conversation went on in tones we couldn't hear in the main newsroom. Finally, after about an hour, the women left, and they surprised several of us by smiling as they passed by. As soon as they had cleared the newsroom, Dave emerged, took a deep breath and lighted a fresh cigarette as he approached my desk. His comment went something like this: "Well, that's over with. They started out saying we should not have published anything. I soon convinced them it was better to have the true story told in the *Tribune* than to let the local gossips garble the facts and magnify the incident to something more dramatic and embarrassing than it already was. The girl wants a job with the *Tribune*."

Dave could be an objective news reporter one day and a highly opinionated writer of critical editorials the next. He went to the heart of the matter in most any discussion. He carried his feelings with him on some occasions, but he could seem surprisingly neutral on others. He could be both traditionalist and innovator. He liked Herbert Hoover in 1932, but he supported Franklin D. Roosevelt in 1936. He seemed always to enjoy the ability of George W. Norris to break with the Republican leadership of both state and nation and get away with it. He supported Norris in his advocacy of the one-house legislature.

Dave's best writing for the *Tribune*, I always thought, was in his news stories. Some of this came in the 1927-28 period when Hastings was enjoying a spurt of industrial expansion. He wrote with zest and promise about new industries, new bus lines, new railroad services and the possibilities of irrigation. His editorials were well reasoned, generally, but they contained few quotable phrases or sentences. Going through the *Tribune* files in the 1970s, I was surprised as I reread his attacks on William Madgett in the 1931 mayoral campaign. Much of the viciousness I had sensed at the time seemed to be lacking. It could be, of course, that my standards of measurement had been altered by seven years of experience as an editorial writer on a metropolitan paper and more years as an elected officeholder.

Dave was a challenging mixture of inconsistencies. He was sentimental in such matters as his Welsh-British ancestry and resentful of anyone (including physicians) who warned him against heavy smoking. He was more cerebral, though, than emotional in most situations. He may have been as practical and conventional as his job and his station in life required. Still he almost always could find a good word for those who cited chinks in the armor of public heroes or discovered flaws in what passed for conventional thinking. He was both practical and visionary in his decision of the late 1930s to install a pump irrigation system on his farm. In this he was every bit as much of a pioneer as his father was in settling there in the 1870s. He was bored by small talk but was polite enough to engage in it when convinced that it was the best he could get from those around him. He was good to be with in some important learning years of my life.

7. Summer of '34

Season of Heat, Drouth, Dismay and a Test of Human Durability

The summer of 1934 at Hastings—and throughout the region—was the hottest and driest on record. To this writing there has been no summer like it.

For that single season the vast farmlands of Nebraska and neighboring states were condemned to the kind of climate that explains the Sonora Desert in Arizona. Rainfall at Hastings for the first eight months of 1934 was comparable to that of a similar period at Tucson. The temperature exceeded 100 degrees on an average of almost every second day between late May and mid-August.

Crops withered and died in the fields. The most defiant of weeds were reduced to naked stems that shivered in the fiery winds. Dust clouds skipped across virgin pastureland with the slightest breeze. Farmers and their wives carried water in pails to save trees that had gone unaided through the rigors of 50 previous summers.

The earth and all upon it seemed to store the heat from the searing daytime sun and release it at night. Tired and sleepless humans deserted stifling bedrooms to seek relief in basements, doorways or on the hard ground outside where a slight breeze might be stirring.

Drouth as a natural disaster is more subtle than a tornado or a flood. It comes on slowly. People tend to postpone the reality. Finally, they react in disbelief, dismay and, sometimes, despondency. The end of a tornado or flood is usually definite and recognizable. The end of a drouth, though, can be stretched through a whole succession of false signals and misplaced hopes.

The recurrent hope in Nebraska in 1934 was in the history of a land where rains eventually had come in years past. There was solace in the realization that the weather knew no favorites. The homes of the rich (a relative term, certainly, in those years) were just about as hot as the homes of the poor. The crops of the big and established farmers went down just as promptly as did those of struggling beginners. The human spirit was sustained by little beyond that sense of widespread sharing which can work in times of trouble as well as in times of triumph and success.

Every time I think of what happened over a period of not more than four months I am reminded of how Justice Oliver Wendell Holmes passed off as "incommunicable" his experiences as a soldier in the Civil War. Misery is hard to describe. And so are frustration, bewilderment, mental fatigue, physical exhaustion and monotony. All of these were the facts of life in central Nebraska between May 1 and September 1 of a year that literally burned itself into my memory.

We should have anticipated some of the trouble. There had been severe drouth in northeast Nebraska and South Dakota, starting two years before, and several carloads of hay had gone from Hastings in 1932 to help Knox County farmers keep their livestock from starving. While the wheat crop had sprouted and got off to a reasonable start in the fall of 1933, it was in precarious condition throughout the winter. December and January brought considerable warm, dry weather. Observant farmers warned of trouble. January brought only a trace of moisture. People in Hastings enjoyed the mild temperature, and some made their way to the golf courses and tennis courts.

Precipitation in February was .82 of an inch, but the total for March fell back to .25 of an inch. Then April came up with only one-tenth of an inch. This was a spring drouth of unprecedented intensity.

There was a dust storm on April 11, and we of the *Daily Tribune* signaled our concern by putting the story under a strong headline on the front page. There was weather news on the front page of almost every issue for the next four months.

By April 20 the high temperature readings were in the eighties, and A. E. Anderson, state and federal crop statistician at Lincoln, issued a guarded statement about the critical condition of crops all over Nebraska.

By the first of May farmers were detecting brown spots in their wheat fields. After a trip into the country one afternoon I approached Henry Smith, general manager of the paper, with the suggestion that we might as well report that the wheat crop was lost. Smith was not quite ready to go along with me, and on his advice that we proceed with caution, I wrote a story for the May 5 paper which dwelt on the fact that the mild weather had hastened maturity of the wheat and that the yields in fields that survived the drouth would be much lighter than normal. Straining to be positive, I summarized the belief of certain observers that a timely rain could save some of the wheat.

On May 7 there was a front-page story under this headline: "Midsummer Temperature Again Today." The reading was 90 degrees at noon, and the afternoon high was 97. After four days of this kind of weather, there was a sharp drop in temperature, but no rain.

The *Tribune's* weather story on May 11 was in the No. 2 spot on the front page, and it was a dispatch from Chicago that described a dust cloud estimated to be 1,500 miles long and 900 miles wide. It had blotted out the sun over Chicago, the Twin Cities, Des Moines, St. Louis and Kansas City.

No one questioned the fact that the dust was a product

of heat and drouth, but somehow we failed to sense the extent to which Great Plains soil could erupt when strong winds moved in. The term "Dust Bowl" had not yet come into the nation's language, but it was evolving through various synonymous forms.

Scanning *Tribune* files in the summer of 1978, I was reminded of the mental anguish, the ambivalence, the distress, even, of having to play the role of daily chronicler of a disaster that gained new significance with each issue of the paper. My town, my community, my career, my life almost, were victims of a freakish streak of weather. I could dislike what was happening, resent it and regret it, but I could not make it go away. As an editor I had to face facts and report them. It was not my job to make the drouth seem less severe than it really was. Still, I sought every possible means to make the bad news bearable.

Thanks to the presence of Harold Cowan, sports editor and general reporter, I could order a change of pace, so to speak. I did that on May 12. Cowan had been turning out occasional pieces in light vein that appeared under the byline of "The Cub Reporter." For the May 12 paper he did a tongue-in-cheek article that started out as follows: "Yesterday I scored the scoop of my career. I unearthed a grizzled old-timer, hibernated and withdrawn into his secluded den, who well remembered the last time it rained in Adams County."

Cowan stretched the interview with his fictional Washington Irving Jenks into about a column of entertaining paragraphs, and when the paper came off the press, we all felt rather good about having found some grounds for humor in the distress around us.

The high temperature on May 20 was 98, a record for that date. There was a drop back to 76 on the twenty-first, and on the twenty-fourth there was a general rain. The precipitation total at Hastings was only .13 of an inch, but there were readings of an inch at Minden, .50 at Alma and

Summer of '34

.41 at Holdrege. That was enough to justify a *Tribune* headline that said, "Showers Relieve Drouth Situation."

A streak of mild days ran through the twenty-sixth, when everybody forgot the weather. That was the day for a non-stop run from Denver to Chicago by the Burlington's new streamlined train, the Zephyr. It went through Hastings in late forenoon—on schedule.

The final three days of May were scorchers, with high readings of 103, 102 and 100 in that order. May 30 (Memorial Day) was a short workday, and my wife and I had arranged to move our goods into a new home we had bought earlier for $4,200. The house was more attractive than the apartment we were leaving, but it was not noticeably cooler. I couldn't help thinking about the debt it represented and the possibility that persistent drouth could put the finishing touches to the already tottering economy of the Hastings area. At $40 a week, I was one of the *Tribune's* higher-paid employees. Companies all around us were cutting out costly personnel.

The opening days of June brought rain to many parts of Nebraska. Not a drop fell at Hastings, but the reports of two inches at Nebraska City and smaller amounts at points all the way from there to the Panhandle counties were enough to inspire a banner headline in the *Tribune*: "Rains Bring Hope for Drouth End."

Hastings eventually got some of the relatively frequent showers, and the total precipitation for June was more than two inches—the most that had fallen in any month that year.

By this time the news included reports of efforts in Washington to provide relief for the drouth-stricken areas. The White House, rather than Congress, was the source of most of the proposals—a good illustration of the way Franklin D. Roosevelt hung onto the leadership image that he had managed to establish in the opening months of his administration. One dispatch told of a plan to put $150 million into a program to buy land that farmers were ready to abandon, provide feed for starving livestock and buy up animals that farmers could no longer save from starvation.

On June 20 the *Tribune* reported almost an inch of rain at Hastings—the heaviest fall of the season. But within two days another cloud formation brought a deposit of dust that firmed up a feeling among Hastings housewives that this invader from the skies demanded new techniques for sealing cracks around doors and windows and otherwise protecting carpets, furniture, dishes and food itself from gritty contamination.

Beyond conventional electric fans, there was no provision for air-conditioning in the average home. Those hot summer days, when dust forced the closing of all windows, speeded up the processes of invention. By midsummer we were hearing of all sorts of devices for cooling a room. An electric fan blowing over a bucket of ice or a tub of water was common. Bed sheets or screens of one kind or another were set up with water dribbling from the top and a fan blowing air across or through the moistened surface.

The forced ingenuity extended into the elementary research shop of the F. Jaden Manufacturing Company, from which eventually came a line of home and office air-conditioners that took the made-in-Hastings label into hundreds of communities across the country. These units were a refinement of crude arrangements that some mechanically inclined men had set up in their Hastings homes during the summer of 1934.

Hastings water, coming from the taps at about 55 degrees, was the coolant. An old automobile radiator, the necessary piping to run water through it and a fan blowing air across the cooled coils completed the mechanism. The water, of course, was discharged where it could benefit grass, trees or flowers.

The Jaden Company's Golden Rod conditioner was

Summer of '34

nothing more than a compact arrangement of radiator, fan and water connections. It was good only where the available water came at a relatively low temperature, as was the case throughout much of Nebraska.

By the end of the summer of 1934 there were a few room air-conditioners in Hastings that bore the brands of national manufacturers and were quite obviously developed from the mechanical refrigerators that had started showing up in kitchens a few years before. The *Tribune* management bought one of these, made by Frigidaire, and installed it in the newsroom.

The newspaper had been the scene of a fire on the night of April 25, and after several weeks of contemplating the damage at the old building on Burlington, the owners had decided to move to quarters in the Stitt Building on Third Street. The news department was assigned space on the second floor, where there was only a flat roof between us and the beating sun. Henry Smith, whose office was adjacent to ours, decided early that this was a good place to try out the new contraption.

The machine we got probably was designed to cool a single room in a home. The refrigeration unit was about the size of those in home refrigerators of the time and the metal frame resembled a small heating stove. It stood near the middle of the room, with no provision for bringing in fresh air or blowing out the old. At the end of a hot day we had a room foul with tobacco smoke and the body odors of as many as eight persons who were rarely cooled to the non-sweating stage.

We cooped ourselves up in that room of perhaps 400 square feet and felt a bit smug as we considered the fact that employees in all other departments were without the luxury of air-conditioning. As unpleasant as the room was by the standards of a later day, it was comfortable in comparison to what it would have been with dust-laden hot winds blowing through open windows and doors.

While there was all sorts of talk in Hastings about ways to cool people off and make life a little easier in 100-degree weather, there was talk at the national level about ways to make it rain. A front-page story in the *Tribune* on June 23 took note of a range of suggestions and quoted a federal meteorologist in Washington to the effect that no proposal coming to his attention seemed worth pursuing.

By June 27 Hastings had experienced 11 days in which the temperature had exceeded 100 degrees. By July 15, when the reading was 108, the season's total of 100-degree days had reached 21.

Going through the *Tribune* files of that awful summer, I found a measure of reassurance that our news staff had written a pretty fair record of the unusual weather and the community's reaction to it. I wasn't sure at the time. Somehow we seemed to be falling back on the weather as a news topic for the simple reason there was little else the public seemed interested in. The rationale was sound; it has been followed by daily papers since their inception. But to those of us managing the flow of news our weather stories seemed repetitious and monotonous.

The heat itself was enervating, but we had to overcome some tangible obstacles, too. The dying crops, the parched lawns, the wilted trees—these had their counterparts in the spirits of people, our staff included. It was far from an ideal situation for the flowering of initiative.

One way to break the monotony of our weather news, of course, was to put Harold Cowan to the task of looking at the heat from the standpoint of his role of "Cub Reporter." In mid-July he wrote a story that ran on the front page under this headline: "Heat Makes Folks Know Each Other." He came up with a combination of fanciful and factual observations, including this sentence: "You'd never have known that Mrs. Fuzzle snored if the heat had not driven her to sleeping with her head in the parlor bay window."

On July 18 the *Tribune* introduced a reporting device that I would not have recalled if I had not explored the files in 1978. With that day's front-page weather story there was a chart showing at a glance that there had been 20 days of temperatures between 100 and 105 degrees, four days with readings between 105 and 110 and one day when the high was above 110. The above-110 day had been the previous Sunday, when the high was 112. This 100-degree chart was a regular front-page feature until the days of abnormally high temperatures totaled 44.

On July 28, a hot and cloudless Saturday, south central Nebraska forgot the heat for a few hours and scanned the skies. The National Geographic Society and the U.S. Army had sent a giant balloon into the air from a base near Rapid City, South Dakota, to record weather at high altitudes. Three men and a collection of instruments were crowded into a pressurized sphere that was expected to seek maximum altitude, float over the Great Plains and come to a landing before getting far enough to the east to be hampered by extensive woodlands.

At an altitude of about 11 miles the bag began to tear, and in a relatively short time the crew members decided their first challenge was to maintain a measure of control until they were near enough to the earth to make a safe jump with parachutes. With a shortwave radio they communicated their plight to ground crews, and their reports aroused speculation that they were floating in the general direction of Hastings. When Silas Lyman, one of the few shortwave listeners in Hastings, got the first hint of this, he called the *Tribune* and our final bulletin for the afternoon papers was based on his reports.

Henry Smith, meanwhile, had let me know that some of our staff members should be on hand for the landing. I alerted Francis Robertson and Elvin McClenahan, the photographers, and more or less commandeered Dean Shaffer and his Chrysler New Yorker to start cruising through the countryside. Somehow we got enough information to suggest the landing would be north of Holdrege. In any event, we arrived at the Reuben Johnson farm, between Holdrege and Loomis, about 30 minutes after the bag and gondola had landed in what was generously referred to as a cornfield.

Reuben Johnson's field was the meeting place of several hundred persons that afternoon—a thousand perhaps. Some came from neighboring farms, some from Holdrege, Loomis, Bertrand and other towns. Several airplanes had come down at the nearest landing strips, bringing news reporters and photographers from Omaha, Lincoln and points farther away. By the time our party arrived there was not a tattered scrap of the thousands of square yards of balloon fabric to be seen anywhere on the ground. It had been the object of the earliest souvenir seekers and probably was torn into a thousand pieces. Someone gave me a piece about 10 inches square.

All three of the men whose excursion had gone awry had made good parachute landings, even though they jumped from relatively low altitudes. All had landed near enough to the balloon that they were on the scene when we arrived. Maj. William E. Kepner, commander of the flight, was answering the questions of reporters. Capt. A. W. Stevens was rummaging through some debris. Kepner would advance to the rank of major general within a few years and be frequently mentioned in the news during World War II. Stevens was the photography expert, and he and Orvil Anderson, second in command, would be more successful in another expedition into the stratosphere a year later, from the same base in South Dakota.

The ground was powder-dry and dust was stirred up by every footstep. There was no evidence of corn in the vicinity of the wreckage, but I took the time to roam beyond the crowd far enough to satisfy myself that Reuben Johnson's field had included no more than brown, sterile stalks for some time. I faintly recall that Mr. Johnson put in a claim for damages, but got nothing to cover any loss of corn. The drouth had taken care of the corn long before the balloon struck.

While Reuben Johnson's corn may have been beyond redemption, there were fields from which some feed could be salvaged, and H. J. Gramlich of Lincoln, state director of the federal cattle buying program, was urging farmers to harvest such fields before further deterioration.

By early August the cattle buying program was going full blast, and some of the saddest stories of the summer were those about farmers delivering cows, calves and steers that were near the point of starvation and barely able to walk. One of the heavy buying points was Roseland, and *Tribune* photographers went there to record the sorry condition of animals that might not have made it through the summer in their dusty pastures.

By the middle of August we of the *Tribune* had proclaimed a possible end of the drouth so many times that the biggest rain of the summer was cautiously described as no more than just that. It started falling about 11 o'clock the night of the fourteenth, which was primary election day in Nebraska. We were at the office in full force, putting the final touches to our election extra that would be on the streets shortly after daybreak.

Before midnight we threw open the windows and shut off our straining air-conditioner. Some of us left our desks and typewriters and stood outside while the rain soaked our shirts. The rain itself justified our conduct. Unconsciously, though, we were celebrating the end of an ordeal such as nobody in the region had ever experienced. The tension seemed to ease after that election night rain. There would be more hot days, but there would be enough rain to revive pastures and encourage the planting of another wheat crop. The price of that hot, dry summer, however, would not be paid in full until another year.

8. First There Was Dust

Then the Rains Descended and the Floods Came

On the night of March 16, 1935, we were all set to put out an "extra" edition of the Hastings *Daily Tribune*. It would feature the state high school Class B basketball finals at the Hastings College gymnasium. The finalists were Mead and Stockham.

The very fact that Hastings was the scene of a state tournament was a matter of considerable civic pride. Basketball playoffs in Nebraska had been pretty much a monopoly of Lincoln interests centering in the University of Nebraska athletic department.

From the standpoint of *Tribune* management the "extra" would be an expression of support for a worthwhile community enterprise. We were confident that players and fans of the teams in the playoff would be avid buyers at 5¢ a copy if we could get the papers to the gym before the players were dressed and gone.

Total sales might reach 300 copies, which wouldn't begin to meet the cost of the operation. But making money wasn't the idea. It was a firm conviction of Henry Smith that we should put ourselves out once in a while to demonstrate full support of events of this kind. We would show the people of Stockham and Mead and elsewhere that a basketball tournament in Hastings could get big-town treatment.

Harold Cowan, sports editor, was at the court-side press table with a direct telephone line to a typist in the

First There Was Dust

Soil in transit

newsroom. A typesetter, makeup man, stereotyper and pressman were on the job. I was to edit the copy, write the headlines.

We were prepared for just about every contingency, with one exception. We were not prepared for a dust storm, and the one that struck that night was the worst in a series that had started about a year earlier.

There was a preliminary game, as I recall, and we were at the office by 7:30 P.M. I was conscious of increasingly high winds, but thought little about them until I was called to the composing room at about 8:20 P.M. The front-page makeup form stood ready to receive the final type and the proper headline from two I had written—one for a Stockham victory and one for a Mead victory. Photoengravings of both teams were at hand, but what the men in the mechanical end of the operation wanted to show me was the thick layer of dust that had collected on the makeup forms and on everything else.

Looking out the big plate glass windows, we could see

that the dust was dimming the street lights. And around the edges of the window panes we could see it suspended in the air that whistled through every crack.

There was so much dust in the air that the men in charge of mechanical equipment feared there could be serious damage to some of the machinery if we tried to operate it. My memory tells me that we didn't even try to print an "extra." (I looked through the *Tribune* files in 1980 and found no evidence that such an issue was printed.)

The dust of that season made much more news, of course, than it might have suppressed on the night of the Class B tourney. All through the following week the *Tribune* ran front-page stories about dust clouds extending from Texas to the Dakotas. Our local reports sometimes distinguished between dust from nearby areas and dust from afar. If it turned out to be red in color when caught in a droplet of rain, we immediately classified it as Texas or Oklahoma dust. The dull gray local dust had been anticipated through the winter and spring, because there had been little replenishment of soil moisture following the disastrous heat and drouth of 1934.

Within three months of the March 16 dust storm that had stopped the presses, so to speak, there would be rains and floods that would inspire a whole series of "extra" editions of the *Tribune*—editions with more to tell—and usually with tragic overtones—than could have been written into Stockham's game with Mead in the Class B basketball finals.

There would be the start of rebuilding in flood-devastated areas and portentous talk of flood control dams in the Republican watershed at points all the way from Wray, Colorado, to Manhattan, Kansas. There would be climactic turns for the better in the long struggle for political recognition of the Tri-County project. Formal reorganization of Nebraska's legislature into a one-house

First There Was Dust 133

body would take place. All in all, 1935 would go down as a year that brought more than dust. For a month or so in March and April, though, there was little else to talk about in Hastings.

There were dust stories on the front page of the *Tribune* almost every day. There had been clouds of dirt over the region in 1934, but in that period of some 30 days in 1935 we experienced enough dust that it was hard for me to believe that most of what I remembered of the "Dust Bowl" was squeezed into those few weeks of March and April. We measured one day's dust against another's by the extent to which it clouded our view of the roofline of the courthouse no more than a block from the *Tribune* newsroom window.

On March 21 a headline said: "Dust Storm Damage Spreads." On March 23 we used the same large type in a front-page headline saying, "Ill Wind Blows Up Big Yarns." This was over one of Harold Cowan's "Cub Reporter" stories, an attempt to give a light touch to news that was basically dismal, disappointing and monotonous. There were practical suggestions in the news about the desirability of wearing gauze masks when outdoors and sealing doors and windows with wet cloths. Jim Good, one of Hastings' few blacks, strolled up and down Second Street one dusty day in a pair of colored glasses with lenses about the size of a dime. This was a reversion to the comedian role he had played in stage appearances in his younger years.

There was rain on April 5, but it was the first in a month and not enough to start speculation as to a shift in weather patterns. One of the worst dustfalls of the season was reported on April 22. It was beginning to rain at scattered points, and by May 1 the state crop report was surprisingly optimistic. On May 18 the *Tribune* reported there had been more rain for the calendar year than had been recorded by the middle of summer in 1934. More than five inches had been recorded at Hastings between May 8 and May 21.

Reports of floods of varying intensity started coming over the press service wires. There was water in the streets of Trenton, Benkelman and Stratton. The Republican River was reported at "flood stage" at McCook on May 29. By May 31 that city was said to be without communication services because of power failures.

The wire services started counting the dead, and the *Tribune* reported on June 1 that fatalities were "near 100." There was a report from Oxford that a family of 11 was missing. The *Tribune* started publishing names of victims, but it was a matter of weeks before fatality figures could be corrected with adjustments for early duplications and for persons who hadn't bothered to get themselves off the "missing" lists.

There were stories from several points of families that refused to heed early warnings. Occupants of farm homes were rescued from rooftops. There was an obvious refusal to believe that the water in tributaries as well as the main stem of the Republican would rise as high as 10 feet around houses that had stood for 40 or 50 years. Cambridge was inundated as a flooding Medicine Creek rushed to the Republican.

The confusion in which we operated at the *Tribune* brought home the fact that we didn't have a staff large enough to cover all the spots where news was developing. Henry Smith came up with the suggestion that we send a man to the upper reaches of the Republican and let him develop a series of stories that would consolidate and summarize the many incidents of which we had received only superficial reports as the rains fell and the destruction spread. Neil McDonald, just home from his first term in the lower house of the Nebraska Legislature, agreed to head for the McCook area and work from there. This was on or about June 2, but the crest of the flood had not yet

First There Was Dust 135

reached Red Cloud, where the river came nearer Hastings than at any other point in its course.

While the river had risen steadily for the length of its course in Nebraska, it became apparent that the flood at its peak would hit the Red Cloud area as a rolling wall of water and debris. Along with a score or more persons from Hastings, Paul Hansell, Elvan McClenahan and other staff personnel went to Red Cloud to greet the flood in its final show of intensity. What they saw from a point on the north-south highway, that would be under water in a matter of minutes, was described by Hansell for *Tribune* readers:

The demolishing wall crawled forward. Almost at its crest was floating one of the large buildings from the CCC camp a short distance up the river. Like a huge houseboat it came, turning lazily in the current.

Only a few hundred feet away, the wall seemed to be racing toward the highway. Hundreds of rabbits and other small animals raced before it and were engulfed as they became exhausted or turned to one side when they saw the waiting people.

Now the edge of the racing water was plainly visible, gathering up everything loose as it came. Spectators scurried back toward higher ground. McClenahan (who took pictures) was one of the last.

In the wake of the rains and flood there was plenty of cleanup work for the *Tribune* staff. What was the cost? Were there any benefits? What lessons were learned?

The loss of human life was still a matter of estimates, but the toll was not as high as some of the early reports had indicated. Ultimately, federal agencies would lump losses along the Republican with those on all branches of the Kansas River system and come up with a death toll of 110 and property loss of $18 million. Most of the deaths and property damage were in Nebraska.

We *Tribune* staff members started looking from the

past disaster to future prospects. We learned from the grave diggers at Parkview Cemetery that the new moisture had penetrated the subsoil to a depth of six feet in some places. This meant there had been complete recovery from the moisture depletion of the previous year and a half. Normally, this would make for a good wheat crop and bright prospects for corn. Through early June the wheat was luxuriant, but the heavy rains had encouraged an infestation of black rust that meant drastic reduction of yields in many fields. Corn got off to a good start in June, but a later prolonged dry spell forced many farmers to cut their corn for forage rather than lose everything.

September came, and with it the necessary action in Washington toward something better than the fragile year-to-year hopes of a region wholly dependent on cycles and whims of weather. Memories of dust and flood and withering crops were pushed into the background as Hastings celebrated the birth of the Tri-County project. This was the dawn of an era of new prosperity and stability, or so people told themselves.

In October the Burlington completed reconstruction of tracks in the Republican Valley that had been destroyed by the June flood. The railroad staged a celebration at McCook, and I was among 50 or more representatives of the news media who were picked up along the line and taken on a special speed run between McCook and Oxford. The train we rode was one of the line's sparkling new Zephyr units, and the highest speed attained was 122 miles an hour. The story of this run was flashed across the country as evidence that the Burlington's main line was open all the way between Chicago and Denver and that the rebuilt roadbed was firm and safe.

Riding to McCook on the special train the night before the celebration, I met for the first time a young man named Foster May. He was an Omaha radio announcer who had been stranded in McCook during the height of

First There Was Dust   137

the flood. He would be singled out the next day as the person who provided McCook for a time with its only communication with the outside world. Within the next five years he would become one of the better-known personalities in Nebraska, and in 1942 he would go down in defeat along with the venerable George Norris, in a three-way race for the United States Senate seat Norris had held since 1912.

Dr. George Condra, state geologist, long-time teacher and researcher at the University of Nebraska and uncontested monarch when it came to matters pertaining to water resources of the state, was among the Burlington's guests on that occasion. At one point he apparently felt under obligation to make a speech. He mounted a baggage truck and started waving and shouting instructions to assemble in front of him. For some unexplained reason a wave of complete indifference ran through the crowd. Nobody stopped to listen, and Condra found himself talking without listeners. Naturally dominant in facial features, physical size and vocal powers, he was at that moment as completely defeated as I ever had seen him.

A long-standing challenge of the Great Plains was summed up in the contrasts and contradictions of 1935. The dust dramatized the waste of a basic resource, the soil. The floods dramatized the need for ways to hold back excess rainwater until it might be put to constructive use. The green wheat fields of June and the six feet of moist soil measured by the grave diggers built hopes that would be blasted, as in many past years, by heat and drouth in July and August.

Thinking back on 1935, I see it as a pivotal year in public thinking about public policy. It was one of those times when men and women, whatever their organized state, are moved by crisis or disaster to start something that logic told them should have been started long before.

A *Tribune* story on July 17 told of talk in Washington

about the need for a reservoir on the Republican. Senator Norris was quoted, and it was apparent that he was ready to turn from his success as champion of the TVA, the Tri-County and other special interests to a genuine effort in behalf of conservation in the whole Republican watershed. Other political personalities were talking in the same tone.

Over the next three decades dams would rise in the Kansas-Republican watershed all the way from Bonny in eastern Colorado to Perry in eastern Kansas. The *Tribune* would be a dedicated chronicler of these developments, but for my remaining five years with the paper the top story on a day-to-day basis had to be the Tri-County project. And that calls for another chapter.

9. The Tri-County Odyssey

A Story of Willful Men Who Went for Water—And Finally Got It

As a college freshman in the mid-1920s I was surprised by the amount of talk I heard in Hastings of the need for irrigation on the rolling plains of south-central Nebraska. I had thought there was sufficient rainfall in the eastern half of the state to grow crops without the watering that had been a drudging part of farm life for me in eastern Colorado.

I was casually curious about a rather primitive research project that P. L. Johnson and others carried out on a vacant lot west of the campus near Ninth Street. They had leveled an area of perhaps 500 square feet, built low dikes around it and on occasion had flooded it to a depth of maybe a foot. While I never bothered to inspect the site in detail or talk with the experimenters, I learned through someone that the object was to study the manner in which water penetrated the tight loess soil of the area. There had been questions as to whether water could be applied to this land in the way it was applied to the lighter and more penetrable soils of the western part of the state.

By the time I had finished college and was established with the *Tribune* I was aware that far-sighted individuals throughout the region had been talking about irrigation for years and had some controversial plans for bringing water from the Platte River to tens of thousands of acres in Adams, Kearney, Phelps, Gosper and perhaps some other counties south of the Platte.

In a matter of months I decided that irrigation was an idea that would not stay away. It had been cropping up in various forms over more than three decades and had survived public skepticism and discouraging reports from feasibility studies. I started familiarizing myself with the history and background of this phoenixlike enthusiasm. Any mention of irrigation was news for the *Tribune*.

There was the story of Joel Hull of Minden, Union Army veteran and dreamer. As far back as 1887 he saw the need for water on the tablelands of Kearney County and looked to the Platte River as a source. A canal, starting near the mouth of Plum Creek in Dawson County, he reasoned, could bring water to the vicinity of Minden and make possible an industrial community of flour and feed mills as well as agricultural production enhanced by irrigation. It was generally agreed that if Hull had found the necessary financing he would have built the canal.

The route proposed for Hull's canal was pretty much the same as that laid out in 1914 by engineers of the U.S. Reclamation Service. The service had responded to pressures starting with a new organization, the Tri-County Supplemental Water Association, which, in turn, had enlisted the support of Nebraskans in Washington, all the way to the secretary of state, William Jennings Bryan.

The reclamation report, prepared by Charles T. Pease, included many negative implications. There were questions as to the water supply and the possibility that landowners downstream from the proposed diversion from the Platte would consider such a project a threat against a water source to which they might establish a claim. There was the further implication that Reclamation was not convinced there was a need. Here was a proposal to irrigate land in an established farming region. These tablelands, dotted with farmsteads, were in direct contrast to the indisputably arid lands where the service was making its reputation. How did one "reclaim" corn

The Tri-County Odyssey

and wheat fields and pastures where cattle grazed? Or so the bureau people seemed to wonder.

Tri-County planners, of course, had acknowledged the existence of an orderly farming economy. They were trying to make up for an overall lack of moisture that was greater than pioneer settlers had anticipated. They had given up on the oft-expressed theory of early land-sale promoters that once the prairie sod was broken and the land put under annual tillage, the region would attract more rain. Water from the Platte, therefore, was looked upon as a logical supplement to rainfall that was short of need—a form of insurance against the loss of crops that might have been saved by just one good rain.

There was great emphasis on the fact that the soil of the region had capacity to store water to depths of several feet and hold it until plant life required it. In 1914 and for the next 20 years the "supplemental water" theory was nourished, fortified and written into the case for the Tri-County project largely on the strength of the story of Charles W. McConaughy and the snowdrifts that formed one winter around corn shocks in a wheat field near Holdrege. McConaughy, grain merchant and mayor of Holdrege, had seen a field of wheat that was marked by a rather orderly pattern of spots where the straw was longer and the heads were bigger than in the rest of the field. He sought out the owner of the land and got an explanation. Shocks of corn had stood in the field during the previous winter, and the bigger wheat marked the places where the shocks had stopped blowing snow and caused it to accumulate in drifts of considerable depth. Where these drifts had been the soil had absorbed and retained much more moisture than in parts of the field where little snow had collected. McConaughy, an ardent advocate of irrigation, pounced on the snowdrift story to strengthen his argument. When the Tri-County project finally came to pass, one of its major units, the reservoir in Keith County, was named for the vigorous, outspoken McConaughy.

The so-called Pease report of the Reclamation Service was made public in October of 1914. It drew mixed reviews, but in the main it was disappointing to Tri-County leaders. McConaughy and others criticized its failure to take note of the "supplemental water" theory as opposed to the theory applied in arid regions, where little or no allowance was made for seasonal rains.

While the Pease report had a devastating effect in some circles, it did not break the spirit of McConaughy, George F. Kingsley of Minden and a few others. They were convinced that Pease had based his findings on inadequate knowledge of the water supply. They were disappointed that the state engineer, Donald D. Price, had signed the report. They went back to Price with a request that he make a new water study. The state engineer was caught in an awkward situation. He was a candidate for reappointment, and he took note of the fact that an employee of the Reclamation Service was among outsiders mentioned as candidates to succeed him. Out of all this came the appointment of George E. Johnson of Falls City as state engineer. This appointment, in retrospect, seems about as fortuitous as any single development in the history of Tri-County.

McConaughy and Kingsley lost no time in getting Johnson involved. In a matter of weeks he had written a new report and filed it with Kingsley. Instead of accepting the Pease plan for a canal that would divert all water directly from the Platte, he came up with plans for two reservoirs on Plum Creek. While he accepted in full the theory of storage in the soil, he saw need for the surface storage the two reservoirs would provide. There was a cool practicality about George Johnson in 1915 that would distinguish him as chief engineer for Tri-County two decades later, when the project was still subject to shifts of opinion, jealousies and political whims as it went

The Tri-County Odyssey

through the final stages of approval by the Public Works Administration. The Plum Creek reservoirs that Johnson recommended were soon accepted as possible sites for generation of electric power.

Enthusiam for the Tri-County plan ebbed some during World War I. Farm prices were good, and 1915 brought the heaviest rainfall in south-central Nebraska that ever had been recorded. Leaders of the movement were not idle. They sought endorsements of various organizations, both political and private, and George Johnson, as state engineer, made at least one trip to Washington in the interest of the project. McConaughy and Kingsley and their allies in the Holdrege and Minden communities kept up the pressure for a new study by the Reclamation Service. They strengthened their case materially, most observers agreed, with a decision in 1915 to bring Adams County and the business interests of Hastings into active involvement. Prior to that the Tri-County label had been interpreted as referring to Kearney, Phelps and Gosper Counties. After that there was a tendency to think of Adams, Kearney and Phelps as the trio, but in fact for the next 15 years there would be active participation by representatives of the four counties. The project headquarters would be at Hastings for many years, including some years after a supreme court ruling virtually eliminated Adams County from the area of basic benefits. Adam Breede committed the *Tribune* to a role of active support of Tri-County in 1921, and that commitment was a factor, certainly, in Hastings' increasing involvement in Tri-County affairs.

In the fall of 1923 Tri-County leaders organized a tour of irrigated areas around Scottsbluff, Nebraska, and Sterling, Colorado. Thirty-three men in eight automobiles traveled more than 700 miles on dirt and gravel roads to get a first-hand view of the hurried activities of the sugar beet harvest in the North and South Platte valleys.

Dave Lewis went along and reported the tour for the *Tribune*. Others from Hastings included Mayor C. G. Ingraham, Louis Stein, W. C. Cooper, Lloyd Thomas, Howard J. Dunn, George Dutton, John Uerling, Steve Swigle and Albert E. Stitt whose "white streak" Essex was the pilot car.

Finally, in 1924, came a new federal report. Its authors were F. F. Smith of the Bureau of Reclamation (the former Reclamation Service) and A. Lincoln Fellows, senior irrigation engineer in the office of Agricultural Engineering, Bureau of Public Roads, Denver. For almost a decade there had been communication between Tri-County spokesmen and various federal officials as to the need and purposes of such a report. George E. Johnson, as state engineer, had made suggestions, as had members of the staff of the University of Nebraska.

The Smith-Fellows report was positive in tone, and it tended to undo some of the mischief of the Pease report of 1914. At the same time, though, it brought into sharper focus some of the realities of the project, including questions that would not be easily answered. Irrigation would mean a new cost-of-production item for farmers. Would a farmer's pledge to buy water place a bonded debt against his land? The Plum Creek power plants were pictured as having capacity to develop far more electricity than could be sold in the immediate vicinity. Private power company executives began pondering what this would mean in the way of competition. There were stirrings of concern in Platte Valley communities. Would Tri-County take so much water that there would be none left to expand irrigation on the flat valley farms where it already had been tried and proved generally beneficial?

For the next 10 years Smith-Fellows would be the principal reference book of Tri-County promoters. It would be cited before the Nebraska Legislature during stormy debate over a bill to create a big public utilities

The Tri-County Odyssey

district that would have power to build and manage irrigation and power facilities. It became important to Nebraska's argument for federal legislation to control tributary streams and prevent a recurrence of the disastrous 1927 flood on the lower Mississippi. The state legislation squeaked through the Senate and died in the House. The national bill was amended to the point all it promised was a survey by the Army Engineers.

And so the story had been building when I came to the *Tribune* in 1928. It had been a story of high hopes and bold dreams, but for every hopeful sign and every new version of the dreams there had been negative or obstructive developments. The story, as it would be for several more years, had been a story of strong-willed men refusing to give up after one long walk after another down deadend streets.

The election of Arthur Weaver as governor in the fall of 1928 set off some political maneuvering that was seen one day as favorable to Tri-County and the next day as unfavorable. A resident of Falls City and active in the Mississippi Valley Association, Weaver was unqualifiedly in favor of improving navigation on the Missouri River. In interior Nebraska there were many who looked upon the pro-navigationists as a threat to irrigation.

I looked upon farmers as the occupational group that ought to see the potential benefits of irrigation if anybody could see them. But some farmers were skeptical, many were indifferent, and a few were outright hostile. There was casual acceptance of the Tri-County effort among business and professional men and women in Hastings, but most of the meaningful comment came from individuals associated with the chamber of commerce or the little group of activists who had joined hands with like-minded groups at Minden and Holdrege.

Here was a movement conceived in the interest of the region's agriculture that would have been long dead if it had had to rely on the kind of leadership offered by the few active farmers involved. That working farmers should be skeptical seemed quite proper to my farmer father in 1930 when I outlined the Tri-County program to him. He had followed the development of irrigation in his home county in Colorado and was convinced that a high percentage of the farmers on the land in Nebraska would not make the adjustment. Most of them, he said, would lose their farms by the time they had learned how to manage the higher costs of irrigation farming. I thought of his comment every time I attended a meeting with reluctant farmers.

Stephen Swigle of Hastings, a retired farmer, joined the Tri-County boosters early and attended countless meetings. E. E. Binfield, who lived on a Hall County farm near Prosser, attended some of the early meetings, but by the late 1920s he had become an avowed critic and opponent of the plan. A man of impressive features and a strong voice, he appeared frequently in the little informal clusters of men on downtown street corners in Hastings. Other men listened to him, but few stepped forward to challenge some of his warnings of what might happen if the Tri-County development took place.

As a member of the lower house of the Nebraska legislature he sponsored an amendment to a piece of key legislation that would have barred any irrigation of lands beyond the watershed of the river from which the water came. The amendment was defeated, and what was known as Senate File 310 in the legislature became the law under which Tri-County eventually evolved into an operating entity. While Binfield continued to appear on Hastings streets and did, in fact, die of a heart attack in downtown Hastings, his allegiance in his final years, so far as Tri-County was concerned, was to Grand Island, seat of the most relentless opposition Tri-County had to contend with.

The Tri-County Odyssey

There had been sporadic challenges of the Tri-County idea almost from the beginning among individuals in the Platte Valley. While there had been little irrigation development east of North Platte until after World War I, there had been enough to make for an uneasiness in certain quarters when word came that Platte water might be channeled in large quantities to the upland areas south of the river, beyond the watershed of the Platte in places.

Tri-County leaders courted the interest and support of civic leaders in North Platte, Lexington, Gothenburg, Kearney and other valley towns. During the late 1920s, when interest was high in getting federal help for flood control projects on tributaries of the Mississippi, there was an Association for the Conservation, Control and Utilization of Our Water Resources that represented a union of the Tri-County Association and the Lower Platte Irrigation Association. President of the association was George P. Kingsley of Minden, vice-president was E. C. Kelso of North Platte, secretary, Ben Neff of Lexington, and treasurer, J. N. Clarke of Hastings.

The Conservation Association was instrumental in convincing Governor Weaver that the state should make a survey of its water resources and its potential sites for storage of flood water. A board of engineers got the assignment. Its chairman was State Engineer Roy Cochran and its chief technical spokesman was Professor Clark Mickey, head of the civil engineering department of the University of Nebraska. During my first two years with the *Tribune* I saw and heard a lot of Clark Mickey and became fascinated with the way W. C. Cooper, secretary of the Hastings Chamber of Commerce, could rattle off the long words of the association name as he borrowed them on frequent occasions to boast that one of the chamber's policy aims was "conservation, control and utilization of our water resources."

The situation was confusing to a young reporter-city

editor, just as it must have been confusing to readers of the *Tribune*, who were pretty much on their own when it came to sorting out the meaning of all the maneuvers, all the challenges and charges, all the criticism and implications of self-seeking. George Kingsley of Minden and C. W. McConaughy of Holdrege and their followers in those cities, as well as in Hastings and elsewhere, wanted irrigation for what it would mean for the economy of the region. The men in North Platte, Gothenburg, Lexington and Kearney who joined the Tri-County leaders in the Conservation Association were not openly fighting Tri-County, but it was hard to overlook a sort of join-them-rather-than-fight-them attitude. There was always the threat of Tri-County's dipping too deeply into the waters of the Platte, on which valley communities had an unmistakable emotional claim, if not a proprietary one.

Grand Island interests, with A. F. Buechler, editor of the *Independent,* as their willing and sometimes self-governing spokesman, wanted to be sure no Platte water got outside the watershed and that there should be no lowering of the water table in the valley. There were strong objections from Grand Island to the idea of generating electric power. The fact that Grand Island was the home of the Central Power Company made it easy to blame the opposition to electricity on the "power trust," a popular term in those days in identifying private power interests whenever they seemed to stand in the way of public ownership.

When the Grand Island *Independent* was sold in 1930 to Oscar Stauffer of Arkansas City, Kansas, more than one person in Hastings suggested that the new ownership might have private power connections. I recall someone trying to run down Stauffer's banking relationships in the hope of finding a link with power interests in Kansas City.

Representative Willis B. Sears of Nebraska introduced a bill in Congress early in 1930 that would bring the federal government into a flood control program for the Mississippi basin and justify federal support in building storage dams on the Platte. Within less than a year the measure had run its course and was shelved.

George Kingsley died in October 1929, and Fred R. Kingsley, his nephew, succeeded to the presidency of the Conservation Association. Looking back on George Kingsley's death and how it coincided with the beginning of the Great Depression, I see it as the start of a period of groping for a new sense of direction for Tri-County. New directions would be two or more years in coming, but they would come not just from new leadership in Tri-County but as a direct result of bold thinking at both state and national levels about irrigation and power projects as part of a fast-moving parade of ideas for revitalizing the economy.

George Norris, up for re-election to the Senate in 1930, was targeted for defeat by powerful leaders of the Republican party at both national and state levels. He survived a shameless attempt to confuse voters in the primary and won decisively over Gilbert Hitchcock in the general election. Firmly aligned already with the supporters of public ownership of power facilities, he would advance to new levels of prestige with the election of Franklin D. Roosevelt to the presidency two years later. The same Nebraska voters who returned Norris to the Senate voted for Democrat Charles Bryan over incumbent Arthur Weaver for governor, and in 1932 they gave Bryan a second term and a legislature dominated by his party. These were portentous events so far as Tri-County was concerned, more portentous, I think, than anyone thought they were at the time.

Just as portentous—and timely—in my opinion, was the gradual emergence of new leaders in the Tri-County movement. These included Dr. Donaldson W. Kingsley, son of George P. Kingsley, and Ralph O. Canaday, whose father, J. S. Canaday, had been with George Kingsley at a Conservation Association meeting at Kearney the day before the latter suffered his fatal heart attack. Dr. Kingsley, after years of study, internships and hospital residencies in the East, began the practice of medicine and surgery at Hastings in 1928. Canaday had practiced law at Bridgeport, seat of the Nebraska Bureau of Irrigation, before joining a Hastings law firm in 1931. These men moved gradually into Tri-County activities, but when the time came for formal organization in 1933 Kingsley was elected president and Canaday was hired as secretary and general counsel of the Central Nebraska Public Power and Irrigation District. These two natives of Minden and George E. Johnson offered a rare combination of temperament, talent and dedication. Johnson, while not a resident of the area until he became an employee of the district, had maintained an interest in Tri-County since 1915 when he studied the project as state engineer. He saw at that time a need for water storage, and it became easy for him to insist that if there was to be storage there should be generation of electric power.

It seemed obvious to me that both Kingsley and Canaday possessed an extra measure of zeal that had to have come from their respective fathers' interest in the project. Canaday's years at Bridgeport gave him familiarity with irrigation problems and irrigation law. Kingsley faced every challenge, every confrontation, every meeting or conference with the seriousness of the surgeon (that he was) entering an operating room. Whatever crises might have bothered him were masked by a normally stern countenance. The three men adapted easily to the changing political climate of the early 1930s, and there was never any question in my mind but that they had a rapport with Senator Norris that was a cut above what could be said of the leadership of any other Nebraska project that needed help in Washington.

The Tri-County Odyssey

Dr. Gene E. Hamaker, in his scholarly review of the early years of Tri-County, cites 1931 and 1932 as a period when the movement seemed to be "in eclipse." At the same time, he points out, there was considerable activity and consolidation of plans on the part of irrigationists in the North Platte-Kearney area. Farmers in the Tri-County area seemed to have lost interest, and on top of all that, as I recall in vivid detail, the business leaders in Hastings were distracted by painful proof of economic depression. In the fall of 1931 the First National Bank went into receivership. Two other financial institutions were closed in a matter of months.

What was happening to the economy in Hastings was happening, of course, all over the nation, and the political reaction in Washington did more than anything of a local nature to bring Tri-County back into public discussion. The Reconstruction Finance Corporation (RFC) was established early in 1932, and within a matter of months Congress extended the agency's powers to permit loans to self-liquidating public works projects. In Nebraska there was immediate attention to the possibility of a hydro-electric project on the Platte River that might qualify for an RFC loan.

In late August there was a meeting at Kearney for the stated purpose of discussing "development of a hydro-electric plant and storage reservoir at Sutherland, Nebraska." To Tri-County people this meant two things: First, their neighbors in the Lower Platte area had progressed in their planning to the point they could present a specific project, even though it included no part of the proposed diversion of water to the Tri-County region. Second, Tri-County had to choose between supporting the Sutherland proposal or breaking with the valley irrigators and trying to come up with a qualifying project of its own.

The record is vague as to whether Tri-County supporters engaged in any formal deliberation of the dilemma. Delegates from Hastings, Minden and Holdrege attended the August meeting and a second meeting just a week later. Out of the second meeting came a new organization, the Platte Valley Reservoirs Association, and the list of officers indicated that Tri-County was a part of it. Harry Williams of Gothenburg was president, Fred R. Kingsley of Minden (president of the inactive Conservation Association) was vice president and Thomas Gass of Kearney was treasurer. C. G. Wallace of Hastings and Adolph Held of Holdrege were board members, along with Carl Gray, president of the Union Pacific, and others.

About the best Tri-County could say at this juncture was that it still had a foot in the door. The articles of incorporation adopted by this new organization were explicit in their statements that the current purposes were to provide irrigation in the Platte Valley, protect the water level of the valley and generate electricity. No one could read them without seeing the heavy hand of Grand Island interests in the drafting. Tri-County leaders returned to their respective communities with a clear understanding they were on the defensive. While the North Platte-Kearney irrigationists—the real initiators and ardent supporters of the Sutherland project—accepted Tri-County support, they recognized that there was enough fear and prejudice in the Grand Island movement to threaten their whole plan.

My most significant memories of this period relate mainly to C. G. Wallace. He had lived at Lexington and was well known there and elsewhere in the Kearney-North Platte region. It was his idea that he could work within the board of the new organization in behalf of Tri-County. He worked hard to maintain communication between Tri-County and the valley interests, and it was safe to presume that he did all he could to discredit A. F. Buechler as a critic of Tri-County. Buechler had singled out Wallace, by innuendo if not by name, for mention in some of his more scathing editorials. One of his references implied that there was a sinister cabal of pro-Tri-County interests that included Fairbanks-Morse. Wallace was a salesman of Fairbanks-Morse electric generating plants.

I am confident that Wallace was instrumental in getting Fred Kingsley to call a meeting of the dormant Conservation Association so that he and W. C. Cooper could introduce a resolution expressing support of the Reservoirs Association. He may have had something to do with an expression of support from the Hastings City Council. Wallace was quicker than some of the others, perhaps, to see merit in giving the Sutherland project a feeling that if it couldn't sell its power at Grand Island it might sell some to the municipal electric system at Hastings.

Wallace visited frequently with me about his activities, and there was never any question in my mind but that he saw the possibility of isolating the obstructionist elements of the Grand Island area from the Platte development program. It was a vain hope.

Of all the years of Tri-County's turbulent pre-natal period there was none, I am sure, into which was crowded as much strategic maneuver, as much quiet intrigue, as much name-calling, as many passionate outbursts or as much suspense as 1933. It was a pivotal year in relations with the Platte Valley cohorts in the Conservation Association and the Reservoirs Association. The Platte organization finally deserted Tri-County under pressure from Grand Island.

The whole question of whether there could be a public power and irrigation district into which Tri-County might fit its plans hung in the balance at Lincoln through heated debate of Senate File 310, the enabling act that was sought by several potential projects, including Sutherland. If Grand Island interests had had their way, they would have written into the new law a prohibition against any project that sought to divert water from one watershed to another. While Tri-County eventually would survive a court ruling that outlawed such diversion in Nebraska, the presence of such a barrier in 1933 could have been fatal.

This was the year in which Dr. D. W. Kingsley and Ralph O. Canaday came to prominence as Tri-County leaders and spokesmen. The two of them were in a Tri-County delegation to an April meeting at Holdrege, where Keith Neville of North Platte announced the Sutherland group had decided against joining Tri-County in a public district and would pursue its case in Washington without further consideration of a unified system.

This was a blow to Tri-County, but it was offset in part by a reviving interest in the possibility the new administration in Washington was genuinely interested in providing funds for public works projects. The very optimism of the Sutherland backers in this regard had been a tonic for Tri-County. While Senator Norris seemed extremely cautious when it came to the differences between Tri-County and Sutherland people, he made it clear in several ways that he favored unification of all Platte projects. It was frequently suggested in private conversations that a power struggle was in the making between Norris and Arthur Mullen of Omaha, Democratic national committeeman and Sutherland's attorney in Washington. Mullen never quite hid his disdain for Tri-County, but there were men in the Tri-County camp who said that in a showdown Norris was more likely to have the ear of Franklin Roosevelt and Harold Ickes than Mullen was.

In a hasty move to establish a public power and irrigation district under the new state enabling act, Tri-County settled for a district made up of three cities—Hastings, Minden and Holdrege. In a matter of months there was another reorganization, and the Central Nebraska Public Power and Irrigation District was formed of four counties—Adams, Kearney, Phelps and Gosper. Dr. Kingsley was elected president in both instances, and Canaday was hired as secretary and chief counsel. The board in final form included Kingsley, Stephen Swigle and John Kipp as directors from Adams; Christian Aabel, Fred R. Kingsley and Andrew Jensen from Kearney; C. W. McConaughy, Ira Sheets and J. W. Taylor from Phelps, and J. S. Fitzsimmons, Claude Smith and F. J. Bean from Gosper.

The Sutherland project—organized as the Platte Valley Public Power and Irrigation District—remained a step ahead of Tri-County all through 1933. It was ahead in filing petitions for creation of its district under the new state law and was much ahead in Washington. Having filed for funds through the Reconstruction Finance Corporation, it did not have to go through the formalities of filing a request with the Public Works Administration when that organization came into being with passage of the National Industrial Recovery Act. Tri-County, however, had to go through a formal request, and its project had to be scrutinized in detail by authorities of the newly-created PWA. It was midsummer before Tri-County decided to apply to PWA. Sutherland's application went straight from RFC to PWA, without hearings. Tri-County's had to go through state and regional PWA offices that were still in the organizational stage. Tri-County's application got to PWA's state advisory board in mid-August.

Somewhere in the rush for approval of their plan in Washington, Sutherland leaders were confronted at Lincoln by questions as to their Platte River water rights. Governor Bryan held up approval of the new Platte Valley District because of these questions. Tri-County spokesmen were quick to restate their claim to a filing that pre-dated Sutherland's. What had been for several years an uneasy partnership of Tri-County and Platte Valley interests had become a spirited rivalry.

Recriminations were heated and pressures on Governor Bryan were intense as the two project groups sought the kind of state recognition that was essential to the good standing of their projects in Washington. One suggestion was that a PWA engineer should determine how the water might be allocated between the districts, but Governor Bryan refused to think of assigning authority over Nebraska water to a federal engineer in Washington. Another suggestion—attributed to C. G. Wallace of Hastings, and generally agreed to by both parties—was that both withdraw their filings and then refile with equal standing. New filings were made, but Robert G. Simmons, former congressman and attorney for Grand Island interests, filed an objection to Tri-County's filing. Shortly thereafter came a finding by Clark Mickey that there were flaws in the way Sutherland anticipated its water needs and there would not be enough water to operate its power plant during seasons of low river flow. PWA came into the picture with a suggestion that Sutherland enlarge its reservoir, and so the jockeying proceeded.

A more or less innocent sufferer from the water rights controversy and seeming stalemate was the so-called Columbus project on the Loup River. Its water rights application had been delayed along with Sutherland's. As in many other situations, this one tended to make of Tri-County the problem child of the entire Nebraska effort to take advantage of PWA funds for emergency public works projects. It is hard to look back on the period and not wonder how any of the projects could have recovered from the confusion and successive application of whatever political balm, anaesthetic or purgative seemed convenient.

Tri-County won approval of the Nebraska advisory board of PWA, and its application got to Washington in

The Tri-County Odyssey

late 1933. By that time, though, PWA spokesmen were saying that current appropriations were exhausted. Tri-County leaders talked of going back to the Reclamation Service for help, and Grand Island interests were saying the time had come to challenge Tri-County's water rights in court. Senator Norris continued to advocate unification of the Tri-County and Sutherland projects.

There came a time in early 1934 when Interior Secretary Harold Ickes declared that if Governor Bryan continued to quibble over the Sutherland and Columbus water rights, PWA would abandon consideration of these and all other projects in Nebraska. Arthur Mullen, the Democratic national committeeman, was quoted to the effect Governor Bryan had better shape up or prepare to retire from the political arena.

Mullen, it turned out, was preparing to retire from his committee post. When the state central committee met to name his successor, the Mullen faction won an easy vote for its choice of Keith Neville of North Platte over William Ritchie of Omaha. Keith Neville had been identified with the Sutherland project from the beginning, and while he had been a fair and friendly negotiator through the years when Tri-County and the Platte Valley group tried to work together, there was no question as to Tri-County's having gained little from the departure of Arthur Mullen. Adding insult to injury, so far as Tri-County was concerned, was the state committee's passage of a resolution urging PWA financing for the Sutherland and Columbus projects without even mentioning Tri-County or the several other Nebraska projects still hoping to qualify for PWA funding.

It is hard to look back on 1934 and remember anything good about it in Nebraska. It was the year of the most extreme combination of heat and drouth the region ever had experienced. Crops and people's spirits withered together. Even before the extreme heat of spring and summer had set in, there were discouraging reports from Washington as to the fate of Tri-County's application for PWA approval and financing. Congressman Terry Carpenter of Scottsbluff told the Hastings Rotary Club that the project required more money than would be available.

PWA sent two engineers to the state in April. One of them was Major C. R. Olberg, a former Bureau of Reclamation employee and more recently involved as a consultant on a mammoth dam construction project in Russia. I visited briefly with him at the Hastings airport before he took off for a tour of the Tri-County area.

The word seeped out gradually after he had returned to Washington. It was good. He saw the possibility of a dam on the North Platte that would back up the entire flow of the river. On the strength of his advice, Tri-County filed an application to store two million acre-feet of water in what would be known as the Keystone Reservoir. There may not be a single event in Tri-County's tortuous history that ranks above this as a landmark.

Quit worrying about whether there is enough water for everybody's needs. Dam the whole river, control it on a year-around basis, and most of the grounds for criticism of Tri-County will be nullified. That was the fresh new thinking in Tri-County circles, even though many months passed before anybody talked about Keystone as any more than part of an alternate plan.

There were repeated reports from Washington that Tri-County's application was on dead center. Many top officials of PWA were openly skeptical, and Secretary Ickes seemed to lack enthusiasm. PWA's engineering division reported adversely on Tri-County in May, and the finance division did likewise in June.

There was some evidence that Washington was getting weak signals from Nebraska. Tri-County leaders and Senator Norris were pressing the case, but there seemed to be little grassroots enthusiasm. Ralph Canaday and

The Tri-County Odyssey

other Tri-County folk called a meeting of chambers of commerce and commercial clubs at Holdrege in March. The need for a region-wide show of interest in and support for Tri-County was explained. On that occasion and at later meetings of what became the South Platte United Chambers of Commerce the case for Tri-County was explained, but in due time the organization could flash word to Washington of its interest in several projects that were taking shape all the way to the headwaters of the Republican River.

L. B. Stiner, Hastings lawyer and a familiar figure in courtrooms of several counties, was the first president of the United Chambers. Whether on orders from Henry Smith or on my own, I started attending the monthly meetings. All the meetings of that first summer were well attended, despite heat, drouth and the generally low morale of business leaders and farmers who had watched a wheat crop burn up in May and a corn crop suffer the same fate by early July.

For my part these meetings were a break in the monotony of a dreary summer. As a matter of fact, L. B. Stiner and I were in the Hastings delegation to just about every meeting for a couple of years, and we usually rode in the same car. J. B. Hillers, veteran realtor, was with us on several occasions, and his and Stiner's reminiscences of their earlier years in Nebraska were interesting and entertaining. Once as we followed Route 6 in the Republican Valley, Hillers recalled that as a boy he had taken a wagonload of wheat to town from his farm home near Indianola. He left home with three silver dollars in his pocket. Somewhere along the way the coins got lost in the wheat. He emptied the wagon, one careful shovelful after another, and finally recovered all his money.

One can only speculate as to the extent the South Platte Chambers stirred public opinion. Most everyone agreed, though, that the organization symbolized the kind of action that could be interpreted effectively in Washington. The primary election in August and the general election in November reflected a rise in Democratic influence in Nebraska. This was an unmistakable vote of confidence in the budding New Deal and could not be completely ignored by those with responsibility for final disposition of Tri-County's case before the Public Works Administration.

Governor Bryan, definitely friendly to Tri-County, sought the Democratic nomination for the United States Senate. He lost to Edward R. Burke in the primary. While Burke was considered to be on the cold side of a professed neutrality so far as Tri-County was concerned, his Republican opponent in November was Robert G. Simmons, whose involvement with Grand Island protesters marked him as openly hostile. Burke won. The new governor was Roy Cochran, a former state engineer. To the best of my recollection, he avoided any show of prejudice against Tri-County, even though his hometown loyalties were to North Platte.

The year of decision turned out to be 1935, but for the first seven months of that year the project seemed to hang in the same balances that had prevailed since 1933. Tri-County's size in relation to other projects, both outside Nebraska and within, made for close questioning in Washington. The whole nation was waiting for congressional action to make new funds available, and Nebraska, with two projects already approved for financing, was a relatively small state. There were suggestions from Sutherland leaders that Tri-County should abandon all the power features of its proposal. There was the steady stream of chronic complaints from Grand Island, of course, and genuine differences of opinion among PWA engineers as to whether there was need for all the power Tri-County, Sutherland and Columbus could produce.

One of the discouraging developments of early 1935 was

a request by Nebraska's new senator, Edward R. Burke, for a new survey of Tri-County, its relations with Sutherland and its possible effect on water disputes between Nebraska and Wyoming and Colorado. It was hard to believe this was more than a delaying tactic, but the survey was ordered by the Bureau of Reclamation and placed in the hands of a former University of Nebraska professor, Dr. O. V. P. Stout. Dr. Stout became ill and died before the survey was completed, and that made for another delay. Others did pick up Stout's work, though, and from it came some data that seemed to answer questions Secretary Ickes had been asking about water supply. The word he got was that there was enough water to meet both Tri-County's and Sutherland's needs.

To strengthen its position, Tri-County revised its funding estimates in August by elimination of the Keystone dam and reduction in size of its power plants. In so doing, it brought its total cost estimate to about $20 million. (Funding for the dam was restored later.)

The action from that date was fast and furious. I doubt that anyone could trace an orderly sequence of developments or spot the exact time and place of the start of this favorable trend of events. There seems to be no question but that Senator Norris had expressed again his impatience with Secretary Ickes and PWA.

The *Tribune* of August 26 proclaimed progress with this headline in red ink: Tri-County Recommended for Federal Works Money.

I like to think I wrote that headline, but at some point in late August or early September I was in the Mary Lanning Memorial Hospital for removal of my appendix. My surgeon was Dr. D. W. Kingsley, for whom these were anxious days. To the best of my recollection the operation took place after August 26. If so, both Kingsley and I were more relaxed than we might have been at any time in the previous two months.

There was considerable confusion as to just what was meant by the "approval" announcement of August 26. While there may have been tacit agreement extending all the way to the White House, there would be anxious moments as the case proceeded through a network of prescribed procedures for allocation of the kind of loans and grants involved.

It was known that Harry Hopkins presumed a sort of dictatorial power over emergency relief projects and that he was not reluctant to dispute decisions of Harold Ickes. Hopkins probably had some reservations about Tri-County, but from all indications Ickes was firm and somewhat belligerent in his final position in support of the project.

Meanwhile, those Nebraskans who had disputed Tri-County's right to a place in the sun had not given up. Even before the approval announcement came from Washington the Sutherland board had authorized a strong objection to some of the findings in the Bureau of Reclamation study of water supply. A. F. Buechler, in the Grand Island *Independent,* conceded that President Roosevelt probably would go along with Tri-County as a special favor to Senator Norris. Arthur Mullen and Senator Burke—the latter finally conceding an open hostility—went to the president himself to register their objections.

There had been enough confidence among Tri-County leaders that all questions would be answered and final approval would be forthcoming within four weeks, and September 27 was selected as the day for a big victory celebration in Hastings. There were some tense moments as the month dragged on. Presidential approval did not come until the day before the scheduled celebration.

I was still convalescing from my appendectomy (doctors kept surgery patients down longer in those days), but I walked part of the distance with the *Tribune* contingent of the parade. Congressman Charles G. Binderup had flown in from Washington, and James E. Lawrence, editor of the Lincoln *Star* and one-time member of the PWA advisory committee in Nebraska, was on hand to speak.

The formal celebration seemed entirely fitting at the time, but as a reflection of what Tri-County meant to Hastings and other communities represented, it fell short. Just what would have been appropriate is not worth arguing at this late date, but anything truly proper and fully meaningful would have had to be more than a victory march with bands playing and flags waving. There was victory to celebrate, of course—victory over the skeptics in Washington, over the jealous interests at Grand Island and elsewhere in the Platte Valley and over the Mullen faction of the Democratic party. But the euphoria of those early fall days transcended any pride of triumph over opponents who could be identified by name or place. What many people seemed to feel was an emancipation of the spirit, a sudden freedom from the grip of economic depression that had been all the more punishing because for two years it had been accompanied by extremes of weather that had tested the very souls of men and women in the best as well as the worst of circumstances.

The cannon shots and trumpet blasts of that September 27 celebration barely had died down when Henry Smith called me in to review the *Tribune's* continued responsibility for making Tri-County meaningful and successful. He recalled our special effort during the heat of the recent summer to provide printed testimonials of scores of farmers supporting Tri-County and how copies of our paper had been carefully delivered to key individuals in Washington. He expressed satisfaction with the results of an effort to which he had given a lot of personal attention, the organization of We-Want-Water Clubs.

The *Tribune* had a vested interest in the project, he

stressed. Our progress could be no greater than that of the total community. We were not to rest on our laurels. The job ahead was to keep the community conscious of Tri-County's presence and its promise. He suggested that a good goal for me was to see that there was something about Tri-County in every issue of the paper.

There was a definite upturn in activity as well as morale as we of the editorial staff took up the task of reporting the existence and activities of a going concern. We described the promptness with which George Johnson put his staff together and prepared to meet some strict deadlines for contract-letting that had been set down by PWA. We told about the survey parties going out from Hastings, Minden and Holdrege to fix the lines and elevations of the major canals. We described the support organization in the new headquarters in the Stitt Building, next-door to the *Tribune*.

We told of the enlistment of engineers and other technicians. Many came from the state highway department at Lincoln. Some came from the Corps of Engineers office at Omaha. No small number of new staff members had been jobless for months, some perhaps for a year.

Some things about the new organization came almost as a shock. It was hard to believe that there would be need for 25 or more new automobiles. No new industry had come to Hastings for years. No new job center with need for scores of men and women had opened. A place where people were being hired every day, where thousands of square feet of office space was being furnished—this was a far cry from the frugality and austerity by which we had been conditioned.

The very novelty of this explosive birth of an institution was stimulating. It was progress and action. It was news. We relished the opportunity and reported the activities with unrestrained enthusiasm.

What we did not take time to note in those days was

that the Tri-County story would someday dovetail into the bigger story of Nebraska's ultimate emergence as a public-power state. The fight to build a project that would subsidize the cost of irrigation with revenues from electric plants was especially appropriate to Nebraska, a state where agriculture was supreme. Some of the intensity of feeling that came from charges and suspicions that private power companies were quietly supporting move after move to discredit Tri-County was contagious.

Year after year, during which there seemed to be an unending supply of barriers to be set in front of the Tri-County movement, there had generated a sort of intuitive reaction to the charge that power companies in Nebraska were not performing in the public interest. Senator Norris, meanwhile, was advocating a national policy of encouraging electric service for rural America, and farmers were slowly coming to the realization that Tri-County might bring them electric lights and power as well as irrigation.

The steps by which the various private power companies ultimately were taken over by public districts cannot be reviewed here. But they cannot be separated from the influence of George Norris at that moment in history and the way in which Tri-County had come to dramatize the struggle for public hydro-electric development.

The story that starts in the 1880s with Joel Hull's inspiration stretched over more than half a century before anyone could point to tangible results. These came in the form of dams, lakes, power plants, canals and other irrigation works that are utilitarian in every sense of that word. There are valid reasons, though, why there should be a lake named McConaughy, a dam named Kingsley and power plants named Canaday and Johnson. These can be viewed as monuments to visionary and willful men. Many others were never thus memorialized, but they were equally visionary and equally willful.

Dr. James L. Sellers, long-time professor of history at the University of Nebraska, wrote an eloquent introduction to Dr. Gene E. Hamaker's detailed history of Tri-County's founding. Among his observations was this paragraph: "This is a tremendous story. If anyone thinks this development was imposed on Nebraska by Washington, he probably will continue to do so, for this is too big an account for him to read."

Let it be said by one who was in the press-box through the decisive stages of a bitter contest that Dr. Sellers was right. Every point was scored the hard way, and never once did anyone believe that the critics and obstructionists, in Washington or anywhere else, would throw the game before the clock ran out.

Epilogue

The Central Nebraska Public Power and Irrigation District was alive and well when I visited its headquarters at Holdrege in 1982. Its annual report identified it as a "public corporation and political subdivision of the State of Nebraska" and listed its major properties as three hydro-electric plants, a two-million-acre-foot storage reservoir and an irrigation delivery system serving 125,000 acres. Its board was made up of representatives of the same four counties that joined in its founding. The irrigated acres fell far short of the estimates of a half-million or more in the 1930s, but the pattern of irrigation development in Nebraska had shifted dramatically to a greater emphasis on pumping systems than on the gravity-flow concepts of the founders. The district was pointing to its storage facilities as important factors in recharging the underground source of water that was being pumped onto vast land areas beyond the bounds of Tri-County. C. J. Hargleroad, district president, was quoted in the 1980 annual report to the effect that Tri-County had "drouth-proofed 600,000 acres."

10. Man in Black

George W. Norris—
For the Poor and Beaten Down

George W. Norris wore dark suits and black ties. And they seemed to harmonize with his personality.

There was a sadness in his eyes and a deadly seriousness in his work. He went to the heart of his subject in the opening sentences of his speeches. He never told jokes. His was a direct, no-nonsense approach to all big issues.

I thought of him every time I heard Johnny Cash in his popular song of the 1960s and 1970s about a "man in black." George Norris, always dressed in black or near-black, seemed to share the burden of the "poor and beaten down"—as the man in the song—and he considered the American farmer to be foremost among those in that condition.

American history will place Norris high among the hundreds who have served in the U. S. Senate. Some have said he belongs among the first 10.

There is no question but that he got where he did because of his interest in and concern for the people of agricultural America. He was one of them. He aspired to no other identification.

Born on an Ohio farm, he taught country school to earn his way through Valparaiso University in Indiana. He was determined to go west and become a lawyer. He tried the state of Washington and didn't like it. His next stop was at Tecumseh, Nebraska, where he tarried a few months before settling in Beaver City, about 200 miles farther west. He served as county attorney and district judge before his election to Congress from a district laced by the fertile valleys of the Republican River and several of its tributaries.

In all of his years in Washington, he shunned the bright lights and gay parties. His dark suit and black tie—his everyday dress—were the limit to which he would accede when the invitation implied formal attire.

George Norris served 10 years in the House of Representatives and 30 in the Senate. He ran as a Republican until 1936, when he found himself so much at odds with party leaders that he ran as an independent.

The tendency toward independence was a part of George Norris almost from the beginning of his public career. He didn't realize the extent to which this spirit of self-determination was straining relations with his party until 1930, when Republican leaders, from Herbert Hoover in the White House to precinct workers in Nebraska, undertook to remove him from the Washington scene.

But by that time Norris had established himself as a man of the people—especially the people of Nebraska's farms and small towns. He had, in a sense, deserted his contemporaries in the leadership of his party.

His last 10 years in the Senate were, in some respects, his most fruitful. It was during these years that one of his ideas blossomed into the Tennessee Valley Authority and another became the basis of the National Rural Electrification Administration.

George Norris left his mark on the government of Nebraska. He, more than any other individual, was responsible for the state's decision to go to a one-house legislature.

He made several notable contributions to the legislative processes in Washington. He led the move to break the power of the speaker of the House, and he was the

Senator George W. Norris

principal author of the Twentieth Amendment to the Constitution, which eliminated the "lame duck" session of Congress.

My 12 years with the *Tribune* covered a period when Senator Norris went through some of his bitterest fights. These were the years, also, of some of his greatest triumphs.

Traveling from Washington to McCook, his hometown, he sometimes stopped in Hastings to consult Dr. E. C. Foote about his eyes. He would come in on the No. 3 some night, stay at the Clarke Hotel, see the doctor the next morning and take the afternoon train to McCook. During my early years at the *Tribune* it was taken for granted that Dave Lewis would try to get an interview during these visits. I recall one time when this took place while the senator ate breakfast in the hotel dining room.

With the election of Franklin D. Roosevelt to the presidency and the improvement of Norris' standing in Washington, there was an obvious change in the senator's relationship with Hastings. Norris had supported the Roosevelt candidacy, and his followers took for granted that the new administration would look more kindly on some of Norris' ideas than Herbert Hoover's administration had. There was a gradual realization in Nebraska that Norris could not logically continue to push for the Tennessee Valley Authority without recognizing the similarities between it and some proposed developments in Nebraska. Among the latter was the Tri-County.

While his personal visits to Hastings seem to have been fewer after 1933 than before that, his importance to the community increased tremendously. He exerted great influence in behalf of several Nebraska power and irrigation projects that could be carried out only with federal funds—the Tri-County among them. In his autobiography Norris refers loosely to these as a "Little TVA."

Dr. D. W. Kingsley, first president of the Central Nebraska Public Power and Irrigation District, the legal entity under which Tri-County was developed, and R. O. Canaday, secretary and chief counsel, were in frequent contact with the senator. His office in Washington was consulted almost daily through a period of many months when the fate of Tri-County hung in delicate balance between certain federal officials and forces in Nebraska that sought to have it declared ineligible for federal funding.

I first saw Senator Norris and heard him speak during the campaign of 1930, when he was the target of one of the most bizarre and amateurish maneuvers in Nebraska political history.

He had been openly critical of the Hoover administration. As a matter of fact, he had come out in support of Al Smith over Hoover in 1928. This was another illustration of his free thinking. Here he was, a Protestant, a Dry, a Republican, supporting a Roman Catholic, a Wet, and a Democrat.

His opponents did some canvassing and discovered that Norris was an overwhelming favorite against any possible candidate in either party for re-election to the Senate. Someone hit upon the idea of creating a legal tangle by running a man of the same name against him in the Republican primary. A younger George W. Norris, willing and gullible, was discovered managing a Skaggs Safeway store at Broken Bow.

Almost immediately there arose the question of whether the second Norris filing had reached the state house in time to qualify him as a candidate.

Very quickly this second Norris became known as "Grocer Norris." A U.S. Senate committee started an investigation of the whole plot. Ultimately, Grocer Norris was disqualified. If his name had appeared on the primary ballot, however, it might have resulted in enough confusion that the third man on the ticket, W. B. Stebbins, could have won. That was the idea from the beginning.

Senator Norris, in his autobiography, wrote in generally mild tones of people who crossed or opposed him in his long political career, but of those who were admittedly involved in the Grocer Norris plot, he wrote with studied scorn. A forgiving man in most situations, he was firmly against a pardon for one of the men who had gone to prison for perjuring himself during investigation of the affair.

C. G. Wallace of Hastings, a devoted Norris supporter, liked to tell of a conversation during which the senator reported on a visit to a Custer County farm on a hot midsummer day. A young mother sat in the shade of a tree, waving a fan over the face of a sleeping child. She was battling some persistent flies as well as the heat, and the senator could not help thinking that a woman in town would be behind screen doors and would have the benefit of an electric fan. The senator was almost intemperate, Wallace said, in expressing his disgust with a system that made electric fans available to most urban dwellers but could not find ways to bring them to the homes of rural America.

The story was highly relevant in the dry and hot mid-1930s, when there was practically no electrification in rural America. In a society that now takes home air-conditioning for granted, in rural communities as well as urban, it is hard to realize that an electric fan could have stood as a symbol of the wide gap between urban and rural living.

Wallace's story has stayed with me over the years as sound evidence that much of the tenacity of George Norris as a lawmaker stemmed from his compassion for the "poor and beaten down."

Richard L. Neuberger and Stephen B. Kahn wrote a biography of Norris in 1937, when he was still near the peak of his career. They chose as the title a word that probably sums up the man about as well as any other—*Integrity*.

I came to respect his integrity in 1940, even though at that moment it seemed to work against a personal ambition. I was seeking desperately to qualify for a Nieman Fellowship at Harvard which would have paid expenses for me and my family for a year of stimulating study. I had interviewed Senator Norris and had covered many meetings at which he spoke. I wasn't sure how well he knew me, so I turned to a close friend of the senator, Dr. D. W. Kingsley, and asked him if he would tell Norris of my application and suggest that a letter from him to the proper people at Harvard would be particularly effective.

I didn't keep a copy of Senator Norris' reply, but the key sentences ran something like this: "If the Harvard people write to ask about the young man, I shall be happy to speak favorably in his behalf. Tell him, though, that I never write voluntary letters of recommendation. I consider this a misuse of the powers of my office."

As a reporter, I had been impressed by the man's blunt independence. As solicitor of a favor, I caught it straight in the face.

One of the senator's many periods of travail came in 1917, when he opposed President Wilson's Armed-Ship Bill—an obvious step toward involvement in World War I. His friends in high places, his supporters among newspaper editors in Nebraska and countless others were confident that his career had crashed. They could not see how a man who went against the prevailing chauvinism could muster enough support to stay in office. Norris was ready to resign from the Senate, but he decided to go to Nebraska—as he often did—to explain his position.

He couldn't find anyone to act as chairman at a meeting he had called at a public hall in Lincoln. And so he called the meeting to order himself and opened with these words: "I have come home to tell you the truth."

His deprecators hadn't reckoned with a number of factors, not the least of which was the presence in Nebraska of many first- and second-generation Germans. They were looking for someone who could talk about affairs in Europe with a little more objectivity, a little more consideration of both sides of the issue than they were hearing from most everyone else in Washington. They helped fill the hall to overflowing.

Interestingly enough, Senator Norris was a supporter of America's going to war with Germany in 1941. His explanation was relatively simple. Our whole way of life seemed to be threatened by Hitler in 1941. He hadn't been able to believe in 1917 that Kaiser Wilhelm was preparing to overthrow the forces of democracy everywhere.

I last saw George W. Norris and heard him speak at Lincoln during World War II. He was then past 80 years of age. He still possessed some of the old fire. But he didn't have what it took to win another campaign. He went back home to McCook after defeat in 1942 and died there two years later.

Fighting Liberal is the title of the autobiography of Senator Norris that was published by MacMillan in 1945. It was written after the senator had gone home to McCook, worn down by his more than 80 years, shaken and somewhat embittered by his defeat in 1942 by Kenneth Wherry of Pawnee City.

I observed the writing of this book from Lincoln, where I was directing the school of journalism of the University of Nebraska. James E. Lawrence, editor of the Lincoln *Star,* taught a night class in newspaper editing and was, in a technical sense, a member of my staff. Since he was 17 years older than I and a widely experienced journalist, I made no attempt to supervise or regulate his activities. Out of respect for my position, nevertheless, he always kept me informed of any shifts in his schedule and of the frequent occasions when a member of the *Star* staff took over his class in his absence.

Early in 1943 he advised me that he was urging Senator Norris to write his memoirs, and he was offering to provide whatever assistance the senator might accept. He made several trips to McCook before getting a commitment from Norris. Eventually he was traveling to McCook regularly to help with the writing. At some stage he told me of his suggestion of a title and of the senator's initial rejection of it. My recollection is that Norris had some reservation about calling himself a "liberal." He would have been more comfortable perhaps with "progressive." In any event, Lawrence was far more of an enthusiast for the project than Norris, and the senator acknowledged this in a prefatory statement in the book as finally published. He went so far as to concede that Lawrence had elaborated on some subjects. That this was taking place came through to me in Lawrence's conversations after each of his trips to McCook. One of his problems was to get the senator to loosen up and accept credit for his many accomplishments.

I haven't the slightest knowledge of how the book fared financially, whether Norris or Lawrence benefited from royalties. My guess is that if there were any profits, they were small.

Jim Lawrence was a man of tremendous ego, but I developed a great deal of admiration for the way he went about making sure that George Norris himself could be credited in history with personal comments on significant events with which he was identified. For Jim Lawrence *Fighting Liberal* was a labor of love. While historians eventually may be able to piece out a record of the Norris career that differs here and there from the autobiography, their job is made easier by the presence of a book that would not have been written if Lawrence had not made up his mind to do all he could to assure Norris a proper place in the annals of a nation.

Jim Lawrence, well into middle age, carried a heavy load at the *Star*. This did not deter him from boarding a night train about once a week, riding to McCook, spending a day with Norris and going back to Lincoln on another night train. He was indefatigable and ever confident that this project in behalf of a friend and idol was worth all he was putting into it.

Lewis Gannett, a prominent journalist, once referred to Norris as "the only honest man in political life in America." He may not have been the only one, but he certainly is hard to overlook in any search for men whose honesty in public life left lasting impressions.

His character was shaped by many things. His parents

worked hard to establish a home on rocky, stump-dotted land in Ohio. His father was a victim of a farm accident while George was still a small boy. An older brother died from a wound suffered while serving in the Union Army. He labored to earn his education.

He knew the pain of drought in the farming areas of western Nebraska, and he knew the helplessness of farmers who could do nothing about low prices when their harvests were abundant. He lived close to farmers and townspeople at Beaver City and McCook. He heard their troubles in intimate detail as he presided over district court at these and neighboring county seats.

He wore the black—if any man ever did—for the poor and beaten down, and he seemed never quite to forget that in his own time he had been among them or close enough to them, at least, to sense their distress, their frustration, their helplessness.

And he never forgot that one of his responsibilities in public office was to do all he could to help such people, to encourage them, defend them and recognize that they had rights as well as did the rich and powerful.

11. The Bell Tolls Later There

Notes on Some Individuals for Whom It Tarried

The healthiest place in the United States for a middle-aged male is a stretch of the Nebraska prairie south of the Platte River, but nobody seems to know why.

So went the first sentence of an article in the May 1969, issue of *Holiday* Magazine. The supporting statistics came from a study by Dr. Herbert L. Sauer, member of the medical faculty at the University of Missouri-Columbia. The magazine article was by Joan Younger Dickinson, and she visited Hastings in search of material with which to warm up the cold facts of Dr. Sauer's research.

The magic zone that can be outlined from the Sauer study is a jagged triangle covering 14 counties and embracing the Nebraska portions of the Big and Little Blue rivers. Hastings sits on a divide between the upper tributaries of each of these streams and near the western point of the triangle. Boosters of the city as a good place to live were quick to take note of this, and so was I. To what extent could I expect my life span to be extended as a result of having breathed the air for 16 years, drunk the water and enjoyed exposure to any other elements that might explain Dr. Sauer's findings? More than anything else, though, the Sauer study sent me on an exploration of my memories. The result is a sort of anthology of the durable, but it is also a roll call of engaging men and women who lived beyond the average of their time.

Pinned to His Brother

Nathaniel Martin, a familiar figure in Hastings, was the grandfather of a college classmate, Bernice Johnston. He died in 1928, and it was not until then that some of us learned that he had been given up for dead after an Indian's arrow had pierced his body in 1862. He was shot in the back as he and a brother, together on a horse, tried to escape from a band of Sioux that had raided the family homestead on the Platte River. Going all the way through Nathaniel's chest, the arrow penetrated the back of his brother. The parents nursed both boys back to health after they had lain bleeding in a barn overnight. The brother with the lesser injury died at the age of 47. Nathaniel died at 79.

Self-Made Mayor

During my early years with the *Tribune* I had frequent encounters with the undisputed claimant to the title of No. 1 elder citizen. Jacob Fisher was a native of Germany whose educational opportunities had been severely limited, but when he got to Hastings (about 1880) he knew enough about American ways that he became postmaster, mayor, baker, bank director and leader in Masonic bodies. He was about 90 years old when I first met him, but nobody was quicker with a response to questions about the state of affairs in the city, the state or the nation. And few men's opinions were more fixed. When Hastings needed make-work projects to ease the pressures of the Great Depression, attention quickly centered on surpluses in the funds of the municipal water and light department, which Fisher had helped establish. One of several investments of those funds was in a lighted fountain honoring the former mayor.

Salesman of Ideas

Charles G. Wallace, during the years of my most frequent association with him, worried about his health, carried pills and compared his aches and pains with those

The Bell Tolls Later There

C.G. Wallace
age 90

of others. He gave in to none of his ailments, though, until he had passed his ninety-fifth birthday.

His memories went back to boyhood on the raw prairies of Furnas and Dawson counties, to the blizzard of 1888 and to a futile attempt to win a piece of Oklahoma land for himself by participating in the dramatic opening of the Cherokee Strip in 1893. He had tried his hand at manufacturing bed springs in Arkansas and at operating an iron foundry in Hastings. When I came to know him, though, he was a highly successful salesman for Fairbanks-Morse.

While his company produced a considerable line of hardware items and probably was best known for its scales, Wallace confined himself to the sale of electric generating plants. To the mayors, administrators and municipal councils of scores of towns and cities he projected much more than the technical details of his company's engines and generators. He sold an idea—the idea of public ownership of the sources of electric current. To a town or small city this meant a compact diesel-powered plant, owned and managed by the local government. To the burgeoning private power companies of the time it meant competition for the central generating services they offered.

During the early 1930s Wallace was a familiar figure in the state house at Lincoln, where bills having to do with the rights of municipalities to finance and build electric plants were repeatedly at issue. During these years as a lobbyist he became known as "Hungry Wallace," a name pinned on him by critics and competitors. Around Hastings, though, he remained "C. G." or "Charlie." At the *Tribune* he appeared regularly with what he considered newsworthy information from the public ownership front. The appearance of a two-or-three sentence report of some town council's vote to buy a generating plant drew his thanks and appreciation.

In the middle and late 1930s the whole state became the battleground between private and public ownership forces. As the major power properties began shifting from private developers to public districts, Wallace found himself riding the new and faster currents. He had aligned himself with the forces of public ownership all the way from the Tennessee Valley Authority to Nebraska's smallest towns. George W. Norris, the father of TVA and the Rural Electrification Act, had been a natural ally from the early days of Wallace's involvement in public ownership. C. G. and his son, Glen, were active supporters of the rural electrification movement as it spread across Nebraska.

In the late 1940s I received a long handwritten letter from Wallace, then approaching 80, wondering if I had any thoughts about the desirability of rerouting the Union Pacific's crack passenger train, the City of St.

Louis, on its daily runs between St. Louis and Denver. Wallace had read that the Union Pacific officials were concerned about what some new flood-control dams on the Kansas River would do to their tracks in the Manhattan-Salina area. The railroad might consider shifting its principal Denver-Kansas City traffic to its Marysville-Hastings-Gibbon line, Wallace reasoned. He probably wrote similar letters to a half-dozen persons. He wrote to me because I was on a newspaper in St. Louis and might be in position to publicize the idea. Anything to promote his hometown usually got C. G.'s attention and his active support.

During a visit to Hastings in October 1952, I got word that C. G. wanted to see me. We met, as I recall, in the middle of a street, and our conversation was brief. He was feeling good about a letter he had written to Adlai Stevenson after Dwight Eisenhower's announcement in a campaign talk that if elected president he would go to Korea in person to tackle problems in our country's relationships there. Wallace's advice to Stevenson was that he should announce that if he (Stevenson) won the presidency he would send Eisenhower as a special envoy to Korea. Wallace thought it was a good idea, and he wanted to tell me about it. He was a fascinating mixture of ideas and action.

Wallace was interesting for the additional reason that he seemed always ready to share details of an experience, even when these might reflect lapses of judgment on his part. Nothing illustrates this better than his long review of a health-seeking hegira that he took in his early sixties. Local physicians had not satisfied him with the explanations of a nagging discomfort in his midsection. Someone suggested he consult a practitioner in Denver, a man who lacked standing in certain professional circles but had managed to comfort and satisfy a lot of patients. Wallace took an overnight train to Denver, but by the time he got there he had decided on a new course of action. Without leaving the railroad station, he arranged to take another long train ride to the Mayo Clinic at Rochester, Minnesota. The Mayo doctors checked him thoroughly and sent him home with instructions to relax and take a light shot of whisky before dinner each evening. "Awful stuff" he said of this medicine, but he started feeling better right away.

Eugene Clair Foote, M.D.

Death came to Eugene Clair Foote shortly after his one-hundredth birthday. Born at Ayr, he had lived all his years in Adams County, except for time spent in medical studies, military service and such excursions as one to India to contribute his services for a given period as eye surgeon in a mission hospital.

Between the years of his twenties and his seventies he was as well known as any citizen of Hastings. He would have been a man of distinction wherever he might have chosen to live and care for the pains and defects of people's eyes, ears, noses and throats.

As a college freshman I consulted him about trouble with my eyes. He tested my sight, prescribed new lenses for my glasses and sent me on my way. The impressions of that visit to his new office building were many. I overheard his conversations with several patients. The voice was strong and clear, the words were reassuring and optimistic. By the time he got to me I was almost awed by the power of his personality.

The climactic moment of that first encounter, however, had to be at the reception desk on my way out. The glasses would be ready in a week or so, I was told, and I would be expected to pay for them. Since I was trying to earn my own way through college, there would be no charge for the examination. I would benefit from that policy for the next four years, and on one occasion in my junior year the charges Dr. Foote waived would be for nasal surgery that occupied him and his nurse for almost an hour. Hundreds of college students of that era could have related similar experiences.

It was impossible to detect in the attitude of any personnel of the Foote Clinic a suggestion that we college students were fitted into the schedule at the convenience of the doctors. Dr. Foote and his associates seemed always to be working from a crowded waiting room, and non-paying students were taken in order or by appointment.

During my years with the *Tribune* the newspapers of the country had not got around to the kind of reporting of medical news that would be commonplace in the second half of the twentieth century. We accepted with only passing complaint the strict limits the medical profession and the hospitals placed on news about their patients. The administrator of the Mary Lanning Memorial Hospital at Hastings would share with us little more than the name of a patient.

The best we could do with a surgery case—with a few exceptions—was to report a "major" or a "minor" operation. Our readers were left to guess whether "minor" surgery for an adult meant dealing with hemorrhoids or skin cancer. A "minor" operation on a child was almost always a tonsillectomy. Only in the rarest of cases did we report that anyone had cancer. When death came to a victim of this disease, we usually attributed it to a "lingering illness."

This closed-door policy on medical news meant that our newspaper failed miserably—as did most other dailies—in reporting many of the day-to-day crises in the lives of a community and its people. Word came to us now and then of the extremity of some of the cases of mastoiditis that were treated by Dr. Foote. Whether the hospital reported them as "major" or "minor" I don't recall, but we were denied any detail beyond what came from family or friends of the patients. We would hear of parents who had come 150 to 400 miles with a pain-ridden child wrapped in blankets and stretched out on the back seat of a side-curtained touring car. (Mastoid troubles usually came in cold weather.) Occasionally we would report that a family from a sandhill community or from somewhere in the upper basin of the Republican River was in town for "medical treatment," but that would be about all. The story that lay behind those cases was that Dr. Foote had developed a reputation for success in the delicate operation by which the infection and pain of mastoiditis could be relieved. In conversations with other physicians in later years I learned that he was exceptionally deft in cutting the opening in the skull and doing what else was necessary to relieve an infection that was dangerously close to the brain. One of his non-medical friends insisted that his skill was not hurt any by the woodworking hobby he pursued in the basement of his home. "He cut a neat hole," my informant said. His father, this person observed, would have appreciated that. He was a cabinetmaker.

Gerontic Athlete

Herbert F. Anderson met the eldest daughter of Dr. and Mrs. E. C. Foote at Hastings College. Their decision to marry led to a revision of his career plans after he had taught and coached for one year in the high school at Cambridge. He returned to Hastings to complete a number of prerequisite courses before enrolling in the medical school of the University of Nebraska at Omaha. In due time he and Clair and their growing family were back in Hastings, and he was a part of the Foote clinic.

He was content for the next several decades to be known as the skilled physician and surgeon that he was. But on retirement he chose a sort of reversion to the athlete of his college years. He and Clair chose to live the year around in the upper reaches of Poudre Canyon, Colorado, where members of the Foote family had spent summer vacations for many years. They sawed wood, built bridges and other structures, made home repairs, climbed steep slopes as occasion suggested and shoveled snow in winter. But for Herb Anderson there was some vitality yet to be expended. He involved himself in national and international track and field competition for older men and became a consistent winner. His point total in a 1981 decathlon for 78-year-olds was a world record. Earlier he had won the decathlon for the 70-75 age group.

At the age of 79 he was competing in the 200 meters, 400 meters, high jump, long jump, javelin throw, discus throw, 400-meter run and pentathlon.

Dr. Mabel Dixon

In 1905 Dr. Mabel Dixon established herself as the first woman dentist in Hastings and the fourth in Nebraska. In 1965, at the age of 84, she was recognized as the oldest woman dentist still in active practice anywhere in the world. She closed her office at the age of 87.

Dr. Dixon never married and involved herself in many community organizations, including the YWCA and the Business and Professional Women's Club. My sharpest memories, though, are of her in the forefront of a campaign against dentists who advertised their services and against a newspaper that was accepting display ads that quoted charges for dental services.

The time was the early 1930s, and the shock waves of the Great Depression were forcing both buyers and sellers of goods and services to a variety of second thoughts. To the brothers Amick, two dentists who had come to Hastings from another town, there was logic in the presumption that hard-pressed individuals with dental problems would like to know in advance the cost of the necessary treatment. The Amicks bought space in the *Tribune,* and so-called "ethical" dentists who may not have spoken to each other for months got busy on their telephones. Some of them called the *Tribune,* and in due time a delegation headed by Dr. Dixon came in for a long discussion with Henry Smith and Dave Lewis.

The whole issue was delicate at best. Within the *Tribune* staff there were strong feelings for and against the acceptance of dentists' advertising dollars. Some of us felt the need for new revenue in about the same way money-pinched individuals were conscious of the need to save a few dollars when time came to have a wisdom tooth extracted or to invest in a gold crown. Just what kind of compromise Smith and Lewis may have worked out with the dentists has faded from my memory. The Amick ads continued to appear, but there may have been some restriction of their content.

Call Me Ben (Sherman, That Is)

I met Ben Sherman when I stopped as a college freshman to buy something from his stock of army and navy surplus materials and related items at a modest store on First Street. He was in his twenties then, with a merchandising career ahead of him that would extend beyond his eightieth birthday.

By the time I joined the *Tribune* staff, Ben had moved his store to the west side of Hastings Avenue between First and Second streets, and his line of merchandise had shifted from the tents, cots and military wearing apparel to men's and boys' clothing. Ben followed the birth notices in the *Tribune*, and saw to it that a pair of "pants" from his store was among the first gifts received by hundreds of boy babies.

As Ben's business expanded during the 1920s and 1930s his patronage of the *Tribune* advertising columns increased, and by the late 1930s he was one of the most consistent advertisers. In the late 1920s he started personalizing his ads with this line: "If you like me, call me Ben." In Hastings that became as well known as the line made nationally famous a few years later by Hallmark Cards: "When you care enough to send the very best."

There were stories of men coming into Ben's store, asking for Ben and explaining they were not looking for merchandise. "I just wanted to say I had called you Ben," was the comment of more than one non-buying visitor.

Tribune personnel always claimed for Herbert Riggert, advertising manager in the late 1920s, credit for selling Ben on use of the slogan in the form adopted. Wherever credit belonged, there was no question as to the fitness of the line. Ben was not the kind to sit in his office with close friends when there were customers on the floor. He was visible and available to anyone entering the store. He had personality, style and quickness of wit. On a cold December morning in the early 1930s I was greeted at the office by word that Ben's store had burned during the night. I headed for the scene and found Ben in the crowd that had gathered around the smoldering walls. He spotted me and started pouring out his feelings. "This is awful," he said at one point, "I just know that some people will say something about a damned Jew who would set his store on fire to collect insurance." Suddenly a feeble smile crossed his face and he added, "But you know, Harold, I wouldn't burn it down just four days before Christmas." Ben was good at turning his humor on himself.

Some 40 years later Ben would face an even worse disaster. This time there was a mysterious explosion that leveled his building and adjacent structures. Ben didn't rebuild, but he didn't retire either. He extended his career in the men's clothing business in Hastings by affiliating with a new Magee's store. I visited with him there in May of 1980. We compared hearing aids and reminisced, but Ben kept an eye on the front door. He was a master of personalized mechandising—from army shoes to Hart Shaffner and Marx.

Charles E. Uerling

Born at Ayr in 1900, Charles E. Uerling was bracketed

with Ben Sherman in the minds of many through their more than 50 years of prominence in business and community leadership. They survived the confusion and financial distress of the early 1930s and were among the younger independent retailers in town when Uerling opened his furniture and appliance business in 1933. (He had spent the previous ten years with the Gaston Music and Furniture Company.) They were close friends and lived in the same neighborhood. They had many things in common, not the least of which was a ready wit. I never think of Charlie Uerling without recalling the story of his induction into the United Commercial Travelers.

U.C.T. was a fraternal insurance organization with traveling salesmen as the backbone of its membership. There was nothing wrong, of course, with soliciting membership among non-travelers, and the Hastings chapter was especially aggressive in this regard. The initial fee was $18.50, and for that the member was protected against accidents and other contingencies.

Full membership did not come until the candidate had been formally initiated in a ceremony that was patterned on the rituals of non-commercial fraternal bodies.

In any event, as the story went, Charlie Uerling arrived at the entrance to the meeting room (the Clarke Hotel ballroom) and was greeted with the required series of formal questions as to his interest in the organization and his qualifications for membership. After two or three questions Uerling came out with this plaintive protest: "Now listen, fellows, if there is any question about this, I'll take my $18.50 and go home." There were no more questions, as I recall.

Alice Brooke, Activist

Alice Brooke identified with a great variety of causes, and most of them related to somebody else's need or distress. Her quickness of movement and brusqueness of speech gave the impression sometimes of impatience with

The Bell Tolls Later There

others' concerns. The truth was that she usually had other people's troubles in mind and far more things to do in a given day than she would find time for. She may have attained her highest level of visibility during the 1930s. Community institutions dear to her heart were on hard times, as were countless individuals who suddenly remembered that Alice Brooke was more interested than most in other people's needs. She was in her late sixties and early seventies then, but there was no retreat for her from the responsibilities of preserving the Red Cross chapter, the Sunnyside Home for the Elderly, the Women's Club, the YWCA, the Adams County Fair, and the Democratic party.

As an ardent Democrat, she welcomed most of the New Deal remedies for the nation's ills. In 1936 she was a delegate and member of the platform committee at the Democratic national convention. While this was a high honor, she took it in stride, just as she had taken her election to the school board in 1914 and to the city council in 1933. She was the first woman in years to serve on the council, and on the night of her swearing in her male colleagues were hard put for ways to welcome her. One of them proposed that her presence might be reason for a rule against smoking in the council chamber. This she seemed to resent, and in words close to these she made her feelings clear: "I don't smoke, but I've been smoked on all my life, and I guess I can stand all the smoke you gentlemen can create. Go ahead and smoke."

Alice Brooke had a profession—optometry—but she didn't practice it much. Her office was at the rear of the family drugstore in the heart of downtown, but she was rarely in it. Her husband, A. H. Brooke, her son, Donovan—and the drugstore—were more supportive of her community activities than was her profession.

The wry humor of A. H. Brooke—and his complete understanding of his wife—came out when she ran for the state legislature in 1930. He placed an advertisement that read as follows:

"I entered the drug business in Hastings 27 years ago, poor but honest, and am still so, but one thing I take credit for: I brought Mrs. Brooke to Hastings—or did she me? Anyway, she has waited on our customers all this time.

"But she has waited on many more people outside the store. There has been no public service or enterprise or trouble or need in Hastings for 27 years but what Mrs. Brooke wanted or tried or did do something....

"Now she is a candidate for the state legislature. If you want her to serve you in Lincoln, or if you want to get her out of town for a spell, vote for her on Tuesday, and if you want to get her away bad enough, get your neighbors to vote for her."

Alice Brooke lost that election. A few years later, after the Democratic resurgence, she might well have won. By that time, though, there was no lower house in the legislature—just a single body with no designations by party.

Nettie Simms

While Alice Brooke seemed always to worry about problems at home, Nettie Simms seemed to make the whole world her concern. Wife of David Simms, lawyer, druggist and Franklin D. Roosevelt's choice for Hastings postmaster, she traveled to Europe and South America, attended the Cause and Cure of War Institute in Washington, visited the League of Nations headquarters in Switzerland, played the role of professional tour guide on occasion and lectured on international issues in various parts of the country.

Tribune staff writers followed her activities more or less routinely, reporting her travels and brief comments on things she had seen and heard. We missed an opportunity, as I think back on those days, to label her as the

Cassandra she truly was. Events verified her fears.

She came back from one of her first trips to Germany with firm convictions that she had seen a country preparing for war. She described in detail the bands of marching boys she saw, carrying sticks instead of guns, but reflecting a militaristic spirit which convinced her that Hitler was preparing his nation for conquest. I remember asking other visitors to Germany if they had seen things to support her forebodings, and most of their responses were little more than a shrug of the shoulders. People talked about Nettie's alarmism at bridge tables and luncheon clubs. For the most part, though, she was a prophet who had to wait for the invasion of Poland and France to endow her with full honors in Hastings.

Nettie Simms and Alice Brooke—they happened to be the only women at a meeting of the chamber of commerce board in 1933 at which the chamber president, W. J. Rinder, was outlining Hastings' response to the National Recovery Act of the Roosevelt New Deal. The NRA, as the implementing agency was called, was designed to enlist business and industry in a voluntary campaign against unemployment. Rinder, declaiming the chamber's commitment to the cause, rose to the heights of showy prose for which he was well known. Here was a challenge, he declared, to "impregnate every man and every woman." He broke off his sentence there, but proceeded to pick up his theme without losing momentum. Some of us glanced at Mrs. Simms and Mrs. Brooke. They had eyes only for the speaker. They were not the kind to see humor in a verbal slip that might divert attention from the main issue.

Nettie lived into her late seventies. Alice just missed her eighty-fifth birthday.

Donaldson Wright Kingsley, M.D.

Donaldson Wright Kingsley was born in Minden in 1899. For a couple of uneasy minutes of a summer day in

1939 I thought he and I might die together within a few miles of Minden.

The anxious moments of that day came with the failure of the engine of Kingsley's Cessna 170 in which he, Robert Lasch of the Omaha *World-Herald* and I were returning from Denver. Flying somewhere between 4,000 and 5,000 feet, we had passed Minden on our right and were within a few minutes of the Hastings airport. The engine coughed intermittently and then quit. Kingsley turned from the controls to various buttons and levers while the plane jerked and twisted. The silence was overwhelming. There were a couple more coughs and that was it.

Lasch and I offered no advice, but we got some reassurance from the pilot's seeming confidence. He spotted a windmill, got the wind direction, and started a 160-degree turn. We already had passed over a field of wheat stubble that he was going to try to land on. As we neared the ground Kingsley toyed with his gadgets again and got the engine started. There was a burst of power that permitted a leveling of the plane as we broke into the high stubble and weeds that brought us to a quick stop.

We were a few hundred yards from Highway 6 and about two miles southwest of Heartwell. It was agreed I should get to the highway and from there to a telephone. Kingsley was certain the manager of the airport at Hastings would come to our rescue, and he was on the scene in less than an hour.

It turned out that the fuel tank was empty, even though the gauge had shown enough to get us to Hastings. The airport manager, Ray Beebe, brought a can of gasoline and flew the plane back to Hastings. I was a ready volunteer to drive his car.

Kingsley, Lasch and I had been on a three-day tour in the interest of the Tri-County project, with which Kingsley had been intimately identified since being elected president of the sponsoring agency, the Central Nebraska

The Bell Tolls Later There

Public Power and Irrigation District. We had planned an aerial tour of the North Platte River all the way from North Platte to its origins in northern Colorado, with stops at Casper, Cheyenne and Denver. Between Scottsbluff and Casper we had encountered rough air, and Lasch became ill. Because of the likelihood of more unpleasant flying along the river's upper reaches, we decided to go from Casper to Cheyenne, where we had an appointment with the governor of Wyoming.

At Denver we visited the Bureau of Reclamation offices and the state capitol, where we conferred briefly with another governor. One of Kingsley's objectives was to head off proposals in both Colorado and Wyoming that might interfere with Nebraska's claim to water that was to be stored behind Tri-County's key dam on the North Platte near Ogallala. I had accompanied the doctor on many of his trips in behalf of the project. This one, however, was the most extensive, and it has turned out to be the best remembered.

I called at his office almost daily through the months and years when there seemed never to be a time that the project was free from crisis. We didn't always talk about water rights, lawsuits and hydroelectric power in our many hours together. I told him often about my aches and pains, the tensions of my job and my fear of ulcers. He would question me as to my eating habits, my exercise routine and whether I was getting along with my wife. Once, when I was about 27, he gave me the somewhat fatalistic advice that at the age of 25 or thereabouts one must expect degenerative diseases to start appearing and that one had better prepare to deal with them in one way or another for the rest of one's life. In 1935 we agreed that he should remove my non-functioning appendix, and so our relationship continued through my final days with the *Tribune*. The medical advice I got (even the operation) didn't cost much. The real bonus of these experiences, though, was in the opportunity to observe an intelligent man of complete dedication to a cause that was in the public interest.

As the Tri-County project became a physical reality the dam at Ogallala was officially named for George P. Kingsley, father of Donaldson. A Minden banker, the father had been an aggressive campaigner for irrigation in the early 1900s. The son, returning to Nebraska in 1928, had joined in the revival of irrigation promotion shortly after launching his medical practice at Hastings. For seven years I was in almost daily contact with this highly trained physician and surgeon (Cornell, Harvard, etc.) who had to slight his professional ambitions to make sure that his father's dream might be eventually realized. While the dam was named for the father, no small share of honor belongs to the son.

In his race with degenerative diseases he stayed ahead beyond his eightieth birthday.

Alva V. King

In 1980, more than 90 years after he was born, Alva V. King narrated a commercial for a Kansas City, Kansas, bank that showed up on the television screens of the region over a period of many months.

For those of us who had known him at Hastings there was no mistaking the voice and the face. He looked and sounded much as he had looked and sounded through the 1930s, when he was pastor of the First Presbyterian Church.

The gist of the commercial was that for many years he had been advised by the bank's trust department in such a way as to keep the income from his estate abreast of the inflationary trends of the time. It was an expression of just what he thought of the bank's services, and he had no reservations about saying what he thought, to whatever extent it might benefit the bank. It sounded much like the churchman I had known at Hastings—who said what he thought about things in the community, sometimes to the discomfort of fellow citizens.

Ellen Harn's Relayed Kiss

In the spring of 1930 the *Tribune* recorded the death of Miss Ellen Harn, who had celebrated her one-hundredth birthday the previous year. A teacher in the Kenesaw area for many years, she was credited with a story that enabled her to say, "Lips that kissed mine were kissed by Washington."

Legend had it that her aunt had handed Gen. George Washington a gourd full of water when he stopped near the family home in Maryland. The general's thanks was a kiss for the youngster, or so the story went. When Ellen Harn died, the 48 United States extended from the Atlantic to the Pacific. When her aunt gave Washington a drink of water, the 13 colonies were no more than the foundation of a nation.

Mabel Stone Lyman

Born at Hastings in 1882, Mabel Stone Lyman came within two years of celebrating her one-hundredth birthday. She had passed the age of 90 before she ceased to startle friends with her annual junkets to far corners of the world.

While she qualifies in her own right for a place in this chapter, I find it impossible to write about her without writing about her husband, Silas B. Lyman. He died while still in his sixties. I remember him as a personality to reckon with as I went about my duties as managing editor of the *Tribune*.

The Lymans had social ties with the Henry Smiths, and Henry Smith was my boss. It seemed to me that Si Lyman took undue advantage of his opportunities to unload on Smith his criticisms of the way my staff and I handled the news. About once every two months Smith would call me in and open the conversation in about these words: "I was talking with Silas last night, and he thinks. . . ." There were times when I looked upon Silas Lyman as a sort of hair shirt. Trained in the law and conservative in habit and thought, he was as critical of the way Smith ran the whole *Tribune* operation sometimes as he was of my editing. I am not certain that Smith didn't look upon him as a hair shirt at times, too. And all because Lena Smith and Mabel Lyman were good friends and fellow club members.

Silas was twice elected to the city council and at one point found himself aligned against the *Tribune* and a large segment of the community. He had chosen to oppose a plan to convert the Samuel Alexander homesite at Seventh and Lincoln into a park. Silas lost that one, but he stuck to his belief that it was wasteful to put public funds into preservation of a landmark of pioneer days. The land was being donated to the city, but Silas was looking at the cost of upkeep.

Frank Elmer Weyer

Frank E. Weyer at the age of 90 was searching for and organizing materials having to do with the history of Hastings College. No man could have been better qualified for the assignment. From 1918 to 1960 he had been a part of the institution as professor and dean. Few men at 90 could match his long record of active involvement in the educational field. Born at Ainsworth, he had earned his bachelor's degree at Hastings and taught in public schools before returning to the college, where he established himself almost immediately as the man in charge of most day-to-day academic activities. He filled that role for 42 years.

He followed his retirement with 10 years as a visiting professor at Campbell College in North Carolina. Back in Hastings and then in his eighties, he took up the role of college historian and did me the honor of commenting on a chapter of this book in which I refer to him as the first personality with whom I had any dealings as a freshman.

John Walter Caldwell

John Walter Caldwell, born at Peoria, Illinois, lived in the magic zone of longevity from infancy until his retirement, first at Bruning, then at Blue Hill and finally at Hastings. He celebrated his one-hundredth birthday in 1980 as a resident of San Bernardino, California. For many years he was known in Hastings as a competent and conscientious carpenter and cabinetmaker. His son, Wendell, who was in college with us a couple of years, chose to follow his father in the construction business and built a compact little house in Hastings after his marriage to Zeta Caldwell. During the winter of 1932-33 Mrs. Hamil and I rented the new home from the younger Caldwells. Times were getting hard, and they had gone to the Scottsbluff area in the hope of finding better employment opportunities. Coming back to Hastings, Wendell was added to the *Tribune* staff as a learner in the printing trade. He was one of two or three additions to the staff in deliberate response to the National Recovery Act of the Roosevelt New Deal. Forsaking his father's craft, he stayed with newspaper work until retirement at Modesto, California.

Myra Grimes

The annual Tapeline issue of the Hastings *Tribune* in 1940 centered on the history of Hastings and the surrounding region. One of the featured pictures was a full-page portrait of Mrs. Myra Grimes, about 80 years old at the time. She had come to the new community at the age of 18 and could recall the night in 1878 when a group of young men from Hastings took teams and wagons to Juniata and loaded up the county records and transferred them to Hastings. It was the climactic incident in a long dispute over the location of a permanent county seat. Mrs. Grimes could remember that she and several other young women sat up that night until the raiding party had returned.

Pauline Ragan

Pauline Shallenberger came to Hastings as a teacher, married John Ragan, a lawyer, reared two sons and, after 60 years in Hastings, went to live with a son in Edmonton, Alberta, where she died at the age of 90 in 1945. She was active in the founding of the Hastings Carnegie Library and the Hastings Woman's Club, the George Eliot Club and the Sunnyside Home. Her husband, a lawyer for the Burlington, arranged for the naming of two branch-line towns as a sort of family memorial—Pauline and Ragan.

Her maiden name was written into Nebraska history by a brother, Ashton C. Shallenberger, who served the state as governor and as a member of the national House of Representatives. *Historical News,* publication of the Adams County Historical Society, called Mrs. Ragan an "intellectual."

Pleasant Lee Johnson

Pleasant Lee Johnson, native of Iowa, had come to Hastings in the 1880s and was an active member of the Hastings College board of trustees during my student years. He had been identified with financial institutions in his younger years, but his interests ranged widely.

He had engaged in the new game of baseball as a student at the University of Iowa, and legend had it that he and his fellow players thought nothing of catching hard throws and long flies without benefit of gloves. His interest in sports was reflected in the fact that he made the initial financial contribution to the building of Hastings College's first gymnasium, a wooden structure that bore his name; it burned during my freshman year.

On a farm near Hansen that was occupied by his son, Bedford, he set out, at an age when most men were considering retirement, to dig an irrigation well and demonstrate the possibilities of improving the land by tapping the water-bearing sands 100 feet or more below the surface. With shovel, windlass and other simple tools, he dug to the level of the sands, but his well never was put into operation. A quarter of a century after his death, though, the farm was served by a new well, and the crops were probably beyond P. L.'s fondest expectations.

The Martis and Others

The signs of durability in an individual generally differ from case to case. In the case of Lloyd J. Marti, friends noted there was no letup in his consumption of strong cigars as he neared his eightieth birthday. This, they reasoned, was as good proof as could be found of an outstanding level of stamina. It is worth noting also, of course, that his parents, Mr. and Mrs. D. B. Marti, had lived far beyond 80, with many of those years having been spent in Adams County. Lloyd, born at Hastings, retired after more than 50 years in the practice of law at Lincoln and two terms as mayor of the city.

At the winter home of Lloyd and Beth Marti in Sun City, Arizona, in 1981 we enjoyed visiting with a number of Nebraskans and ex-Nebraskans. Among those definitely qualified for listing in this chapter were Patricia (Mrs. Harold) Johnson and Fay Hulsker. The latter confessed he was well past 75, but he had the look of a man nearing his first eligibility for Social Security.

Of Beth Marti, hostess on that occasion, it must be recorded that she had reached the qualifying age. Native of Alexandria and our neighbor in Hastings through most of the 1930s, she could look back on a lifetime in or near the magic circle of longer living.

Other close neighbors during our six years on Cedar Street in Hastings were Mr. and Mrs. Howard Harse and Mr. and Mrs. Clifford Hunt. Both men were veterans of World War I. Howard Harse, then living at the Sunnyside Home, walked the mile or more to greet me at a downtown store where I was autographing books in October 1976. He was said to be near 90 then. Clifford Hunt, past 80, was active and visible in Hastings in 1982.

12. Pearson the Poser

Or the Many Faces of Idaho Bill

On a spring day in 1924 I went out the door of the high school in Sterling, Colorado, just as a two-seated, topless Model-T Ford rolled by with a full-grown bear, half-standing, half-sitting, in the rear section.

The driver, with all the nonchalance of a farmer on his way to a downtown store, was almost as much a surprise as the bear. He wore a mammoth western hat, a long goatee and a mustache. Gray hair flowed under his hat.

Several of us gazed in awe. We observed that the bear was pretty well tied into place, but it ran through my mind that the animal was fully half as big as the car.

Next day the Sterling *Advocate* carried an article about these unusual visitors. The man identified himself as an outdoorsman and adventurer of some repute, I recall, but I quickly forgot what name he gave. He told how the bear had broken one of his chains or ropes a few days earlier and had upset the car when it tried to jump out. The driver had suffered a leg injury, and this explained the pair of crutches we saw at his side as he drove past the high school.

About five months later I stood on the campus of Hastings College and watched a herd of some 30 horses move down the street under the supervision of four or five riders. One rider stood out, and after a second look I knew he was the man who had come through Sterling with a bear in the back seat of his car. In due time I was to learn

"Idaho Bill" in full dress

that Hastings was the part-time home of this individual, that he was generally known as Barney Pearson and was sometimes called "Idaho Bill."

For the next 15 years I would see quite a bit of the man. If there is such a thing as a working impostor, he fits the description as well as anyone I ever knew. When he died in 1942, the death certificate showed his occupation as "actor." Barney would have liked that. He was never one to challenge any tag or description that might enhance or romanticize his career.

Most certainly he was no John Barrymore, but in ways that were crudely comical at times and in claims that were often patently unbelievable, he built and lived a legend and never seemed to tire of strutting across his imaginary stage. Some who followed his career to the end say he actually played some bit parts in Western movies about the time of the outbreak of World War II He had passed three score and ten by then and was a seasoned poser if not a polished dramatist.

Some of the accomplishments he listed for himself had a tinge of reality. He was often in the company of wild animals, though most who knew him were inclined to doubt his stories of adventurous captures. The bear I saw him with in Sterling in 1924 could have been the 700-pound cinnamon he was publicly credited with having presented to President Coolidge in the Black Hills three years later. The horses I saw him driving past the Hastings College campus probably belonged among the props of a Wild West show with which he was now and then identified.

The Hastings *Tribune,* when I went to work as a reporter in 1928, was extremely bearish on Barney. His comings and goings, I was told, were not news. This seemed to be the unanimous opinion of Henry G. Smith, Dave Lewis and Marie Herrin, and who was I to quarrel with these three veterans who pretty well determined what was fit or unfit for print in the years immediately following the death of Adam Breede, the paper's founder? How Adam had viewed Barney was never explained to me. I suspect, though, that he was more tolerant of this ubiquitous buffoon than were Smith, Lewis and Herrin. After all, Adam and Barney were somewhat alike. Each enjoyed the limelight.

Pearson the Poser

By the early 1930s we were publicizing some of Barney's activities, and a policy of somewhat sparing attention to him continued through my years as managing editor. It was hard to outlaw Barney as a news subject in a city where everybody talked about him. It was especially hard to ignore a brush or two he had with the law and such things as his appearance once with a Cord sedan and two strange young women.

Harold Cowan, sports editor and general reporter, loved to talk with and write about Barney. He had just the right tongue-in-cheek touch to keep Barney's exploits in proper perspective, and while he never seemed to be trying to bury Barney, he wrote with enough skill that everybody knew it was not the *Tribune's* intent to praise the guy unduly or dress him in a cloak of respectability beyond what he deserved.

A few weeks after Barney died in 1942, Cowan, then working for the Omaha *World-Herald,* wrote a feature article which started as follows:

"Barney 'Idaho Bill' Pearson died in Los Angeles the other day, and it may be that death will at last call his hand. It may show him simply as an eccentric, a royal-flush humbug or truly, as he said, an exemplar of the Old West and once consort of Buffalo Bill, Deadwood Dick, Pawnee Bill, Doc Carver and other famous frontiersmen."

Historical News, publication of the Adams County Historical Society, dug up some facts on Barney's origin and early life and printed the following in a 1977 issue:

> Bonde R. Pearson was four years old when his parents emigrated from Sweden in 1872 and settled on a homestead ten miles southeast of Hastings. He grew up on the farm with his brother and sister; another sister had died and was buried there.
>
> As soon as he was grown, Barney shed the farm and his name—for he was never called Bonde again. He

headed west, buying and selling horses. Eventually he landed in Pueblo, Colorado, where he became the first man to drive the town's spirited fire horses. There, too, he met and married Sarah (Sadie) Trifty on May 3, 1891. Later the two of them and Mildred, their daughter, moved to Hastings, where Barney continued his horse dealings, buying wild ones in Wyoming, Montana and Idaho, shipping them to Hastings and selling them.

Barney hit the headlines with a splash after July 29, 1906, for that was the night he stood outside his home at 109 East Fifth and fired his shotgun through the dining room window, plugging Walter McCulla in the left side and hip as he stood talking on the telephone. Barney's wife was in the room, and another man was in the living room. Three other persons had been there....

The murder trial began on December 7, 1906, before a full house and ended a week later when the judge discharged the jury; it had deliberated for 52 hours without reaching a verdict. The second trial was quicker, for on May 10, 1907 after an hour and a half of deliberation the jury had voted for acquittal.

Subsequent to all this, Barney's wife won a divorce suit, and he entered on a period of absence from Hastings.

When he came back, several years later, he was no longer the journeyman trainer and trader of horses. The farmers of Adams and adjoining counties who once had looked to him for young and untamed work stock were somewhat awed by his buckskin shirts and other western paraphernalia, and they listened with more than casual interest to his stories of having acquired a ranch and a nickname in the wilds of Idaho.

Somewhere along the line he had met William F. (Buffalo Bill) Cody and Teddy Roosevelt. When the latter came to town in 1912 as the Bull Moose candidate for president, he asked that Idaho Bill ride with him to the railroad station. This was obviously a big surprise to the local bigwigs who still looked on Barney as a farm boy turned horse trader whose dubious claim to local fame was that he had killed a man.

There were those who said Barney's ego had been enormously fattened by his ability to speak casually in faraway places about having used a gun to dispose of a man who had been unduly attentive to his wife. I am inclined to think there was something to this. He was not without some feeling, it seemed, that now and then he had to prove himself.

I recall distinctly the importance he attached to a stained and faded letter which he said he had received from Buffalo Bill. The date was of a period when Cody was still associated with his Wild West Show and the content of the letter had to do with Barney's offer to supply Cody with some horses. The letter had been sent from Cody, Wyoming. The handwriting, on lined paper, seemed genuine.

Barney pulled this from his pocket during a visit to the *Tribune* after the appearance of a story about him that he didn't like. It could have been the time we told how he was taken to police court following a tussle with a red-haired waitress. The testimony indicated he had given her a watch and was trying to get it back after she had made some remark to the effect that she didn't want anything to do with him.

His display of the Cody letter struck me as the ultimate in his belief that we of the *Tribune* should not stoop to publicizing a little squabble between a man of stature and an obscure waitress. The words with which he extended the letter for my inspection were all but irrelevant to the situation. But that was the way with a lot of Barney's efforts to explain himself. He was, in all truth, a man of very limited powers of verbal expression. What some might have considered the wisdom of brevity in his monosyllabic comments was in reality a disclosure of how short he was of words.

But what he lacked in vocabulary and fluidity of speech he managed to make up for in his physical appearance and dress. And he must have been a good horse trader or he would not have acquired the money that he seems to have had in convenient amounts from the years of his youth.

Just how many wild animals he had at one time or another, besides the cinnamon bear, no one ever bothered to record. But he developed a formula for making them pay their way. He took a bear and a mountain lion on tour in the early 1920s and got all sorts of publicity in Chicago, Indianapolis and other places. His strategy in a strange city was to go straight to the chief of police. His dress, his goatee, his big hat and long hair—these seemed to charm police officers after he had uttered a few words about buffalo, Indians and other things western. What he usually got from those visits, obviously, was the privilege of setting up his truck and cages at some popular street corner, with full immunity from city ordinances that would have worked against any ordinary applicant for such a permit. In most cases his arrival at police headquarters would arouse the interest of newspaper reporters, and Barney would feed them his full line. This helped bring people to see him and his animals.

On one of his tours with a Dodge truck and some kind of wildcat he said he had captured in Mexico he landed in Pittsburgh. A Hastings businessman saw him there and came home to report that the curious stood in long lines waiting to pay 25¢ for the privilege of seeing what Barney was passing off as the "missing link" in the evolution of man from monkeys.

During the early 1930s, when most everyone was feeling the pinch of the Great Depression, Barney took to flaunting a $1,000 bill. He would eat a 35¢ meal and then

Pearson the Poser

peel this bill from a simulated roll and offer it to the cashier. There were few cash registers anywhere with that much money in them, and the brief drama would end with Barney's digging some coins from his pocket and departing with a suggestion that restaurants ought to be able to take care of their trade better than that.

Christ Cosmos, proprietor of the Queen City Cafe, tired of Barney's act and got set for him. He accepted the bill one morning and started counting out change. Barney quickly retrieved his bill and, from all reports, this stunt was dropped permanently from his repertoire.

He came to the *Tribune* once for help in preparing some material to hand out when curious crowds assembled around his truck. He made sure, as was his custom, to ask for the highest-ranking person in the organization, and that was Henry Smith.

Barney had brought a picture of himself on a rearing horse and wanted it to be the central illustration of a printed piece that would tell all about him in the simplest way possible. When he had gone, Smith called me in, explained the situation and suggested we print a card about four by eight inches. Barney had made sure Smith understood he was to be identified with Buffalo Bill, the Old West, Indians, big-game hunting and so forth. As Smith instructed me to write some copy and lay out the card, he suggested, somewhat in jest, that we refer to Barney as a "lecturer," along with everything else.

When Barney returned a few days later, he studied the proof carefully and then, placing his finger on the word, looked up and remarked, "I sure like that 'lecturer.'" And so I claim some credit for having helped him expand his credentials.

For several years he drove a Cord sedan, with front-wheel drive, that attracted attention wherever he went. He showed up in Hastings once with the Cord and two young women. They were around town a day or two and then headed for Denver. A few days later the Denver *Post* published a long story, with pictures, about Barney and some bizarre developments after the party's arrival in Denver. The sum of what happened seemed to be that the girls had worked Barney into providing transportation to Denver. But once there, they turned on him in various ways, with the consummate act being the shearing of his hair and whiskers while he slept.

He was quite a while living down this escapade. In Hastings later he insisted he had cut his own hair and whiskers. The two women at some stage filed, or threatened to file, a breach-of-promise suit.

During a gangland trial in New York in the late 1930s, he was pictured by one of the newspapers (just one) as being on hand as an old friend of the father of the alleged sweetheart of a somewhat notorious defendant. He and the girl, Hope Dare, made good newspaper copy, but only that one newspaper seemed to find any real relationship between them and the issues before the court.

New York friends sent me clippings from this newspaper. One picture I recall was of Barney in his hotel room, dressed in his best western finery, including a leopard vest. A pistol lay on the table in front of him.

I met him on a Hastings street a few weeks later and quizzed him as to just how he got to New York. His replies were typically evasive. He conceded that *they* had provided his hotel room and had kept him pretty well out of sight. I had to conclude on my own that *they* were some enterprising newsmen who looked upon Barney as one who could liven up their stories about the trial. While his relationship with Hope Dare's father was supposed to have been in Idaho, there was nothing in the stories about her in other papers to suggest Hope ever had been west of Mt. Pleasant, Iowa.

When I asked Barney where he had been since the end of the trial, he welcomed the change of subject. He threw out his chest and said he had been in India "shootin' bingles." I made some quick calculations and asked him how he could have gone to India and back in the two or three weeks into which he was trying to squeeze this episode. (There was little transoceanic flying in those days.) I can't recall that he explained his mode of travel or offered any detail as to what he did with the "bingles." He was a great one to let stories fade into an inconclusive end.

In the final years of his life Barney had developed a new base of operations—Los Angeles. *Life* Magazine, rounding up some of that city's unusual characters for a two-page layout in 1941, or thereabouts, included a picture of him.

Barney's decision to locate more or less permanently in Los Angeles did not mean any playing down of his identity with a rather non-specific locale in the wilder parts of Idaho and adjoining states. But the brief lines with his picture in *Life* took no note of his identity with the dirt-farming country of central Nebraska. Never, in fact, did he seem to tell newspaper reporters about the place of his boyhood, the place he returned to regularly—Hastings, in Adams County—where he was better known than anywhere else in the world. Barney wouldn't have used the words, but Hastings and Adams County were too prosaic and commonplace for him.

This denial of his origins seemed not to bother people around Hastings. Barney was, in fact, a prophet with limited honor in his home community. But he was by no means obscure.

When Clarence M. Pierson came from Polk County to attend Hastings College in the late 1920s, it was a matter of only a few months until fellow students had tagged him as "Barney." He played on the football team, attended law school at the University of Nebraska and attained prominence as a Lincoln attorney. Through it all, he never shook off his college nickname. This illustrates, I think, the extent to which Barney "Idaho Bill" Pearson was an established character around Hastings. It illustrates also, I suspect, the perverse humor that has run high among college students for generations.

Death caught up with Idaho Bill in November 1942, when he was 74 years old, and his body was brought to Hastings for burial. *Historical News* lists the following as pallbearers: Howard Pratt, George Anderson, John Tooley, Vern Magnuson, Walter Knicely and Henry Stamer—a bank president, a manufacturing company executive, men active in real estate, insurance and farming. Few men dying in Hastings in that era could have been honored by a more prestigious list of citizens.

But even after the burial, word came of a final moment of tense drama in the Pearson saga. Two women engaged in a "controversy about him," as *Historical News* put it. One was described as an "older woman" who had become enamored of him while painting his portrait. He was reported to have given her his Cord automobile and some cash in the hope she would remove herself from the picture, so to speak. The other was a "younger woman" who said she and Barney had been planning marriage. He was supposed to have given her some money.

When the estate was finally settled, there was a balance of $2,451 for Barney's daughter. To some who could recall the days when he drove the Cord and pulled a $1,000 bill from his boot and waved it before startled restaurant cashiers this was a surprise. It seemed to verify, though, the statement on the death certificate. Barney really was an actor.

13. A Medley of Memories

Of Street Talk, Legends and News Behind the News

It is hard to look back on 12 years at the news center of a community without an urge to reconstruct certain events. Some things, one reasons, were treated all too casually. Some were not treated at all. Incidents reported in stilted and guarded language invite freshening with the idiom of a later generation. Some things that were pushed aside as gossip or hearsay may still lack verification, but the ingredients of a lively yarn are still there.

The shifts of perspective after as many as 50 years can mean a complete reordering of news elements. When a young man was tried for rape in Hastings, the story ran for days in the *Tribune*. The important fact in retrospect, however, is not the offense or anything about the personalities involved, but in the way the trial provided a springboard for a rival newspaper.

For almost two decades the court battles over the estate of John O'Connor made headlines, but the story element that survives has to do with the manner in which O'Connor's body was preserved for viewing by people from far places in the hope they might establish relationship and thus qualify for some of the sizable fortune he had left. And so we look back on these and other stories:

Rape at the Rock Pile

Times were hard for newspapers as well as other businesses in Hastings in the middle 1930s. Advertising linage had dropped off in both the *Tribune* and the Adams County *Democrat,* a weekly published by W. W. Maltman. Both institutions were hurt by a decline in commercial printing sales, and both had laid off employees. Both were searching for ways to make up for the losses. Maltman hit upon the idea of going after a larger share of the community's advertising dollars by way of a low-cost paper he could distribute citywide five mornings a week. And thus was born the *Morning Spotlight,* a tabloid printed on pink paper.

Confining its circulation to the city, the *Spotlight* could offer a per-line advertising rate well below the lowest rate the *Tribune* could afford. Some merchants quickly took advantage of this. They didn't see the need of paying for circulation in Red Cloud, Clay Center, Minden and other towns where the *Tribune* was delivered every weekday.

While we at the *Tribune* spoke derisively of that "pink sheet" that was getting more attention than we thought it deserved, I was aware from the beginning that Maltman had at least one thing going for him. He had hired Marvin Cruse to handle most of his newswriting. Marvin had worked at the *Tribune* for perhaps a year and had been laid off in one of the *Tribune's* first economy moves of the early 1930s. He was motivated as much as any person could have been to compete with the *Tribune* news staff. More than that, he had spent his period of unemployment studying shorthand and typing at one of the local business colleges. He was a prolific producer.

Marvin and the *Spotlight* took full advantage of their late-evening deadlines. Little that happened after 2 P.M. found its way into the day's issue of the *Tribune.* But the next morning's *Spotlight* could wait for news developing well beyond the dinner hour. While the *Tribune* had to close its forms in mid-afternoon, the *Spotlight* could wait until closing time at public offices before starting its roundup of the day's news. Whereas the *Tribune* rarely

A Medley of Memories

covered much that went on in district court after noon, the *Spotlight* reached its readers each morning with full coverage of the afternoon's testimony. There were many times during the opening months of the *Spotlight's* existence when this handicap came home to us at the *Tribune,* but our readers seemed not to mind. Then came the case of the alleged rape at the "rock pile."

Some young men from a Civilian Conservation Corps camp on the Little Blue had been in Hastings for a night, seeking diversion from their weekly routine. One of them had been with a local girl, and on their way home there had been an incident at what was referred to as the "rock pile" (near the Burlington yards) that resulted in her going to authorities with the charge she had been raped.

The *Spotlight's* first reports of the incident served notice that Marvin Cruse was ready to write more explicitly about rape than had been the *Tribune's* custom. It was the accepted wisdom of most dailies of the time that a "family newspaper" avoided four-letter words and descriptive terms that might help the young to clear understanding of what these words meant. Rape in itself was an acceptable word, and it was looked upon as sufficiently legalistic as not to be shocking.

The trial of this former high school quarterback from a small Nebraska town became a trial for the *Tribune*. Cruse reported in what seemed unrestrained detail the questioning and cross-questioning of the principals, the police and the medical experts. The trial ran for only a few days, but it seemed interminable to us at the *Tribune*. While we may have let down the bars a little to keep close to Cruse's raw recitations of what was charged, what was denied and what was explained by the police and medical witnesses, we agonized over the simplest decisions. How much easier it would have been if we were not being measured each day against "that rag of a *Spotlight*." A few readers called to commend us for our restraint, but there was plenty of evidence that Marvin Cruse's new journalistic standards were meeting with approval. The truth is that this was the first time in my period with the *Tribune* that the staff was exposed to local competition.

When the rape trial was over, it was apparent to me that it had afforded the *Spotlight* an opportunity to force its presence on the community. People were talking about it—some in anger or disgust, but many in awe. We would not take the *Spotlight* and Marvin Cruse lightly for the next several years. (The little paper was taken over in 1942 by the *Tribune* and terminated.)

Marvin Cruse visited our home in St. Louis shortly after the close of World War II, and it was interesting to hear from him how the proficiency in shorthand and typing that had made him such a menace to the *Tribune* in the 1930s had got him into a headquarters company for army service that included involvement in the Battle of the Bulge.

Mummy in Street Clothes

Sidney Trobough, 19 years old at the time, was charged in late 1928 with killing his wife. After three trials, the third on a change of venue to Webster County, he went to the penitentiary for manslaughter.

I remember much less about the details of the Trobough case than about the way it introduced me to one of the most bizarre aspects of one of the most bizarre cases in the history of Nebraska courts.

The day after the shooting I was invited by a law enforcement officer to accompany him to the Livingston Brothers funeral home to view the body of the frail little woman with a bullet hole in her lower neck. I would have to look back on this as a sort of ghoulish expedition if it were not for what came out when I asked about the rather unusual receptacle in which the body had been placed for viewing. It was little more than a long drawer that came out of a thick wall about two feet above floor level. The

A Medley of Memories

Livingstons, Walter and Ed, referred to it as a "vault," and it took only one question from me to start them talking about how convenient this arrangement had been during the more than two years when it was their responsibility to preserve and display the body of John O'Connor.

I had heard about the O'Connor case and had written about it. I hadn't heard until that day in 1928 that O'Connor's body had occupied this same pull-out drawer for more than two years and that the Livingstons had ushered literally hundreds of men and women past the vault to look down on the lifeless features.

O'Connor had died in Hastings in 1913. People knew him as a kind of recluse. They knew he repaired shoes but few knew how well he had saved and invested his money until after his death. He left an estate estimated to be worth more than $100,000—a fortune in those days—and when the word got out, there was a deluge of claims and inquiries. O'Connors in all parts of the country and some in Ireland took note. Many came to Hastings in person. Some sent lawyers or retained local lawyers. Wills and letters were introduced by claimants, and for a time it appeared one of the wills would stand up. In the end, though, this document was ruled fraudulent by the Nebraska Supreme Court.

For the first two years of these legal scrambles the courts had blocked burial of the body. Through that period there was every sort of visitor to the Livingston vault. Some were suspected of having sought the help of artists in doctoring photographs to make them resemble the face of John O'Connor.

Through all this the Livingstons had not been inattentive to their own accomplishments and the considerable opportunity for publicity. At some point near the end of the holding period they stood the corpse on its feet and took positions on either side for a photograph. On my visit to their establishment in 1928 they displayed a soiled and faded survivor of the reproductions of this picture, with a few lines of type explaining that the middle man was two years dead and that the Livingstons had used their own special formulation of embalming fluid when they prepared the body for its long role as a sort of mummy in street clothes. There is no question but that John O'Connor stood up real well for the Livingstons.

District Judge Lewis M. Blackledge, in a 1932 entry that closed the books on 19 years of litigation over the estate, opened with these words, "Poor old John," and followed with an eloquent review of how the case had kept coming back into court "after fiction itself could not conceive of a new question to arise." He ruled that the state of Nebraska would get everything after Adams County was paid $4,000 to cover the cost of court actions, and presumably the embalming.

Revenge Via a Tainted Lady?

The story was told in Hastings of a woman who came to town in the early years of the twentieth century and left a trail of syphilis that shortened the lives of several men of some standing in the community. One heard a dozen versions of the story, some with elements of intrigue.

Most versions referred to the woman as having come from Chicago, and most took for granted that she had been domiciled for a time at the Bostwick Hotel. Several narrators established a villain in the person of a young man who had been hurt by the obvious intent of a socially active circle of young blades to exclude him from its activities. This fellow was supposed to have induced the prostitute to come to Hastings and arranged to make sure that whose who had snubbed him got word of her presence, her good looks and her interests. Those carrying the fiction to the extreme implied that he knew of the lady's infection and got some satisfaction as he made note of likely victims.

A Medley of Memories

It was not uncommon to hear certain persons' illnesses referred to as paresis, and some people would explain in low tones that this was a softening of the brain that could have been caused by syphilis. Several times during my 12 years with the *Tribune* we had occasion to summarize the life of James Laird, by all odds the flashiest citizen of Hastings in the late 1880s. He was a Civil War hero, congressman and defense lawyer in the bitter trial of I. P. Olive. His early death was explained in ambiguous language generally, but when Dorothy Weyer-Creigh compiled her monumental history of Adams County in the 1970s, there was no mincing of words. She reported that he died of syphilis.

Raconteur Par Excellence

Walter Crow was a good storyteller. But it took more than a year of regular calls at his office in the courthouse to detect this and the rather deep vein of sentimentalism that he covered with stern formality and measured words. He was the county attorney from 1922 to 1930.

Born in England, he had grown up on a farm in southern Adams County and studied law in Hastings. His memories covered the emergence of Adams County from its frontier state. He had read extensively in English literature and could quote Shakespeare and the Bible in his pleas to juries. He seemed at his eloquent best, though, when the two of us sat behind closed doors in his office.

Among his heroes were two or three attorneys who were in their prime while he was still reading law in the office of John C. Stevens. He reviewed one day the burial service for one of these men, a professed atheist. His words mainly were his reconstruction of the oration another lawyer, with deep roots in a local church, delivered at the graveside. The speaker couldn't refrain from comment on the deceased's coolness toward religion. He noted this and then asked the assembled friends and relatives to look westward toward a lowering sun. Appraise the beauties of this prairie landscape, he said, and ask if any man could love the wonders of nature, as the deceased had, and not have some belief in a supreme being.

Walter appreciated people of action, people who didn't mince words and were quick to act in times of crisis. He illustrated his point with a story about a farm family that had prospered through its early years in the county and lived in a large house near the Little Blue. A hired girl occupied an upstairs room, and a teenaged son had pestered her with suggestions that he would like to slip into her room some night and join her in bed. The girl went to the housewife and mother to complain. She implied that if the youth persisted, she might pack up and leave. The mother, knowing good kitchen help when she had it, was quick with a solution, "Tell him you'll be waiting for him at 10 o'clock tonight," she said, "But don't tell him you'll be sleeping somewhere else." The mother took the hired girl's bed, and, sure enough, the young man stole into the room at the appointed hour. After the youth had slipped under the covers, she turned, placed her hand on his shoulder and asked, "What do you want, son?" The response was quick and frantic. "Just kill me, Mamma. Just kill me dead."

Or so Walter told the story.

One day I went into the waiting room of Walter's office just as a tall, thin woman of perhaps 35 was coming out. I thought I detected a worried look on her face as she brushed past me. Approaching Walter's desk, I noted a smile on his face, and his first words were accompanied by a chuckle. "That woman is in trouble, but I can't help laughing," he said. "She was out last night with a man, and he left her in a pretty awkward position." Then he went on to explain that they had parked their car on a country road and had ended up making love behind an osage orange hedge. The man died on location. Someone had told her she had better give a detailed report to the

A Medley of Memories

county attorney. At some point Walter had asked her to tell him just when the man expired. Her answer, as he reported to me, was, "jist when, sir, jist when."

The *Tribune* reported the man's death, but avoided any implication of awkwardness in the circumstances.

Close friends of Walter Crow told of his modest home on the east side in which he had preserved all he could to remind him of the few years of a happy marriage, including the full wardrobe of the wife who had come to an untimely death.

Teeth in the Sewer

The story of the woman who lost her teeth during the Nebraska PEO Sisterhood convention in Hastings in 1932 was at least a week late when it appeared in the *Tribune,* but it put a new reporter named Harold Cowan on solid ground with Henry Smith and the rest of us.

A woman called and said she would tell us a "funny story" if we would keep her name out of anything we published. She got the necessary assurance, and Cowan got the job of talking with her.

One of the principal speakers at the annual banquet, main event of the PEO meeting, became ill while on an automobile tour of the city, hastened to the home where she was staying and went through a vomiting spell. Suddenly she realized that when she flushed the toilet she had given up her dentures along with her lunch.

Her hostess called a plumber. He said there was just a chance the teeth could be intercepted before they were swept into the main sewer.

There was frantic digging near the street. The plumber cracked a hole in the sewer and asked for a gentle flow of water from the house. Finally, as Cowan put it, the teeth came "grinning into view." And after some cleansing they were ready to grin at the banquet audience.

From that day we counted on Cowan when a story required a humorous touch.

Ed Wilken's Worried Walk

It was the day before a city election, and Ed Wilken, a new reporter, had put together a story based on street talk about what the contending mayoral candidates might do with the right to fill the more lucrative jobs it was the mayor's right to fill.

The first copies of the paper had been on sale but a few minutes when Henry Smith came to the newsroom to ask what we had done to offend Peter Murphy. Operator of a liquor store, he had been listed as a likely choice for fire chief in the event C. J. Ingraham defeated William Harm.

Why should Murphy think he had been damaged? Why should he have demanded that Smith order somebody out to pick up the papers before they got further circulation? Ed and I assured Smith there were plenty of reports that Murphy was in line for the job if Ingraham were elected.

Smith looked at me and my 140 pounds and then at Ed and his 220. "Ed," he said, "you are bigger than Harold. Why don't you walk down and see Pete?"

Murphy was alone in the store when Ed walked in and said, "I'm a reporter from the *Tribune,* and I wrote that article." Murphy hesitated for a couple of seconds. "That was a helluva thing to write," he said, and turned away.

Ed Wilken recalls this incident as one of the most memorable we shared during our half-dozen years together. He remembers Henry Smith's emphasis on his physical superiority and how this worried him as he walked the two-and-a-half blocks to confront an enraged reader. Was he facing possible physical combat? I remember it, I suspect, as one of those rare occasions when Smith saw an opportunity to give a new reporter a new and beneficial experience.

Bootleggers and "Confisticators"

Raymond L. Crosson was the sheriff of Adams County during my early years with the *Tribune*. He had been police chief in Hastings before and after a long stint with

A Medley of Memories

the National Guard on the Mexican border and in the army in World War I. He came out of the service with the rank of major and was looked up to by ex-servicemen and law enforcement officers throughout central Nebraska. He was exemplary in many ways. He avoided vulgarities in his speech, but he got attention with a voice trained to boom out with the authority of a company commander.

Whenever sheriffs and policemen got together in the late 1920s and early 1930s they were bound to talk about the problems of enforcing Prohibition laws. They talked much of their raids on producers and sellers of illegal "stuff" and about what they did with the bottles, barrels, stills and other paraphernalia seized in a typical raid.

Raymond Crosson was a meticulous follower of the rules laid down by prosecuting attorneys. He was so meticulous, in fact, that he tried to dictate to us reporters the language we would use in writing stories about the arrest of some unlucky dealer in illicit liquors. "I got something for you," he would say on my arrival at his office. Then he would start his narration with the unmistakable implication that he knew the exact form in which the story should appear in print. On more than a score of occasions he opened with these words: "Armed with a search warrant, Sheriff Crosson and (any others involved) entered a home on East Sixth Street, etc." He had learned early in the Prohibition era that the search warrant was vital.

At some stage in the typical report of a liquor raid there would be reference to the still, the bottled goods or whatever other evidence might be collected. Crosson considered that these actions were best explained with the word *confiscate*. As it turned out, though, he had misread the word from the beginning and had fixed it in his mind with an extra syllable. What he did was *confisticate* the stuff, and when he said *confisticate* (accent on the second syllable), it was with so much authority that others followed suit. Sheriffs and policemen in central Nebraska were saying "confisticate" in their discussions of liquor raids, and I came to the conclusion that they were following Raymond Crosson's example. He was that much of a model for his fellow officers.

Bramble and the Big Bank Robbery

It's entirely possible that John Bramble said confisticate along with Raymond Crosson. He was Crosson's deputy when I started covering the courthouse. I recall his telling about a wealthy brother-in-law's sea-going "yak," but Bramble's claim to a place in my memories has to do with his appointment as chief of police in 1929.

The appointment was the prerogative of the mayor, but it required city council approval. For some reason the council, which included several who had years of service behind them, took offense at the rather exuberant spirit in which Davis launched his administration. His trouble may well have started with a statement that he was going to preside over council proceedings in the manner he had perfected as head of the school board. Some of those councilmen considered running the school board a little below such easy comparison. In any event, a majority said no to John Bramble as Davis' chief.

The matter dragged on while City Attorney Charles Bruckman explained that while Bramble was functioning as the "de facto" chief, he was not the "de jure" chief, and that could mean problems. Ultimately, Bramble was confirmed in his job, and his years as chief seemed to give the office a little more life and action than the terms of any of the several other chiefs I observed.

As much as anything else, though, Davis' allusion to his school board experience stayed with me as a lesson in human behavior. I thought of the incident as I looked upon Jimmy Carter in the White House almost 50 years later and how many of his troubles seemed to trace to his bold promise he would run the United States from the

A Medley of Memories

lessons learned in running Georgia.

The most dramatic incident of the Bramble years came in February 1931. Officers and employees of the Hastings National Bank, arriving for the day's work, were greeted by four masked gunmen and escorted immediately to the basement and held until one of the officers, H. E. Nelson, was taken upstairs to the vault when the time lock went off at 8:30. The men got away with some $27,000, and officers of the law from several counties hurried to Hastings to get a first-hand review of what had looked like a perfectly planned and executed robbery.

By the time the first bank employees had freed themselves there had been time for the bandits to put quite a bit of space between them and the outskirts of Hastings, and the general presumption was that they were speeding toward a distant rendezvous.

Just how attention happened to center that night on a modest house on East Sixth Street has been explained in various ways. Some said Bramble and his fellow officers really believed the robbers could be the occupants of that house. I was never convinced that the ensuing raid was based on more than the possibility the "strange" occupants of the place were bootleggers. Most any officer of the law in those days seemed to have a backlog of suspected liquor-law violators. It was not uncommon for Bramble to raid such places when visiting lawmen were around to share the excitement. The very manner in which the East Sixth Street house was raided was enough to convince me that John Bramble was not expecting to find bank robbers there.

The house was surrounded, in proper fashion, and three policemen went to the door. A pajama-clad man greeted them, invited them in and, with a machine gun to back his word, made them lie on the floor while he put on his clothes. Eventually the robbers broke for their cars, with two Hastings policemen, Frank Yetman and J. L. Wood, as hostages. The sound of gunshots aroused the whole neighborhood, but when the smoke had cleared, there was only one casualty on the site. That was Volcott Condit of Lincoln, on hand as a representative of the Nebraska Bankers Association. (He was the son of Nebraska's last state sheriff.)

The fact that the bandits in their getaway had time to take the keys from two police cars and get their own cars out of nearby garages was just one of the elements in the story that made one wonder if Bramble really expected to find the bank robbers. Most certainly, he wasn't prepared for them.

Next day it came out that Wood had been released near Grafton and Yetman near Sylvan Grove, Kansas, and that one of the bandits, with a serious gunshot wound in the abdomen, had been picked up, along with a woman and a baby, at Belvidere. The man turned out to be James Thomas, a Texan with a jail record. He spent some time in the Mary Lanning Memorial Hospital and was back in jail in the courthouse ready for trial when he got his hands on some tools and sawed his way out of his cell one night. He didn't get out of the courthouse, though, and was hiding behind some boxes on a shelf in the treasurer's office when officers nabbed him.

Eventually, all the robbers were accounted for, one being victim of a murder in Missouri, and most of the money was recovered. Leon Davis, 11-year-old son of the mayor, got credit for finding several thousand dollars in the upholstery of one of the getaway cars.

The morning Jim Thomas was found hiding in the treasurer's office, according to one version of the story, one of the officers called to investigate was so nervous he pulled the trigger of his pistol unexpectedly and put a bullet through the courthouse floor. His version was that he wanted to make sure Thomas knew armed men were coming for him.

A Medley of Memories 225

Bramble developed an aggressive police force and something of a personal reputation as an investigator of events beyond normal police routine. He abandoned the department's motorcycle and put a patrolman in a sleek Ford roadster. His men—especially Tommy Dryden, an early driver of the roadster—developed an uncanny ability to spot the automobile of individuals for whom police departments across the country had sent out requests for help in finding. East-west traffic on Highway 6 went through the heart of Hastings, and men in that early patrol car, with little concern for search and seizure constraints, got their hands on an amazing number of individuals wanted by the law in other states. Each such arrest made a story for the *Tribune*.

One day the chief emerged from a conference with a local physician. Curious as to what had gone on behind closed doors, I asked Bramble what his visitor had wanted. His response threw some light on a topic of current gossip. Some months earlier there had been an excursion by Shriners of Tehama Temple to some kind of conclave in a distant city. What went on was never a matter of record, but more than one local household was upset by an anonymous letter that some wives of delegates had received. I never saw the letter, but Bramble, as I recall, had been shown a copy of it that morning and asked if he could help trace the authorship. Nothing ever came of the incident, but it was obvious that some of the Shriners would like to have got hands on the writer of that letter.

Neighboring Editors

Fred Howard of the Clay County *Sun* at Clay Center was in all probability the neighboring editor whose writings I followed closest of the score or more whose papers came to the *Tribune* office.

Fred used a higher grade of newsprint than was used by any other paper of the region, and he insisted on using copper halftones for reproduction of photographs. His paper looked good physically, and it read well, too. And what I read with greatest interest and no little professional envy was Fred's personal column. It ran the full depth of the front page in most issues and usually carried over to an inside page.

In keeping with a widespread practice of columnists of the time, Fred usually limited each topic to a paragraph. He started with short quips and ended with rather lengthy paragraphs that were more narrative than aphoristic. In almost every column these longer paragraphs included sketchy accounts of what Fred had heard from or about two fictional characters. One was called "Clarice of the Lingeries" and the other was referred to as "Miss Lobelia of the South Side." Comments attributed to them suggested now and then that they were to be found in Hastings. There were obscure references to visitors from neighboring towns.

It was hard to avoid the conclusion that Fred allowed these characters to enlarge on events that had their origin in gossip or hearsay that had reached his ears. It was a fair guess that some of the episodes described would be recognized as variations on real happenings. There were those who said Fred Howard knew just enough about events in his community to keep people wondering just when he would let Miss Lobelia or Clarice blurt out some stories that could prove embarrassing to individuals in the community. Whatever his motives, Fred wrote a column that was widely read.

The Grand Island *Independent,* published just 25 miles away, was the daily against which we of the *Tribune* were inclined to measure our performance most regularly. We were in a somewhat smaller city, and our circulation figures and advertising linage reports usually put us a step behind the *Independent* in the statistical columns. We prided ourselves, though, in being far ahead in the use of

A Medley of Memories

pictures and in our coverage of news from the far corners of our circulation area. We pointed out from time to time that while we tried to have a local story on the front page every day, the *Independent* usually was content to turn its front page over to the telegraph editor and concentrate its local news on a couple of inside pages.

The *Independent* editor, A. F. Buechler, was a veteran of perhaps 30 years in journalism by the time I became managing editor of the *Tribune*. He was a vigorous and articulate critic of the so-called Tri-County project, on the ground that it called for diversion of water from the valley of the Platte River.

The *Tribune* was the loudest supporting voice of the Tri-County project, and I was responsible for making sure that that voice was not drowned out by the *Independent's* criticism. There were times when Gus Buechler haunted me in unpleasant dreams, even though I knew him as a gentle man of the best intentions.

14. Fred A. Seaton

Observations on the Start of a Notable Nebraska Career

When I look back on 1936, I have to list it among my years of greatest expectations. The Tri-County project was taking shape. The shock waves of the Great Depression were subsiding. The economy of Hastings was definitely on an upturn. Henry Smith and Dave Lewis were discussing ways to gain controlling ownership of the *Tribune* and assuring me that they would make it easy for me to acquire some ownership along with them. Mabel and I were anticipating our first child.

As I thought about ultimate involvement in the paper's ownership, I took for granted that Smith and Lewis had judged properly the attitude of the surviving blood relatives of Adam Breede. He had left a two-sevenths interest in the paper to Smith, one-seventh to Lewis and the remaining four-sevenths to a brother and sister, David Breede and Louise Engel. A third sister, Mrs. Edward Cline of Lincoln, now spoke for that controlling interest. Her son, Adelbert Cline, had been in charge of circulation and graphic arts services at the *Tribune* since about 1934. The fact that he and his wife had lived most of the time at the Clarke Hotel suggested that he had no intention to establish a permanent residence in Hastings. Smith and Lewis, I am confident, had concluded that in due time the Breede heirs would listen to any legitimate proposal the two might make to acquire complete control. At some point in late 1936 they got word that the Clines would insist on outright sale of the total property and would oppose any plan of Smith and Lewis to retain their ownership. In a matter of weeks a Kansas City broker was listing the *Tribune* as a newspaper for sale.

Prospective buyers started showing up. Smith and Lewis seemed both pleased and surprised. They were apologetic to some extent in discussions with me, but reassuring in their belief that any purchaser would want me to stick around. I was only 30, but I was older in years and experience than other members of the news staff.

Robert Kennedy, advertising manager, and Ray Neff, mechanical superintendent, both talked with me about the possibility of organizing an employee group to buy the paper. Smith and Lewis had cautioned that the Breede interests would be opposed to that. Kennedy and I talked with Howard Pratt and O. A. Riley at the Hastings National Bank and found them hesitant to undertake the financing of a newspaper. We avoided talking with officers of the City National, because Smith was a director there and would not have appreciated our seeming disrespect for his advice against the kind of move we had in mind.

Few of the men who looked at the paper as prospective buyers took time to talk with staff members. One who went through the newsroom was identified later as Fay Seaton of Manhattan, Kansas, publisher of the Manhattan *Mercury* and *Chronicle*. In a matter of two or three weeks he was back with members of his family, and the word was out that they were the new owners of the *Tribune,* and Fred A. Seaton, the older of two sons, was to come to Hastings as general manager.

As we prepared for his arrival we picked up bits of information. Born in Washington, D.C., he had grown up in Manhattan and had attended Kansas State. He had been active in the state organization of young Republicans and had been on Alf Landon's staff through the presidential campaign of 1936. These and other experiences, along with poise and eloquence as a speaker, caused some Kansans to view him as a likely candidate for governor in some future election.

Not the least of my concerns related to the fact that this committed Republican, fresh from a presidential campaign in which his candidate had won the electoral votes of only two states, was taking over a newspaper that had supported the opposition. With Smith and Lewis leaving, I would remain as the principal apologist for or defender of that record.

Fred Seaton's coming to Hastings in the summer of 1937 was not without some similarity to the way the winds sweep into Nebraska from Kansas. Those breezes from the south can be hot or cold, but they are never without enough force and character to establish their presence.

Fred's plan of conquest, if he had one, relied heavily on the strength of his personality. He toured the *Tribune* departments almost daily during those first few weeks, getting employees' names and chatting briefly. He was quick to make a mid-morning coffee break a part of his daily ritual, and he invited me and one or two others to join him at a nearby restaurant when our schedules permitted. Drinking coffee with the boss—that was something new for old *Tribune* hands at any level.

He asked many questions about the way we did things, and his comments reflected some surprise at the extent to which we had tried to make the *Tribune* serve a region extending into all or parts of 10 Nebraska counties and two Kansas counties. Our photography and photoengraving services were new to him, as were several pieces of printing equipment. In reality, the *Tribune* was one of the best equipped small-city dailies in the Midwest.

Fred seemed to appreciate what he had to work with, but he did not disguise the fact that his father (back in Manhattan) looked upon this new property as burdened with some unnecessary frills. The father paid periodic visits to Hastings and spent hours poring over the account books. On at least three occasions, following such visits, Fred went through a sort of ritualistic report of his father's concern about the size of my salary. It had been $52.50 a week when the paper was sold and remained at that level for three years. Fay had discovered on one of his examinations of the books that my pay had been increased shortly before the sale. The fact that Fred did not follow these reports of his father's feelings with some expression of his own opinions left me puzzled, and that Fay never took the time to visit with me as to any of his concerns or questions was downright disturbing. I was in no position, I concluded, to force a frank discussion of whether both Fred and Fay felt I was a more costly employee than the paper could afford. I was inclined to believe Fred valued my experience and ability higher than his father did. The latter, I would conclude eventually, kept comparing Hastings salaries with what he had been paying bright young Kansas State students as part-time employees during those depression years.

Fred's break from his Kansas past seemed at times to be clear and complete, but he could wax nostalgic on such experiences as those he had had as an aide to Alf Landon and as a volunteer assistant and publicist in the athletic department at Kansas State. He had savored a brief period of greatness for Kansas State football through the coaching regimes of Bo McMillan and Lynn Waldorf. He knew the name of every player who had worn the purple in those golden years, and he talked knowingly of how he and others had worked with this or that player on the practice field. Kansas State football unquestionably had been one of his great enthusiasms.

That Fred had been widely known and popular in Kansas was attested to by a steady stream of visitors to Hastings from all parts of the neighboring state. Some were cronies of his college days, some were political associates, many were Republican newspaper editors and publishers from the western part of the state who could drive to and from Hastings in one day.

One Saturday two young men in a car with a Kansas license stopped at the *Tribune* and asked for Fred. When they had gone, he identified them as business acquaintances from Manhattan on a weekend spree. They had heard there were houses of prostitution in our neighboring city, Grand Island, and were looking for information as to how they might locate such a place. Fred made a telephone call or two, as I recall, and passed along whatever information he obtained. I cite the incident less for its singularity than for its contribution to my growing awareness of the affability of the man. He wore the old-school colors of a wide variety of individuals he had met in Kansas, and he was gradually building the same kind of relationships in Nebraska.

Sooner or later a number of younger men and women on Kansas newspapers were inquiring about jobs in Hastings. For most of my three years with Fred I consulted him before filling any vacancy on the news staff. Usually he had a Kansas candidate for most any opening on the paper. George Hart came from Eldorado to be our telegraph editor for a time. He went to Iowa State as a journalism instructor, was called up as an army reservist and became an early casualty of World War II. Helen Hemphill, from a newspaper family at Clay Center, joined us in 1938 or 1939 and remained with the paper until retirement in the early 1970s. A young man in the 1940 graduating class at Kansas State came for an interview. Fred and I agreed to put him on the staff on August 1. Meanwhile, I decided to join the Associated Press in New York on that day, and when Roy Fisher became head of the school of journalism at the University of Missouri some 30 years later, I could claim credit for

Fred A. Seaton 233

having chosen him for his first job after college.

Ken Fredel, who had worked on the paper at Fort Scott and elsewhere in Kansas, did a short turn with the *Tribune* while I was there and came back after I had left. Carl Rott, another Kansan, succeeded me as managing editor in 1940 and later went to Sheridan, Wyoming, to manage a daily that had been added to the growing Seaton chain.

One of the biggest surprises for me during Fred's first year or so at the helm was his almost complete avoidance of comment on the paper's past political positions. This was in many respects a tribute to his ability to size up the public mind in a given situation and adjust to it. What he encountered in Hastings in the late 1930s was an almost complete eclipse of the Republican party. Enthusiasm for New Deal programs—especially the Tri-County project—ran high. While there was a hard core of traditional Republicans in the city, there were many who found it convenient to ally themselves with Senator Norris, the apostate Republican, without having to proclaim support of the Democratic party. Fred made it clear at some time during his first year that he was an unqualified supporter of Norris.

For most everybody in the community Fred Seaton, as head man of the local daily, was a far different character than Henry Smith. A man of minimum exhibitionism, Smith had gone for nine years without having slapped a back or told a laugh-provoking story over a cup of coffee in a local restaurant. Within a matter of weeks Fred was meeting local merchants for coffee at mid-morning and in little clusters of three to six individuals his voice rang out more often than any other. For his new acquaintances this was an exhilarating experience. Where else could they get first-hand reports on what went on in Cleveland hotel rooms during the Republican convention of 1936? Who but one who had worked under him could repeat better the wise sayings of Alf Landon? (Fred always referred to Landon as "the governor.")

Fred's conversations were spiced with an easy flow of axiom and analogy. He frankly conceded that he and other associates in politically dry Kansas had tended to "drink wet while voting dry." On at least a dozen occasions I heard him size up somebody's discomfort or embarrassment in a given situation by likening it to the feelings of "the bastard son at the family reunion."

It didn't occur to me at the time, but it became eventually clear that Fred had brought back to the *Tribune* a personal dimension that had been missing since the days of Adam Breede. While distinctly different in many ways, the two men were quite alike in their willingness to project their powerful personalities and let these relate to the paper in whatever way the observer might choose.

There is no question but that Fred brought to the *Tribune* a fresh brand of salesmanship. He didn't write up orders for advertisements. He didn't solicit in a direct sense. But he was selling himself and the paper at every opportunity. He revived some old gimmicks of small-city advertising promotion, including the "signature ad" that had been frowned upon by Henry Smith. Usually a full page would be used, with some lines at the top proclaiming the importance of an event or project. Individuals and small businesses would be sold the space of a signature. With up to 100 of these at a dollar or more per name, the paper got a good return. One year there was some emphasis on Constitution Day. I remember Fred's promoting a signature page and some of the salespeople's general confusion as to just what Constitution Day was.

While Fred asked questions now and then about events making news, he offered little advice as to the nature and extent of our coverage. He seemed almost awed at times by the emphasis we put on problems of our agricultural economy. I spent a lot of time explaining the Tri-County project, still in its construction stages, and its importance to Hastings and the whole *Tribune* territory. I thought I saw in these discussions a difference between Hastings and Manhattan from the standpoint of a news medium. Whereas Manhattan had Kansas State College as a sort of foundation of the local economy, Hastings had to look to the agricultural welfare of several counties.

Observing the work of Ed Wilken, our agricultural editor, Fred suggested several times that we might buy a farm, put Ed in charge of it and develop our own demonstration center. When Ed and I insisted that any farm demonstration near Hastings should include deep-well irrigation, Fred demurred. He was surprised by our contention that an irrigation system valued at near the purchase price of the land would be worth every penny spent. I remember his saying once that his father had a farm near Manhattan and nobody ever mentioned irrigating it.

Fred made little effort to involve himself in day-to-day management of the news department. He wrote an occasional editorial, usually on an issue of national interest. His inspiration often came from a Washington research service to which he subscribed. I wrote most of the editorials dealing with state and local issues. After a year or more had elapsed, it dawned on me that I had about as much leeway as I had had under Smith.

He suggested one day that I might consider restyling the paper, changing from a traditional typeface to the increasingly popular sans-serif types. A few papers across the country had been doing this, and the results were generally acclaimed. What seemed especially appealing to Fred was the fact that we could alter the appearance of the paper without buying any new type. With the clean solid-line Vogue and Tempo faces we had in the shop and our flush-left headlines, we came up with pages showing more white space and a generally airy appearance.

The next step—and this was pretty much on my own—was to further distinguish the *Tribune's* front page with what was called "circus makeup." There was an example to follow in the Minneapolis *Star,* recently purchased by the Cowles interests and edited by Basil "Stuffy" Walters, who had transferred from the Cowles-owned Des Moines *Register* and *Tribune.* On the traditional front page the flag, or name line, of the paper was centered at the top. The *Star* would push this line down to the middle of the page sometimes. It would put it to the left or right and place a picture at one corner or the other of the top of the page. We borrowed some of these tricks and treated our readers to variety in the appearance of their papers. The fact that the *Tribune* had its own photography and engraving services enabled us to do things with pictures that other small dailies could not do on a day-to-day basis.

The physical dressing-up that we gave the paper during Fred's first two years contributed materially to the ultimate achievement of my 12 years with the paper. One day in early 1939, as I recall, Fred showed me a report in *Editor & Publisher* of a newspaper contest. "Why can't we win some honors of this kind?" he asked. I was ready with a response that ran something like this: "It will take some effort and some money, but I think we are putting out a paper that will stand up against others of its size anywhere in the country. I'm willing to try, if you will agree that I can ask for a little extra effort now and then on the part of other employees, and a little extra cost."

The extra cost, I explained, would be mainly in an occasional replating of a page to eliminate a defect in an otherwise well laid-out paper. This might be an ink smudge, a misspelled word or some other mistake not caught in the normal procedures.

Fred gave the go-ahead, and I set as an ultimate goal

the 1939-40 contests sponsored by the National Editorial Association. Meanwhile, there were some other contests worth considering. At the midwinter meeting of the Inland Daily Press Association in 1940 the *Tribune* won first place among dailies of between 5,000 and 10,000 circulation for typographic makeup and first with a news photo of a checker tournament.

When we received the rules of the 1940 N.E.A. contest, we decided there was an opportunity to win recognition in just about every category. When the awards were announced in midspring, the *Tribune* was winner of first place in general excellence, typography, newspaper production and its job printing exhibit; second place in the contest for special editions, and third place for the quality of its editorial page. While there had not been a sweepstakes contest as such, the judges announced that the *Tribune's* multiple winnings suggested its designation as "America's Outstanding Small-City Daily Newspaper." That line was added to the *Tribune* masthead as soon as I got home from the New York convention where the awards were presented. It remained for several years after I had gone.

Thumbing through the *Tribune* files of that period in recent years, I have had to conclude that whatever we achieved in putting out an attention-getting newspaper at Hastings was helped immeasurably by the times. War was spreading over Europe. Americans, while more comfortable and confident than they had been in the depths of the Great Depression, were wondering about a future that included such possibilities as a precedent-breaking third term for the president who had led them through most of the 1930s. Television had not come along to take the shock value out of newspaper headlines. Radio newscasting had attained a degree of maturity, but its glory days would come with the worst months of the war, and these were still ahead. If that 1939-40 period was a high-water mark for the *Tribune,* it was partly because we had taken advantage of a sort of high-water period for all daily newspapers.

The trip to the N.E.A. convention provided my first look at New York. I traveled by train at the *Tribune's* expense and covered the cost of a hotel room with a *Tribune* due bill. As per agreement with Fred, other expenses were my own. I found time for a visit to the Associated Press offices in Rockefeller Center where an interview had been set up with Joe Wing, head of the feature service. In this I was acting on the suggestion of William T. "Bill" McCleery, who had grown up in Hastings and had worked at the *Tribune* during summers while attending the University of Nebraska. Bill had headed the AP feature service for a while but had chosen to transfer to *PM,* the off-beat newspaper founded by Marshall Field, Jr. in New York. I told Wing I might be interested in a job with the Associated Press, but he thought my minimum salary requirement of $80 a week was a little high.

The *Tribune's* sweep of the N.E.A. awards got mention in the *New York Times,* in an editorial comment as well as in a detailed news story. The convention managers had reported Fred Seaton as editor of the *Tribune,* with a sort of secondary reference to me as the one who had come to accept the awards. This may have affected me more than I realized at the time. In any event, I left the convention pretty well assured that what counted among a majority of these small-city daily and weekly representatives was business management much more than editorial craftsmanship. I had talked with few delegates who did not have some ownership in the papers they represented, and the person with a new idea for selling advertising seemed to get more attention than the one with a suggestion for making a newspaper interesting and effective. (An exception was Hodding Carter of Greenville, Mississippi, well

Fred A. Seaton 239

on his way then to becoming one of the best known small-city publisher-editors in the country.)

Two nights and a day on the trains back to Hastings allowed time for a lot of thought about my future. I felt good about the *Tribune's* winnings, but I could not dismiss the fact that my contribution had been a year of 70- and 80-hour weeks, many nights and Sundays away from my wife and young sons. There had been little time for reading or any other efforts to improve myself for anything but the job at hand.

My mind told me that I had just about exhausted all the career potential of a small-city editor on a paper that somebody else owned. Fred had talked of adding another paper or two to the Seaton ownership and had suggested I might go to one of these as general manager. Some of the papers that might be available seemed to offer less of a challenge than I had faced at Hastings. For the moment I could identify with a newspaper of nationally recognized standing. The *Tribune* had reached a pinnacle, but so, it seemed, had I. Where did we go from there? By the time I got off the train I had made up my mind that the time had come for a change. I relayed my thoughts to Mabel, and she agreed that we should face the prospect of a move.

Around the first of July a letter came from Joe Wing of the Associated Press. He had talked with his superiors and was ready to offer me a job at the $80 a week I had specified. The starting date would be the first Monday in August. Mabel and I had agreed we would sell the house and furniture, take a furnished apartment in New York and see what happened. With this decision already having been made, I advised Fred of the offer and my acceptance.

It did not occur to me at the time, of course, but our parting marked the end of a three-year period during which I had been privileged to observe on a day-to-day basis Fred Seaton's start toward recognition among notable Nebraskans of the twentieth century. He would be

United States senator, White House adviser, cabinet member, candidate for governor. He would identify with a select group around Dwight Eisenhower that would break the 20-year spell of the New Deal in Washington. Interestingly enough, the Kansas connections that he had seemed to sever when he came to the *Tribune* in 1937 served him well in the long run, because Kansas influence probably outranked that of any other state in the manipulations that brought Eisenhower to the front among potential candidates for the presidency in 1952.

The story of most any person who has achieved prominence in the political field has its up chapters and its down chapters. I always have felt that Fred Seaton was coming out of a down period when he arrived at Hastings to take over the *Tribune*. A little more than half a year had passed since he was in the midst of the Landon campaign, with the right to hope that success for his candidate would mean he could write his own ticket, almost, to a responsible and challenging job in Washington, possibly in the White House.

The campaign had provided an alternative, he reminded us on several occasions. Prominent men he met had suggested that whether Landon won or lost, Fred should come east. More than one major corporation would welcome a young man of his talents and experience, they had implied. Discussion of these might-have-beens usually ended with the comment that Fay Seaton, his father, wanted him and his brother, Richard, to join in an extension of the family's newspaper holdings. (He referred sometimes to the examples of Oscar Stauffer, who was building a chain of papers from Arkansas City, Kansas, and the Harris family that had expanded into several cities from Ottawa, Kansas.) And so Fred was in Hastings with the challenge of the first Seaton expansion project, in an agricultural area that had been plagued for five years by depression and drouth. And he was troubled some, I felt, by the fact that the glories of Republicanism were not trumpeted as loudly there as they had been in Kansas.

By August of 1940, when I left for New York, Fred had established himself in Hastings. He had accepted in stride the *Tribune's* new recognition, and with minor investments by some of us on the *Tribune* staff, had put together a company to launch a new radio station in Hastings. While he had dabbled very little in local or state politics to that point, I was convinced that running the best little newspaper in the country or controlling several such newspapers, along with other communications properties, was not his ultimate ambition. I suspected then, and I believe now, that what he hoped to build at Hastings was the base from which eventually would come another move into politics. Call it public service, government or what have you, the lure is much the same, once one has tasted the fruit or merely sat with the dispensers of power.

Political achievers in our society come in every shape and size, and their behavioristic traits run the gamut. Some are good students of government and firm in their convictions as to what should be done in a given situation. Some are good planners and strategists, good organizers. Some have the gift of compromise and know just when to use it. Some need help in this. Some prefer to labor behind the scenes and never aspire to public office. The ones we know best are the ones who have what it takes to win at the polls. Some of these are better at winning than at understanding the functions of the offices to which they are elected. Some are so good at winning that they could not survive if it were not for the back-room strategists and out-front staffs that help them live up to their campaign promises or ignore those impossible to fulfill.

What Fred Seaton did as publisher after I left Hastings was pretty much beyond my range of observation. In one way or another, though, I managed to keep fairly close tabs on him as a politician. His over-all record places him near the top as strategist, planner and manager. He was beaten once as a candidate for the Nebraska Senate (legislature) and in the campaign for governor that pretty well closed his political career. The national offices he held were by appointment. He was in many respects a direct opposite of Dwight Eisenhower, with whose success he identified. Fred had a familiarity with history and political theory and an uncanny ability to measure political personalities. Most observers gave Eisenhower low marks in these areas, but he was seemingly unbeatable at the polls.

There is both paradox and irony in the fact that Fred Seaton moved into the national political spotlight as the backer of a man who was destined to become a legendary loser. In 1948, while in his fourth year in the Nebraska Senate, he accepted the chairmanship of the committee to work for the nomination of Harold Stassen, former governor of Minnesota, in the Nebraska presidential primary. In a field that included such luminaries as Thomas Dewey, Robert Taft, Arthur Vandenberg and Douglas McArthur, Stassen came out the victor. There was an immediate surge of national interest in the man who could manage such a victory, and Seaton was quickly enlisted to help Stassen win support in other states.

On a Saturday morning that summer he called me at the St. Louis *Star-Times,* where I worked at that time, and said he was down the street at the Jefferson Hotel and would have time to visit if I could get away for an hour or two. As soon as I had taken care of my Saturday morning duties I joined him in a room near the meeting hall where Missouri Republicans were in state convention to name their favorite presidential candidate. He was there to advise the supporters of Stassen.

There was an almost steady stream of runners from the

convention floor to his room. Somebody would come in almost in a state of panic because of what a speaker had said in criticism of Stassen. Fred would listen, ask a question or two and then send the messenger back with a reassuring comment, such as "Oh, just let him talk. He can't do any damage. You can answer that when the time comes." In more than one instance he turned to me after the informant had left and asked if I knew anything about the critic who had been quoted. Usually I didn't. What Fred demonstrated to me that day was his ability to play the role of the ship captain in time of crisis or the business leader who keeps his followers looking at the big picture rather than bothersome details. He was a prophet immensely respected by those Missouri Republicans he hadn't known before that summer day.

In the fall of 1962 I was involved in planning the formal dedication of a multi-million-dollar nitrogen fertilizer plant that Consumers Cooperative Association (later to be known as Farmland Industries) had built on the outskirts of Hastings. There would be tours of the plant, starting in the early forenoon, and at noontime a beef barbecue and short program at Duncan Field, about two miles away.

Special invitations had gone to Governor Frank Morrison, other state officials and business and civic leaders in Hastings. Fred Seaton, who had been nominated by Nebraska Republicans to oppose Morrison's re-election in November, was high on the list of invitees, and he was among the first to arrive at the plant office where special guests were to be greeted by CCA executives and board members from Kansas City and other places.

Governor Morrison had assured us he would be on hand, but nearly an hour had gone by and still he had not appeared at the office. Finally, we got word that he was at the barbecue site, and I set out to find him. He was there, all right, beaming with the pleasure of having found what amounted to a captive audience to be dealt with, one person at a time. He was working his way down the lines where early arrivals were waiting for the serving to start.

When I told him there were important people waiting for him at the plant, he assured me there would be plenty of time to talk with the CCA leaders and others while eating with them. He was not running away from this potential harvest of votes.

Just how many votes Morrison picked up as he shook hands along the barbecue lines is pure speculation, but it is safe to say that his hand-to-hand tactics contributed to his winning margin of some 20,000 votes in the election a few weeks later. It is pure speculation also to say that Fred Seaton learned more about Nebraska's agricultural economy by visiting with the dignitaries at the nitrogen plant than Morrison learned from his brief exchanges with persons whose names he forgot as fast as he heard them.

The incident demonstrates, if anything, a tendency of Fred Seaton the politician to be more interested in strategy than tactics. He gravitated toward the people of power and influence, at the expense sometimes of his standing with the rank and file.

Alexis de Tocqueville, the young Frenchman who put a finger on a long list of traits that characterized Americans in 1831, observed that in the winning of votes "one has to descend to maneuvers that disgust distinguished men. You have to haunt the taverns, dispute with the populace: that's what they call electioneering in America."

The picture in 1962 could not have been as dreary as the one de Tocqueville painted in the 1830s, but electioneering of the kind Frank Morrison practiced that day on the chow lines was never Fred Seaton's long suit. Fred was attracted more to the established centers of influence in our democratic society than to the raw sources of it.

Seaton's service as a United States senator started in

1951 when Gov. Val Peterson named him to fill out the term of Kenneth Wherry, who died in office. Whether by prior agreement with Peterson or otherwise, Seaton made it known shortly after taking office that he would not seek the office in the 1952 election. This disavowal, whatever its motivation, pretty well cleared the way for his early involvement in the plan that won the Republican presidential nomination for Dwight D. Eisenhower and sent him to the White House. Sixteen years after the disappointments of the Landon campaign, Fred Seaton was on a winning team and would be rewarded.

His first job in the new administration was as assistant secretary of defense for legislative and public affairs. Friends credited him with having helped the secretary, Charles E. "Engine Charlie" Wilson, former head of General Motors, over some political rough spots. Seaton spoke out more frankly against some of the ravings of Sen. Joseph R. McCarthy than did many others when the senator from Wisconsin seemed at times to have intimidated the whole federal structure. He served for some time as liaison man between the White House and Congress, giving special attention to legislation pertaining to agriculture and national defense. When Douglas McKay, secretary of the interior, resigned to run for the Senate in 1956, Eisenhower turned to Fred Seaton as a replacement.

Seaton's four-plus years as head of Interior were without question his years of greatest achievement. He was credited with sound judgment and a spirit of compromise in dealing with delicate issues that had plagued the administration of his predecessor. Dr. Eugene Trani, for several years on the faculty of the University of Nebraska and more recently vice-chancellor of the University of Missouri-Kansas City, made a study of all secretaries of the interior between 1849 and 1969. He gives Fred Seaton a high rating. One sentence from his comments: "Seaton neutralized the department (politically) and moved the department forward on a broad program of resource development, perhaps his most important achievement." Dr. Trani notes that Seaton's appointment was welcomed by Wayne Morse, outspoken Oregon senator, critic of McKay and the person McKay was wishing to unseat when he resigned from the secretaryship.

Fred Seaton left his mark on the city of Hastings and the state of Nebraska. Biographers often overlook what a powerful political personality can mean to the careers of men and women who come into the range of his acquaintance. Floyd Dominy, who grew up in Hastings, became commissioner of the Bureau of Reclamation in the Department of the Interior during Seaton's secretaryship. Robert K. Gray, another Hastings native, became a White House staff member and remained in Washington as a nationally recognized public relations professional. David A. Hamil, my brother, had served with Fred on the Hastings College board of trustees. He benefited, I am confident, from Fred's favor when his name came up in 1956 as a candidate for administrator of rural electrification in the Department of Agriculture. Other cases could be cited.

Twice during the years between my leaving the *Tribune* and Fred's death in 1974 we discussed the possibility of my rejoining his organization as manager-editor of one of a growing family of newspapers. He laid out an attractive proposal in the late 1940s, but I couldn't bring myself or my wife to the belief we would be happy in a relatively small high-plains community after five years in St. Louis. On a later occasion I communicated with Fred about a report that a much larger paper in the Midwest was for sale and that I would enjoy the challenge of managing it. This paper was larger than any in the Seaton chain, and Fred came to a rather quick decision that he wasn't ready to concentrate as much of the family investment in one property as this would have required.

In 1971, on my retirement from Farmland Industries, I was supplied with a file of letters I had never seen—letters written by individuals who were contacted when I was under consideration for the job I had held for 20 years. One of the letters was from Fred, and I was both humbled and flattered by what he had written: "... this organization would hire him (me) in a minute if it were possible to attract him back."

While we had certain philosophical and ideological differences in our three years together, it must be said, I guess, that we understood each other. I trust the foregoing is a fair appraisal of the personality and traits that carried Fred Seaton to attainments matched by few individuals in the history of Nebraska.

15. A Year with the AP

While Newspapers Still Were the Heart of Journalism

My experience with the Associated Press in New York turned out to be a sort of interlude. Within seven months after I had boarded the Burlington Zephyr at Hastings, with no small measure of misgiving, I was considering a return to Nebraska.

Just as Mabel and I were getting adjusted to apartment living in upper Manhattan and I was beginning to feel comfortable in my work in Rockefeller Center, a letter came from Chancellor C. S. Boucher of the University of Nebraska. The university, he said, was looking for someone to head its school of journalism, and he wanted to know if I would be interested in applying for the job. Mabel and I were quick to agree that we would give full consideration to the proposal. In a matter of a week or so I had worked out plans to take the week's vacation I was entitled to after six months with the Associated Press and go to Lincoln for interviews.

An immediate concern was that my superiors at the Associated Press might choose to terminate me if and when I agreed to go back to Nebraska. For them, therefore, I discussed only one portion of my vacation plans. I wanted to spend some time in Washington, which I did. But I took the train from there to Lincoln.

My day in Lincoln included conferences with Boucher and Dr. C. H. Oldfather, dean of the college of arts and sciences, of which the school of journalism was a part.

There was a meeting with these two and Joe and Fred Seacrist of the Lincoln *Journal* ownership and James E. Lawrence, editor of the Lincoln *Star*.

I do not recall the exact schedule of events, but they included some time together before a luncheon at the Cornhusker Hotel. The usual adjournment to the men's room before we went to lunch was interrupted for me by an encounter with an acquaintance in the hotel lobby. By the time I reached the basement two or more of my fellow conferees were standing at the urinals and I heard one of the Seacrists say, "I think that fellow can do what we want done." Everything seemed to gain momentum from that point, and by the end of the day Chancellor Boucher had assured me the job was mine, provided no objections were raised when he discussed the appointment with some of the persons I had given as references and some members of the board of regents. Just before I headed for the station and another trip to Chicago on the Burlington Zephyr he called to ask if it would be all right to designate me as director of university publicity as well as head of the school of journalism. In the euphoria of the moment I agreed to accept the additional responsibility without asking if it would mean any more than the $3,400 we had agreed upon as salary for the first year.

There was never a step-by-step review of just how I had come under consideration for the directorship, but I was pretty well convinced that the chancellor's first move was at the suggestion of Lawrence.

Gayle C. Walker, the director for about eight years and still relatively young, had developed health problems. Boucher, in discussing the situation with newspaper editors and publishers, had got the suggestion from several that he try to find someone from the working press, preferably in Nebraska. Lawrence and I had worked together in the state association of Associated Press editors, and he knew the *Tribune* as one of the few newspapers that had agreed with his paper's position in support of the change to a unicameral legislature and of the Tri-County project and other public works projects of the New Deal era. For at least a dozen years Lawrence had been teaching a twice-a-week night class in newspaper editing at the school of journalism. Whether that was discussed on my visit to Lincoln I can't recall, but there was never any thought that I should question his right to continue doing that.

Back in New York, with unqualified support from Mabel, I drafted my letter of acceptance. Boucher responded with assurance there would be no public announcement until mid-June or thereabouts and I settled back into my 40-hour-week routine with the Associated Press. That 40-hour week had been quite a change for me. There had been few weeks in my 12 years with the *Tribune* when I had not worked from 50 to 70 hours.

Once committed to leaving New York in late summer, I went through a whole series of reappraisals of my decision. Was I running away from a greater opportunity? Was I leaving a job that offered more self-improvement and ultimate advancement than there would be at the university?

While I may never have answered these questions to my full satisfaction, I found myself looking forward to a return to Nebraska. For the first time since we had arrived in New York, I began to appreciate some of the people around me, though, and some of the experiences living in New York afforded. In fact, I started laying out some projects for the remaining months. One of these was to walk the perimeter of Manhattan Island. I started on a Sunday afternoon in early April, walking from the vicinity of 115th Street to the vicinity of 34th Street, as I recall. This took me past the dock where the French liner *Normandy* had capsized after a hasty crossing of the Atlantic to avoid falling into the hands of the Germans as they overran France. Next day at the feature desk I told one of my colleagues, Ray Peacock, about my plan to circumnavigate the island, and he immediately asked if he might join me the following Sunday. I was happy for his company, and in three Sundays we had rounded the southern tip and made our way to my starting place. There were areas, of course, where we had to be content with getting no nearer than two blocks of the water's edge. But by sticking as close as we could to the water we saw much that we would not have seen from cars or busses or even the few elevated trains that still ran.

Sensing somewhat vaguely that in my new role as teacher of journalism I should be able to discuss intelligently the whole field of news reporting and editing, I began to look more closely at things and people around me. New York at that time was the journalism capital of the world. Newspapers still were both symbol and substance in any discussion of news and news dissemination. Those still appearing in New York offered the full range of content and sensationalism. The *Times,* the *Daily News,* the *Mirror,* the *Journal-American,* the *Herald Tribune,* the *World-Telegram,* the *Post,* the *Sun*—they were all appearing on the newsstands and in the hands of people who read newspapers while standing in crowded subways and on street corners or sitting on park benches. The Associated Press had started some special services for radio news broadcasters, but the emphasis still was on serving the print media, mainly the daily papers.

On the rather rare occasions when three or four of us from the feature service would venture at lunchtime into one of the higher-priced restaurants of the neighborhood, we would identify sometimes a group from *Time* and *Life* whose offices were also in Rockefeller Center. The general feeling among AP people was that these magazine people were better paid. They seemed to be better dressed.

Most of the days our noon-hour retreat would be to one

of perhaps a dozen little places along 52nd Street where a substantial lunch could be had for about 50 cents. We always tipped, of course, usually a nickel.

I never made a count of the staff of the feature service, but it ran somewhere in the neighborhood of 30. My going-away memento, presented at an after-work dinner at a place called "Louie's," was my portrait in crayon by one of the artists, Howell Dodd. Around the picture were 40 signatures. The names included the staff of the photo library that adjoined the big room over which the artists, writers and other feature service folk were deployed.

The faces that went with those signatures still are familiar. There was Joe Wing, of course, the department manager. He had worked for the AP at Lincoln, and his wife had been secretary to the publisher of the Lincoln *Star*. My immediate supervisor was Gardner Soule. Son of a Houston lawyer, graduate of Rice, he had done graduate work in journalism at Columbia. We hit it off from the start, and I was honored to serve as best man at his wedding within a few months after we first met. Gardner served in the navy during World War II, became managing editor of *Better Homes and Gardens* at Des Moines and then chose to return to New York and a free-lance writing career. He is the only associate of that year in New York with whom I kept in contact over the next 40 years. Ray Peacock, who had come into New York from the Milwaukee bureau at about the same time I joined the staff, left to become a public relations man for the Ringling Brothers Circus. He died, as I recall, in the late 1940s.

Joe Morton, who worked with Peacock and me as copy and layout editors under Soule's supervision, was a native of St. Joseph, Missouri. He had attended the University of Nebraska and had worked in the Nebraska bureau of the AP before going to Cleveland and then to New York. With the outbreak of World War II he joined the

A Year with the AP

correspondent corps of the AP and wrote at least one article for the *Saturday Evening Post* from material gathered while on assignment in Africa. He came to his death while accompanying a highly specialized military party that was dropped behind enemy lines in southeastern Europe.

Few syndicated features for sports pages were better known in those days than the cartoons of "Pap" Paprocki. Sports personalities were never disappointed on seeing him for the first time. With the rugged look of a wrestler or football lineman, he seemed to belong among the subjects of his work. As Christmas approached, I wrestled with the problem of developing a greeting card that would have a touch of New York about it. Lifting a pen and ink sketch of the Empire State Building from an advertisement, I approached Pap, and in about five minutes he had hung a holly wreath over the tower, and our card was ready for the printer.

Hank Barrow, who did editorial cartoons for the feature service, ended up in Omaha as cartoonist for the *World-Herald*.

At a somewhat isolated desk in an otherwise crowded room, Vance Packard wrestled with the responsibilities for a weekend feature that went out by the fastest available mail service for Sunday papers wanting a full-page summary of the week's news around the world. His worries were real, because it never was until the final hours that he could be sure that a major development would not call for replacement of large chunks of his original plan with a summary of a new invasion in Europe, a typhoon, a train wreck or some other event.

Vance seemed to sense a community of interest when he learned that I had come from a farm. His roots were in rural Pennsylvania. During my early weeks in New York, before Mabel and the boys arrived, I had dinner with him and his wife, Virginia, at their Long Island apartment.

He left the AP shortly after I did and worked on *Collier's* Magazine until its demise. Suddenly deprived of a medium for his far-ranging explorations of social customs, mores, prejudices and human behavior in general, he started writing books. Between the 1950s and the 1970s his books appeared at regular intervals and were generally acclaimed. The titles included *The Hidden Persuaders, The Status Seekers, The Sexual Wilderness, The Waste Makers, A Nation of Strangers.*

One of the signatures on the memento of my year with the AP is that of Helen Sopot-Lubell. Her husband was Samuel Lubell, who became a popular critic and analyst of the American scene, his writings appearing in various magazines and newspapers during and after World War II.

John Selby, a veteran of about 10 years with the Kansas City *Star* and five or more with the AP, wore the robes of seniority (and a higher pay level) without seeming to look down on us more lowly members of the feature staff. He was the author of an award-winning novel, *Sam*, and was working on another, *Island in the Corn*, that would draw on memories of his boyhood at Gallatin, Missouri. Eventually he would leave the AP for an editing job with Rinehart and Company, book publishers.

One day I observed Joe Wing's calling Selby to his desk (out in the open with the others) and the development of a heated conversation. We would learn later that Wing was disturbed by something Selby had written in a review of a new book by Anne Morrow-Lindbergh. The book, little more than a pamphlet, was *Wave of the Future,* and it reflected some of the views of the author's husband, Charles A. Lindbergh, who was identified with a growing movement for strict neutrality in the war that was spreading over Europe.

It was obvious that Selby didn't like the book. He had

A Year with the AP

opened his review with a statement that he had started reading after getting settled in his commuter train at Westport. Before the train got out of Connecticut, he wrote, he felt the need for fresh air and went to the rear of the coach to get it. I recall second-hand reports of all this, but I don't remember just how much of Selby's original wording remained in the version the AP finally distributed. Selby didn't attend the going-away party at Louie's, but his distinctive signature stands out on the memento of my year with the feature service.

The packets of materials that went to hundreds of daily newspapers from the feature service included stories and pictures dealing with a wide variety of subjects. Adelaide Kerr, always dressed as though starting for a stroll down Fifth Avenue, wrote fashion features. Dillon Graham headed a small staff that sent materials for the sports pages. George Tucker wrote a daily column that centered on things seen and heard in New York entertainment circles. Tucker was better on subject matter than technique. His spelling was atrocious, and Joe Morton, who edited his copy most of the time, made joking references from time to time to the complimentary theater and night club tickets he exacted from Tucker as compensation for keeping his copy up to AP standards. One thing about George—he could get the tickets when most any of us asked him to get them.

The Associated Press was highly regarded by the newspaper publishers of the country. Working journalists, though, often expressed impatience with its conservatism. There was a general understanding among newspaper wire editors that while one could rely on the AP's accuracy, one often looked to the United Press for more lively treatment of a given story.

What I got from my year in New York was a close-up view of the organization and delivery of national and world news and an opportunity to rub shoulders with an amazingly diverse collection of working reporters and editors. These associations would strengthen my standing as director of the journalism school at Nebraska. Within a matter of weeks after I arrived in Lincoln there would be a visit to the campus by Howard Blakeslee, the Associated Press' veteran science editor. These relationships would in one way or another continue through the rest of my working years.

16. Lincoln Years

Campus Life Rewarding, Even in Wartime

My three years at the University of Nebraska would have been quite different had it not been for the intrusion of World War II. Still, the disruptions of wartime did not mean erasure of all benefits and pleasures one should expect from being part of an academic community.

I look back on those years as contributing as much to my personal development as would have an equal period of structured study toward an advanced degree. I was surprised by the extent teaching can be educational to the teacher as well as the taught. But the greatest reward of those campus years came from association with administrators and faculty members and involvement in a variety of community activities. Lincoln was a good place to live, and to the best of my knowledge, it still is.

Staff and faculty at the university, from Chancellor C. S. Boucher down, never once hinted that my standing as director of the school of journalism was in any way limited by the fact that my only degree was a bachelor's in liberal arts from a modest little college. Some deans and department heads seemed eager to test ideas on this fresh recruit from the outside world. Dr. George Rosenlof, registrar, saw to it that I was invited into the Rotary Club. Dean C. H. Oldfather of the arts and sciences college sponsored my membership in a men's study group that proclaimed its distinction in its name. It was simply The Club, or as some would put it "The *The Club*." Dr.

Nels A. Bengston, head of a new program (the Junior Division) for helping freshmen adjust to academic routine, picked me early as someone to whom he could send certain "problem" students for special counseling.

Our home for the first year was a modest cottage on Holdrege Street, near the College of Agriculture, or east campus, as it came to be called. It was our good fortune that a next-door neighbor was Mrs. E. A. Burnett, widow of the man who had been university chancellor from 1928 to 1938, following long service as dean of agriculture. Mrs. Burnett helped Mabel get acquainted in the neighborhood and eventually sponsored her membership in Sorosis, a women's club that probably matched The Club in the prominence of the names of some of its members. In any event, those early months in Lincoln were made easy by the cordiality of the community.

It dawned on me during my first month that the warm welcome was a valuable offset to some cold realities of my situation. I was more of a symbol of change than I had expected to be. I was part of a drama directed by a new chancellor who had had a couple of years to analyze his responsibilities, his problems and his opportunities. C. S. Boucher had come from West Virginia to find a university that had been in pretty much of a holding pattern through almost a decade of depression and a series of cropless years for Nebraska farmers. He was ready in the fall of 1941 to assert his dissatisfaction with certain people and certain practices and attitudes.

Two men on the journalism faculty, Robert Crawford and Lawrence Pike, had handled various writing and public relations duties for the previous chancellor. Boucher had decided early to isolate them from any relationships with his office, and the implied message to me in a couple of conferences was that anything I did to encourage the departure of either would win points in my rating as an administrator.

Carroll Chouinard, a relative newcomer, had started looking around as soon as the chancellor announced in midsummer that I would replace him as director of the publicity office. Within a few days after my arrival in Lincoln he announced he was leaving to take a job in Chicago.

For Gayle Walker, the man I was replacing as director of the school of journalism, the change was bound to be distasteful. He was staying on to do some teaching, but he would have no other responsibilities. No one could have been more cooperative and helpful to me as I struggled to answer questions that dealt with situations and problems I knew little about. In a matter of weeks, though, Walker suffered a heart attack and died.

The school of journalism was a part of the college of arts and sciences and subject to its regulations and standards. The dean of the college, Dr. C. H. Oldfather, made it clear from the start that I would be subject to a minimum of supervision so long as I abided by the basic rules. He was a historian, quick to reminisce and philosophize. His management style seemed to find summary in a casual observation when I dropped into his office one day. Pointing to a somewhat cluttered desk, he spoke in about these words: "I learned long ago that one need not rush through the day's mail and try to respond to every letter. Wait a week and many won't need a response."

Some of the customs and traditions of the school of journalism were not exactly to his liking, he made clear in our early conferences. But just as clear was his admonition that he counted on me to let change come with a minimum of shock and friction. I felt comfortable with Dean Oldfather for all my three years on the campus.

My relations with Chancellor Boucher were more in my role as director of the university publicity office than as a member of the academic staff. By the standards of a later generation, the university administration of that era enjoyed a sort of touch-me-not relationship with the news media. Meetings of the board of regents were rarely attended by reporters and only at the invitation of the chancellor and the board. I do not recall that I ever attended a regents' meeting. When the meetings were over, Boucher prepared a summary of the actions, and these were transposed into a formal news release and delivered to the newspapers and radio stations.

It was my good fortune that Richard (Dick) DeBrown, who had grown up in Lincoln and was a recent graduate of the university, was on hand to direct the routine of the publicity office. He wrote most of the news releases from the chancellor's office and did it in such a way as to minimize my involvement with questions as to what should or should not be reported as to the actions and policies of the board of regents or the university administration. Dick left at or near the end of my first year to take a job in Washington. A second good break came my way when I managed to enlist Ralph Reeder to fill in at the publicity office. Reeder had been editing the magazine of the alumni association and was thoroughly familiar with activities throughout the university. In due time he would leave for service as a naval officer. Reeder and I had many common interests, and we kept in touch with each other through his years (as an extension service editor) at Purdue and mine at Farmland Industries.

The offices, classrooms and photo laboratories of the school of journalism were in University Hall. The once-dominant structure had been sliced down to a basement and one floor. It was immediately north of the newer administration building, where the publicity office shared space with the university editor's office.

The position of university editor had been left vacant with Chouinard's resignation. He had been editor as well as publicity director. Within a matter of weeks after my arrival the editorial post was filled by Miss Emily Schoss-

Lincoln Years 261

berger, a native of Austria, who had been editing publications at Fordham University in New York. The first major publication project to come under Miss Schossberger's supervision was a book on J. Sterling Morton by James C. Olson, who had written it in connection with his work on a doctorate in history. After military service in World War II, Olson would come back to Nebraska and serve as head of the history department and dean of the graduate school before moving to the chancellorship of the Kansas City unit of the University of Missouri and eventually to the presidency of Missouri's four-campus system.

It is hard to look back on those early months in Lincoln and understand the seeming oblivion to the threat that war hung over the nation. There were daily reports of the growing intensity of combat in Europe, and we were aware that our government was preparing for all sorts of eventualities at the military level. Yet the national mood was ambivalent. Men and women took sides on campus issues, the America-First movement, the question of leasing military bases and other activities designed specifically to aid the cause of the Allies. One heard few all-out suggestions, though, that the United States should become fully involved in the fight against German belligerence and expansionism.

Pearl Harbor brought an abrupt end to the speculation and ambiguity. In a matter of hours the national mood had crystalized in support of war. What this would mean to the lives of countless millions of Americans was more a matter of individual conjecture than public discussion. For those young men who had accepted their role as likely candidates for calls to military duty—and university students were among the most likely—what they would be doing and where they would be going was less a question of what than of how soon.

By the time classes were resumed following the Christmas-New Year's break the university had settled into a sort of wartime tempo.

Chancellor Boucher put out the word that he expected all divisions of the university to start thinking of how best we could respond to the new conditions and demands of a nation at war. We of the journalism staff came up with the idea that there might be need for some special training we could offer to the smaller newspapers of the state. Reporters as a group were usually male, usually quite young and thus subject to military duty. Why not look for women within existing staffs and train them to handle routine newswriting and editing duties? How about helping older men from the mechanical staffs learn something about writing, editing and the sale of advertising? By early spring we were publicizing a short course that would be offered in June. We heard from several score editors and publishers, and when the course opened, there were perhaps 15 persons ready to enroll. Several were Lincoln residents, including Bill DeVriendt, who had been a salesman for several years for his family's photoengraving establishment in Lincoln. He made it clear that his interest was more in broadening his acquaintance with journalistic terms and philosophies than in sharpening any writing skills. An ebullient, witty individual, he livened many of our sessions with his comments and questions. Several women came in from small weeklies, and one man who had been selling advertising for a small paper was on hand to prepare himself to take over editorial responsibilities, as I recall. The project was less than a howling success in its overall dimensions, but it seemed to satisfy those who enrolled. Several of the enrollees kept in touch with me as they put into practice some of the ideas picked up in our classes. Bill DeVriendt became a regular caller at my office, and his relationships with the journalism faculty were a factor, certainly, when his firm was awarded the contract for engravings in the

Lincoln Years

1944 *Cornhusker* (student annual).

One incident in those early days of searching for ways to adapt to new conditions and new needs of a nation at war was a brief conference in my office with Dr. Mabel Lee, director of women's physical education. She had made up her mind, she said, that women were going to be taking on all sorts of jobs and responsibilities that would call for physical strength and endurance. There would be work in munitions plants and other places that would call for lifting and carrying. She wanted her programs to put emphasis on development of muscles of the shoulders and back, she said. Then in a sort of aside she observed, "There is going to be need for more plain hard labor than for grace and elegance in getting in and out of a car."

Far from the least of wartime influences on life in Lincoln was the establishment of a major army air base immediately west of downtown at the site of the municipal airport. The influx of staff and trainees more than offset the loss of students at the university and created serious shortages of housing at various levels.

Two members of the Kappa Kappa Gamma sorority came to my office one day for advice on how to handle a problem that they preferred not to take to the office of the dean of women. A young woman wearing a Kappa pin had come to the house with a story about having come to Lincoln to find work and needing a place to live temporarily. She was accepted as a guest, with few questions being asked. In a matter of days, though, some of the sorority members became suspicious. They started checking and came to the conclusion that their guest was not a Kappa from Louisiana State, as she had claimed, and was not listed in the membership of any other chapter. There had been some listening in on telephone conversations leading to a conclusion that the young woman had come to town as the girlfriend of an officer at the air base. The sorority was providing a low-cost domicile for a migrant mistress, or so the girls suspected. After I had heard the story in detail, my visitors asked what they should do. To the best of my recollection, I said, "Tell her to get out." My visitors came back a few days later to say the problem had been solved; the girl had left, and they were relieved of any further fear they would have to appeal to the dean's office.

A far more serious disciplinary problem confronted me in my final year as head of the school of journalism. Horace Basinger, who had replaced Lawrence Pike as instructor in photography, said he had confiscated a collection of negatives one of the male students had made of one of the freshman girls in the beginning photography class. They included a dozen or more poses in the nude. The picture-taker was within a matter of weeks of entering military service, and we suspected he had hit upon a plan to take with him a collection of photos that might be marketable at training camp. In any event, we called him to my office, lectured him (saying something, I am certain, about our right to withhold approval of credits for a semester's study). He turned his negatives over to Basinger, and we considered the case closed. I always suspected that he held back some negatives and that the daring poses of a Nebraska banker's daughter got some attention in military circles.

The Love Library building, first major addition to the downtown campus for many years, was in the final stages of construction when war came. In a matter of months its vast interior was revised to provide a dormitory (or barrack) for occupancy by military units sent to the campus for special courses to qualify men for army commissions.

For some of us the war meant a lot of soul searching. In my middle thirties, I was beyond the age of men caught in the early military draft. But the services could use men of my age and experience as commissioned officers, and a number of Nebraska faculty members headed in that direction. Some had been subject to call as reserve officers. Some were singled out and literally invited to apply for commissions because of special professional skills.

In March of 1942 I responded to a call for men to apply for commissions in the Army Air Corps. I was asked to report to an office in Omaha and prepare to take a physical examination. My interviewer, wearing the insignia of a major, impressed me as one who had been stung a bit by the splendor of his rank and authority. At one point he expressed concern that some applicants for commissions were more interested in getting away from home and family responsibilities than in serving their country. My response was that I hadn't come to Omaha to hear him or anyone else question my interests and motives. He bristled a bit, and I always have thought that something he wrote in my record was what brought an abrupt end to two subsequent inquiries into the possibility I might enter the army as a second lieutenant. A try for a navy commission went smoothly until I failed to pass the eye examination.

In the spring of 1944 it turned out that faulty eyesight would not keep me from serving as a second-class seaman. There had been a request that all draft boards go through their rolls and reclassify any men who might help fill new manpower quotas for all the services. My draft board (in New York) asked me to report to the Lincoln board for reconsideration of the exempt status I had enjoyed up to that time.

There were about 150 men in a contingent that went by train to Omaha for two days of examinations. When I was asked what service I preferred, I chose the navy. The papers I took home classified me as a second-class seaman and indicated I would be notified as to where I should report for training.

When I reported my new standing to Dean Oldfather and others at the university, they filed a request that I not be called until after the end of the school year. Around the campus, though, there was a general assumption that I would be leaving soon. Some of the students threw a party and presented me with a traditional navy cap.

Within less than a month, though, there was a letter from my draft board which stated that I was exempt from further consideration by the military services. This, it turned out, had come from a decision in Washington that the latest combing of the draft lists had flooded the services with candidates who, because of age and physical disabilities mainly, simply could not be absorbed. I remember that the group with which I traveled to Omaha for examinations included men who talked of heart conditions and displayed such things as elastic knee bandages they had to wear because of football injuries.

For the first time in more than two years I was free from the likelihood of a mandatory call to military service. There was a sudden realization that I could start thinking of where I might be and what I might be doing when the war ended. I had every confidence in my ability to stay as long as I might wish at the university. While assuring myself as to good standing with my colleagues and superiors, I had to face some other questions. If I planned to remain in the academic field, I should be thinking about graduate study and advanced degrees. I was an established professional journalist in the minds of Nebraska editors and the Nebraska public, but what did I have as an academician that would sell in New York, California or even Iowa? Nebraska, a small state with limited resources, was hardly the place to think of acquiring a reputation by building a journalism school beyond the needs of the state. This was not the place to think of catching up with the journalism schools at Missouri, Northwestern or Stanford.

I was in a receptive mood, therefore, when a letter came from Walter Christenson, editor of the editorial pages of the Omaha *World-Herald*. He inquired as to my interest in working with his staff during the coming summer and projected the possibility of a permanent position there if we could come to agreement after the summer experience.

I was quick to agree to working in Omaha during the summer. It would be my first opportunity to be a full-time editorial writer, and the pay would be better than I had received as a part-time copy editor at the Lincoln *Journal* during the summer of 1942 and better than I received as a rewrite man with the United Press in Washington during the summer of 1943. I assured Christenson that I would let him know by August 1 if I was interested in a permanent position.

I look back on that summer with the *World-Herald* and wonder sometimes why I chose not to accept permanent employment there. Working conditions were close to perfect. There was no pressure. Christenson made a suggestion now and then as to a topic inviting editorial attention, but in the main I pretty well decided what I would write about. There was a tacit understanding that I would avoid writing on the major issues of the day, especially those situations that called for expression for or against the Franklin D. Roosevelt presidency and certain New Deal agencies and policies. This was the year when Roosevelt went beyond precedent for a second time and sought a fourth term in the White House.

Our work space was a suite of offices on an upper floor of the World-Herald Building, well isolated from the hubbub and traffic of the newsroom. Christenson and Harvey Newbranch, former editor and winner of a Pulitzer Prize for an editorial written in 1919, occupied the inner office. Roland Jones, another veteran of many years with the paper, managed the flow of copy to the composing room, edited letters to the editor and editorial page columns and wrote an occasional editorial. He was in the outer office with me. There was a third desk in our room that was occupied from time to time by someone on a special assignment, as I recall.

One day a middle-aged man showed up and asked for

Harvey Newbranch. He introduced himself as a clergyman assigned to a mission post on an Indian reservation in South Dakota and offered a hurried explanation of why he was in our office. A Nebraska native and brother of a professor at the state university, he had been a regular reader of the *World-Herald* in years past. He remembered Harvey Newbranch's prize-winning editorial. He had admired the paper's stand on various issues and had dreamed of the day when he might meet Newbranch in person. Circumstances had brought him to Omaha. This was his opportunity. Jones or I conveyed the message to Newbranch, and he came into our office with the obvious intent of making the visit as short as possible.

The conversation, every word of which I heard, took an immediate turn against the presumptions of the visitor. The *World-Herald* no longer could be called a supporter of the New Deal, Newbranch explained with considerable emphasis. It was obvious after this explanation that the missionary had come to praise and not to argue. He chose to do neither. In a matter of minutes he thanked Newbranch for taking time to see him and was on his way. I can only guess what went through his mind as he reviewed that conversation. He remembered the *World-Herald* when Gilbert Hitchcock, as publisher as well as United States senator, exemplified what some have called Wilsonian liberalism. The paper had supported the New Deal in its early years, but by 1936 it was ready to support Alf Landon against Franklin Roosevelt. Most certainly it was not pleading for a fourth term in that summer of 1944. This bothered me as I weighed the question of whether to accept permanent employment with the paper.

Looking back on it, that exposition by Harvey Newbranch was an important contribution to the case I had been building against staying on at the *World-Herald*. My thinking about national political issues had gone through tortuous processes during my years at Hastings. I had not voted for Roosevelt in 1932, but by 1936 I had convinced myself that his New Deal was much more clearly directed at the problems of Nebraska than anything recommended by the Republican leadership of the time. I voted for Roosevelt in 1936 and changed my registration from Republican to Democrat in 1938. There was no question but that I stood a good chance of being uncomfortable in the role of editorial writer for a newspaper that had taken so definite a stand on national political issues as Harvey Newbranch described during those few minutes with the missionary from South Dakota.

Within a matter of days there came another letter that opened a whole new line of thought as to my future. It was from Ernest Kirschten, editor of the editorial page of the St. Louis *Star-Times*. He had been in touch with Carlyle Hodgkin, farm editor of the *World-Herald,* and had inquired as to Hodgkin's interest in filling a place on his editorial-page staff. Carlyle had rejected the idea he might try his hand at editorial writing, but he had said something in a letter he wrote Kirschten to the effect that I might be interested, and Kirschten had moved immediately to inquire. He explained that the *Star-Times* was a paper with "liberal" leanings and that my leanings, as described by Hodgkin, were what he was looking for in candidates for the job.

With the St. Louis inquiry at hand, I decided to advise Christenson I would not be interested in a permanent job at the *World-Herald*. I spent a weekend in St. Louis, visiting at some length with Elzey Roberts, publisher of the *Star-Times,* as well as with Kirschten. Within a few days after I got back to Lincoln, Kirschten sent a one-year contract and suggested he would like to have me on the job by October 1. Before making a decision I talked with several university people and was surprised by the enthusiasm with which most of my associates appraised my opportunity. Dr. John D. Clark, dean of the college of

Lincoln Years

business administration, was especially encouraging. His advice was in about these words: "Too many Americans make the mistake of believing in the myth of the rolling stone that gathers no moss. There are times in one's life when one can gather a lot more moss by rolling. And the best time to roll is when you are young."

Arrangements were made to put the school of journalism under F. G. Blood, a professor of advertising in the college of business administration, and the publicity office under George Round, who for several years had handled publicity for the college of agriculture. On the first Monday of October 1944, I reported for work at the *Star-Times* in St. Louis.

Epilogue

Dr. John D. Clark, mentioned in this chapter, came to the university at the same time I did—in the fall of 1941. A graduate of Nebraska, he had practiced law in Cheyenne and had served as vice-president of Standard Oil Company of Indiana in Chicago. While still in his middle years he had earned a doctorate in economics at Johns Hopkins and had taught at Denver before being named dean of business administration at Nebraska. In 1949 he would be one of three men named by President Truman to the newly created Council of Economic Advisers at the White House.

Among mementos of my three years at the university is a promotion piece designed to remind high school seniors in 1944 that the university was still a going concern. One of two students pictured on the cover is Harold Andersen, one of the few males attending journalism classes at the time. At this writing he is president of the Omaha *World-Herald*.

Two students who were in journalism classes all three of my years on the campus—June Jamieson-Hughes and Joan Martz-Rees—have been fellow residents of Kansas

City for many years. June was one of the students who sought my advice on the problem of an unwelcome guest at the Kappa house.